Rhetoric and the Politics of Workplace Innovation

Struggling with Empowerment and Modernization

Martin Beirne

Professor of Management and Organisational Behaviour, Adam Smith Business School, University of Glasgow, UK

Edward Elgar

Cheltenham, UK • Northampton, MA, USA

Published by
Edward Elgar Publishing Limited
The Lypiatts
15 Lansdown Road
Cheltenham
Glos GL50 2JA
UK

Edward Elgar Publishing, Inc.
William Pratt House
9 Dewey Court
Northampton
Massachusetts 01060
USA

A catalogue record for this book
is available from the British Library

Library of Congress Control Number: 2013935027

This book is available electronically in the ElgarOnline.com Business Subject Collection, E-ISBN 978 1 78254 834 8

ISBN 978 0 85793 000 2 (cased)

Typeset by Columns Design XML Ltd, Reading
Printed and bound in Great Britain by T.J. International Ltd, Padstow

Contents

PART II ENABLING, ENACTING AND REGULATING

Foreword

This book emerged from a series of conversations during the summer of 2010 about the value of updating an earlier contribution, viz., *Empowerment and Innovation: Managers, Principles and Reflective Practice*. That was written in 2005, and initially published in 2006, pursuing an ambition to connect critical academic research on the nature and impact of employee participation schemes with practical efforts to improve the governance of modern organizations, enhance employment relations and experiences, and deliver more inclusive and effective ways of organizing and managing work.

Presented against a general backdrop of weak and insubstantial employee participation, certainly in Britain, and amid a profusion of designer models and prescriptions for top-driven participative working, *Empowerment and Innovation* called for a discourse on applied research that was sensitive to tacit knowledge and the self-improving and adapting activities of local work groups. Combining social realism with measured optimism, it drew upon some of the earliest references to empowerment, as an enabling framework to help disadvantaged people assert themselves and exert an autonomous influence on their own life experiences. It also dovetailed with earlier generations of scholarship, including action research (for example, by Trist and his colleagues on British coal mines), partly to demonstrate how employee self-activity can represent a dynamic and innovative force for work organizations, though also to illuminate some of the options, obstacles and struggles that confront those who would seriously strive to achieve participation. *Empowerment and Innovation*, in this respect, aimed for an engaged rather than detached form of scholarship that could speak to everyday concerns in a broad range of organizations. It was written with an interest in academic activism, in broad-ranging ideas about progressive change at work, and with a view to reaching and supporting principled practitioners, including actual and prospective managers, as well as colleagues in the research community and students in higher education.

Evidently, general interest in this sort of critical-practical approach to matters of organizing, managing and working remains buoyant, although contextual conditions have sharpened significantly since *Empowerment and Innovation* was first published. The terms on which relevant debates are conducted and practical change projects introduced have also shifted substantially, raising basic concerns about the prospects for meaningful innovation, and even doubts about the lexicon of progressive intervention. *Empowerment* is now a more contentious and problematic appellation, as the first chapter will explain. A quick review of recent developments will confirm that much has changed over the past eight years or so, requiring something other than a second edition or fresh statement of earlier arguments to promote the research-based empowering activism antici-pated in *Empowerment and Innovation*.

Casting a reflective eye over analyses of economic events (Cowan, 2011; Cho and Newhouse, 2011; Vaitilingam, 2011), the financial crises and scandals that triggered and sustained the Great Recession (from 2007 through 2012) exacted a heavy toll on workplace relations and the nature and experience of employment. As private and public sector organ-izations struggled to deal with the deepest slump since the 1930s, large numbers of managers and executives lowered their sights, or at least found an outlet for traditional concerns. The cheapening, controlling and intensifying priorities that dominated twentieth-century management thinking, especially during recessionary periods, blatantly and unapolo-getically influenced restructuring and modernizing strategies across the globe. More innovative, progressive and participative responses were difficult to detect, denting the expectation in some policy-making arenas that economic shock would force organizational transformations and deliver socially responsible management behaviour (European Commis-sion, 2010, 2011).

Of course, there were some fresh examples of participative working, perhaps most obviously at Audi, with the production arrangements introduced at Neckarsulm, Germany, for the R8 sports car. These offered a variation on group technology, reminiscent of the dock assembly approach to manufacturing applied at Volvo's Kalmar factory in the 1970s (Audi, 2007a, b; see also Chapter 2). Emerging cars move through a series of interconnected production cells, where highly skilled work teams complete distinctive elements of the final product on relatively long task cycles. Employee reports seem to indicate that this work is challenging yet rewarding, providing genuine opportunities for discre-tionary effort, skill development and job satisfaction while exceeding the quality and flexibility outcomes of traditional job structures, a view endorsed by Neckarsulm managers and engineers (Audi, 2007b).

Such positive judgements about work and employment have been scare since the Great Recession, with darker views of modernizing strategies and practices offered by large populations of workers across a broad range of organizations and countries. A disempowering logic has influenced reactions to economic and financial difficulties in some of the most prominent employers around the world.

At one level, participative work arrangements and empowerment schemes, some of them celebrated for their effectiveness and presented as models for future competitive advantage just a few years prior to the Great Recession, were terminated. A notable example of this occurred in the United States, where two cellular production facilities operated by the kitchen appliance manufacturer, Maytag, one in Newton, Iowa, the other in Jackson, Tennessee, were closed. Through 2001, empowered work groups in these factories were heralded for their ability to respond rapidly and efficiently to fluctuating demand in key markets, particularly those for high-quality products that were considered to be strategically important for continuing sales in a globally competitive industry (*The Economist*, 2001). After competitor, Whirlpool, acquired Maytag in 2006, this assessment was rejected. The Newton plant was closed towards the end of 2007, followed by the Jackson factory in August 2009. Whirlpool executives regularly insisted that these were high-cost facilities, and were not economically viable given falling profits and global recession. Selected Maytag products were redesigned to be built on Whirlpool machine chassis at lower wage, non-union factories in Ohio and Mexico (Uchitelle, 2007; Hewett, 2008).

These developments are far from novel, of course, and do not signal the failure of participative forms of organization and management. As Swedish research on the closure of Volvo's group technology plants at Kalmar and Uddevalla during the early 1990s demonstrates, competing management ideologies and organizational power politics can have a greater bearing upon events of this nature than economic processes or the determination of the marketplace (a full account is provided in Chapter 2). Evidence about commercial gains and social benefits that genuinely flow from participative working can be lost or downplayed in struggles between controlling and empowering values and inclinations, as in the Volvo case where company performance figures actually favoured the plants that were closed (Sandberg, 1993, 1995). Nonetheless, executives and managers who were committed to participative working lost out in a power struggle with traditionalists at Gothenburg, who had their own position bolstered as a result of company merger and partnership ties at that time. These opponents of group technology issued statements about the relative inefficiency of the Kalmar and Uddevalla factories, presenting essentially the same justification as the Whirlpool executives (and numerous others) some 16 years later, although in this instance their public relations announcements actually contradicted company figures released shortly before the closures were announced (Sandberg, 1993). Executive claims to authoritative comment are undermined by this episode, which demonstrates that the course of organizational change is mediated by political processes rather than set by markets and economics.

The political clash between competing management values and practical impulses remains important for modernization, and can be detected in some of the most ambitious projects of recent times, though with the cheapening, controlling and intensifying logic of twentieth-century orthodoxy exerting greater influence. The UK Royal Mail provides a good example. With severe constraints on public finances in the aftermath of the Great Recession, Royal Mail executives were pressurized by various government ministers to accelerate long-running change programmes and deliver fundamental improvements in the efficiency and responsiveness of their letters operation (Hooper, 2010; Beirne, 2011). Poor industrial relations had marred previous initiatives dating back to the 1990s, as executive overtures to union partnership agreements and direct employee involvement in the search for greater efficiencies were undercut by recurring attempts to force change through the mechanization and automation of sorting processes, alteration of delivery patterns and rationalization of the distribution network (Noon et al., 2000; Gall, 2005). Despite expressed commitments on the part of key executives to create better jobs and ensure co-operative decision-making, feelings of insecurity and work intensification fostered distrust and collective resistance, including strike action that frustrated, and occasionally thwarted, management plans (Beale, 2003; Gall, 2003).

The executive agenda for modernization following the Great Recession continued to express these schizophrenic tendencies, prioritizing both a 'leaner' letters business and a culture of commitment, cooperation and consensual industrial relations. The view from the top suggested that these were complementary elements of an integrated plan, first stabilizing the business with an efficient platform of work technologies and rationalized jobs, then establishing a constructive partnership with workers and trade unions (Hooper, 2010). In practice, however, unilateral and forceful management action towards the former rendered the latter problematic. Postal workers, and indeed some managers – especially those in support functions – raised questions about the direction and impact of change, highlighting personal pressures that sat uneasily with executive claims about 'pulling together to sustain the business' (Beirne, 2011). Against a background of Mail Centre closures, job losses and heavier workloads through 2009, feelings of stress and vulnerability accentuated divisions between executives and others, and soured employee relations (BBC,

2009; Channel 4, 2010). For those at the sharp end of Royal Mail modernization, regular references to participation and partnership by members of the senior management group amounted to empty rhetoric or little more than a gloss on heavy-handed rationalization.

Again, the Royal Mail case is not unusual. Top-driven change programmes are often torn between rationalistic and participative tendencies (Vallas, 2003a, b; Vidal, 2007), although this is not invariably the case. Employee experiences with restructuring in other major organizations have no gloss at all.

More basic efficiency drives were also evident through the Great Recession, especially with off-shoring and social dumping, terms which cover the flight of capital to areas or countries where labour costs are low and the social responsibilities on employers are considered to be attractively light or unobtrusive. This approach informed the Maytag closures, noted earlier, and subsequent relocation of Whirlpool production from Indiana to another non-union site in Mexico during 2012 (Greenhouse, 2010). China has also been a popular destination, attracting arguably the highest levels of investment in off-shoring and outsourcing in recent decades, with numerous multinational corporations creating their own facilities or establishing extensive sub-contracting networks.

Controversy has often surrounded the employment and labour control policies associated with these off-shoring and outsourcing decisions, certainly in Scotland where the much-discussed relocation of IBM manufacturing from Greenock to factories in Eastern Europe through the turn of the millennium was linked to a shift away from attractive jobs with generous benefits to much weaker terms and conditions (*The Greenock Telegraph*, 2006). In 2010, a series of well-publicized strikes at Honda and Toyota production plants in Foshan, Zhongshan and Tianjin (Jacobs, 2010), together with 11 distressing suicides at the Shenzhen electronics factory operated by Taiwanese firm Foxconn Technology (BBC, 2010; Barboza, 2010; Hurd, 2012), highlighted similar concerns about employment opportunities and the quality of working life in China. Insights into the everyday pressures of high-intensity, low-cost manufacturing, together with employee reactions to long hours, low pay and monotony – including absenteeism and turnover as well as collective resistance – added impetus to long-running political debates about the wider consequences of exploitative and abusive workplace relations. Particular attention was given to the impact on well-qualified younger workers who cover a high proportion of these poor quality jobs, in the West as well as the East, in services and manufacturing, in Apple retail outlets in the United States and in the Chinese Foxconn factory that manufactures their products, for example (Keep and Mayhew, 2010; Cho and Newhouse, 2011; Segal, 2012).

Against this background, with rationalizing, cheapening and intensifying tendencies so prominent in the aftermath of the Great Recession, it would be naïve and insensitive to associate organizational change with meaningful and substantial employee empowerment. Prescriptive writers, management consultants and futurologists have not been deterred, however.

The guidance literature on empowerment remains highly optimistic, presenting it as a viable alternative to hierarchy and the only way of cultivating the key qualities – including front-line flexibility and responsiveness – needed to thrive in the knowledge economy (Carter, 2009; Fernandez and Moldogaziev, 2011). Some of the cruder versions of this seem oblivious to the effects of recession, ideology and managerial politics, insisting that traditional 'command and control' structures are breaking down and that organizations are reinventing themselves to provide greater freedoms and opportunities for their workers (Owen, 2009). This sort of determined optimism, and facility for assertion and exaggeration, characterized many earlier publications on participation and empowerment (including Slater and Bennis, 1964 and Purser and Cabana, 1998). It has also been challenged effectively and repeatedly by historical and empirical research (perhaps most famously by Ramsay, 1977, 1980). At this juncture, however, it signals a remarkable disconnection from the experiences of people affected by recession, suggesting almost a bunker mentality that shuts out any unpalatable or awkward realities.

Other promotional accounts at least acknowledge the continuing influence of management orthodoxy and, indeed, the role that remote, insular and self-serving leadership played in triggering and perpetuating the financial and economic difficulties of recent years (Cooper, 2011). Arguments for empowerment as a means of recovering from recession have tapped into wider demands for ethical leadership and socially responsible management, suggesting that orthodox policies and practices are out of touch with contemporary pressures and social values (Gadman and Cooper, 2009). From here, rationalistic preoccupations are anachronistic, and the challenge is to persuade practitioners to relinquish them for more conducive, effective and empowering practices. The Great Recession revealed the stranglehold that orthodox assumptions have on management thinking, despite the abundant literature on empowerment and participation. Hence, the call is for evidence-based management that can displace outdated assumptions and demonstrate the positive outcomes and performance advantages that flow from empowering management.

Unfortunately, the studies cited in support of this transformative project tend to be narrowly managerialist in orientation, concentrating on management roles, top-driven change and traditional measures of corporate performance. Cooper (2011), for instance, looks to Kotter and Cohen's (2002) linkage between managed empowerment and successful restructuring, and to Sirota, Mischkind and Meltzer's (2005) account of the stock-market benefits that can be realized if managers engender pride, camaraderie and equity among their employees. There is little in these texts to account for independent employee aims and interpretations, or to anticipate how contrasting and conflicting interests between stakeholders (particularly groups of managers and workers) may affect the course of empowerment initiatives. Instead, a unitary view predominates. Empowerment is reduced to a rational calculation about the most effective means of achieving conventional ends, on the assumption that this will be sufficient to encourage managers, as adaptive economic agents, to change the way they relate to employees.

Studies from the critical end of the management-studies spectrum continue to offer more nuanced insights into the tensions and constraints, challenges and negotiations, that influence work and empowerment in practice, correcting for the narrow agenda of prescriptive managerialism (Edwards and Collinson, 2002; Harley et al., 2005). Greater attention is given to the internal dynamics and realpolitik of empowering and modernizing management, recognizing the potential for slippage and for top-driven schemes to 'snap-back' to rationalism, or degenerate in terms of process and content to what Legge (1978) described as 'conformist innovation' (Spreitzer and Doneson, 2008; Beirne, 2008, 2011).

Organizational responses to the Great Recession have underlined the importance of extending critical research to provide independent insights into the cross-national, intricately networked and highly political nature of corporate modernizing and restructuring activities. Multinational academic ties and collaborative projects are now essential to appreciate how global interdependencies really affect work and employment, and to establish the precise nature and impact of local practices, experiences and reactions in different geographical contexts. With tighter international networks, critical scholars will be better placed to unearth the details of corporate service agreements and commercial alliances, and also to question the business interests and momentum behind prescriptive managerialism.

More extensive relational research on workplaces around the world can be expected to have a significant effect in refocusing public and practitioner attention, shining a spotlight on the everyday realities of modernization, loosening the appeal of mythical and rhetorical images, and substituting actual life experiences for idealized notions of what ought to be happening within work organizations. Unitary frames of reference should be breached to a greater extent, stimulating wider discussions about principled rather than just evidence-based research, provoking interest in what constitutes desirable, feasible, acceptable and appropriate modernization, and making it increasingly difficult for people to take such issues for granted or leave them for incumbent leaders and managers to decide (Alvesson and Willmott, 1992; Collins, 2000).

Initial critical analyses of the Great Recession concentrated on underlying causes, and also employee experiences of sub-contracting and off-shoring, widening the focus from traditional industrialized countries via comparative studies of India and China, for example (O'Reilly et al., 2011). Progress in illuminating some of the key developments – including accumulating evidence about the large-scale rationalization and degradation of managerial as well as employee jobs (Hassard et al., 2009, 2011) – opened other areas for investigation, notably the significance of similarly impoverished work experiences for expressions of discontent among workers and managers (Beirne, 2011). The coping, adapting, resisting and self-empowering activities of the various populations of workers and managers at the sharp end of modernization remain relatively under-researched, however. This is an important area for further investigation, particularly as it relates to applied research and the prospects for developing a principled academic activism that can support authentic (rather than curtailing and controlling attempts at) employee empowerment.

The local knowledge and interventions of front-line staff were central to earlier generations of practically focused scholarship. Theorist-practitioners such as Kurt Lewin (1946), Eric Trist et al. (1963), Philip Selznick (1966), Tom Burns (1967) and Bjorn Gustavsen (1979) developed their academic work from a keen appreciation of employee experiences and propensity to act informally to change working practices and contest the rationalizing tendencies of management orthodoxy. Recognizing that pressures and options for organizational innovation emerge at different levels, and that attainable improvements need to connect with employee insights and aspirations, these researchers aligned themselves with 'natural work groups' (Fincham, 1989) rather than favour links to executive or management teams. They were not addressing problems that were narrowly defined by managers or shareholders. Instead, they channelled their scholarship towards practical activities that offered some potential to improve that situation of the wider population within work organizations, and they pursued this 'greater good' by aligning social science with the activism of employees themselves (to a greater or lesser extent), locating and supporting grassroots changes that often emerged out of difficult or oppressive work situations.

The early research conducted by Trist and his colleagues on innovative forms of job design and group working in the British coal mines perhaps offers the clearest example of this logic of empowering academic practice (Trist et al., 1963). The 'composite coal-getting teams' that are famously associated with this fieldwork relied on changes pioneered by miners themselves, in opposition to managerial and engineering decisions, although this is often neglected in textbook discussions that reduce the project to a top-down, outside-in, consultancy exercise. Nonetheless, workers were primary collaborators in applied research that was decentralized and negotiated rather than subject to external 'expert' determination. Gustavsen subsequently expressed the underpinning logic of this empowering academic activism: The 'liberation of work must be done by the workers themselves. The role of social research is to act as support and resource in such a process' (1979, p. 349).

I have argued elsewhere (Beirne, 2008) that critical research has lost some of the radicalism and concern for practical activism that is evident in this classical scholarship, becoming more detached and coldly evaluative. *Empowerment and Innovation* offered some initial thoughts about the reasons for this, and reflections about the implications, arguing for a fresh appreciation of earlier priorities and more developed forms of critical academic practice. Despite some journal and policy discussion (Payne, 2010, 2011, 2012; Willmott, 2012), very little has changed on this front, which is why the Foreword to *Empowerment and Innovation* is reproduced below. The arguments remain pertinent, although some of the obstacles to re-balancing scholarship along these lines now seem more difficult to overcome.

Academic work has also been affected by rationalistic impulses and far-reaching managerialism in recent years, certainly in Britain. This has contributed to a narrowing of scholarship and the cultivation of what Mingers and Willmott (2010) call an academic monoculture that stifles diversity and originality and discourages younger researchers in particular from looking beyond analysis and explanation to address practical matters of innovating or changing work organizations. The roots of this lie in the funding arrangements for British universities and the effect of financial and commercial priorities on senior management efforts to influence research ratings and grant income.

Research assessment exercises that affect the distribution of public funds to universities have increasingly privileged publication in particular sets of academic journals, prioritizing specific editorial policies and discounting other forms of output, including books, research mono-graphs, conference presentations and practitioner workshops, for example. Journal ranking lists, impact factors and citation-based metrics are used to calibrate academic work, and these have been tied to incentive structures, targets and annual appraisal schemes as institutions resort to managerialism and attempt to control output, intensify working and increase productivity (Willmott, 1998).

Ironically, as research assessment processes have developed an 'impact' category that supposedly recognizes contributions to practitioner communities and work organizations beyond academe, the priority accorded to journal lists and attendant managerialism at an institutional level has actually discouraged wider engagement and research-based practice. The achievements of researchers are gauged by the approval of peer reviewers who judge their journal submissions according to aca-demic values and the genre of scholarship perpetuated by the most highly ranked, 'elite' journals (Mingers and Willmott, 2010). This is com-pounded by the metrics and managerialism, which encourage 'the game to be played' with work on familiar topics, in established disciplinary silos, with conventional theories and accepted methodologies (Adler and Harzing, 2009).

Initial reports about the human impact of these rationalizing, intensify-ing and controlling processes in higher education correspond closely with studies of similar developments in other sectors, highlighting feelings of vulnerability, growing stress and slipping morale within academic com-munities (Barry et al., 2001). Researchers are expressing a sense of disempowerment, with fracture lines emerging between vice principals and a broad range of academics, from lecturers to professors (Morgan, 2012). There are also signs that 'bothered' academics are resisting, adapting and articulating more open and enriching notions of scholarship. In an early study of reactions to managerialism in the university sector, Barry et al. (2001) discovered that subject leaders and research co-ordinators who considered that university executives were behaving in an unpalatable or disingenuous fashion were intervening to moderate the 'harsher effects' of directed change as it moved down the hierarchy (p. 98). On an independent basis, they were acting to promote more collegiate managerial behaviour and sustain their alternative view of what scholarship involves.

These similarities in experiencing and also reacting to top-driven change will hopefully encourage increasing numbers of critical research-ers to look beyond their own immediate employment and relate to like-minded practitioners (managers and workers) as potential collabora-tors in empowering projects, rather than just survey respondents or interviewees. The ability of critical researchers to identify with the people they study in terms of predicament and reaction, from a shared sense of life at the sharp end of managerialism, may help to rekindle something of the spirit and activism of the classical scholarship noted above.

Of course, there are risks in this as well. Personal and professional dilemmas are attached to empowering projects, and these range beyond the issues and concerns that exercised academics in the past. Employment considerations and institutional affiliation have a greater bearing upon academic decisions, since attempts to breach the restrictions posed by approved journal output cut against the grain of university managerialism. Anxieties about academic freedom and independence from financial and commercial pressures previously centred on relations with external organizations and the dangers of dealing with managers who expect applied research to be congenial, useful on their own terms rather than challenging vested interests or established practices (Brown, 1967; Eldridge, 1981). Academics are now more likely to confront conservative influences and challenges to research orientations within their own employing organizations. Establishing a safe environment for practically focused empowering projects therefore involves more than negotiating access agreements and collaborative arrangements that maintain the integrity of applied research in host organizations (Beirne, 2008). It probably means claiming and defending space for academic activism in personal appraisal interviews and annual 'development' plans as well.

Whether all of this stimulates interest and nurtures an empowering activism among like-minded critical researchers, workers and managers or has an inhibiting effect is open to question. However, the logic that moved classical scholars such as Lewin and Burns remains compelling. It seems impossible to understand contemporary work organizations and their modernizing strategies without trying to change them. This book aims to promote the broader sense of purpose and practical agenda that characterized classical critical scholarship, and to encourage emerging and established critics of management and organization, whether in education or employment, to find new and effective ways of increasing the congruence between empowering values and work experiences. It remains positive about the scope for 'making a difference', and confident that sufficient enthusiasm exists among people in a large number of organizations who are in a position, and have the determination, to become activists for change.

The chapters that follow combine a sober assessment of constraints and difficulties with a measured sense of space for action and progressive intervention. Following the same logic and structure as *Empowerment and Innovation*, critical research is linked to three levels of practical engagement over the course of the presentation. The first concentrates on critical thinking and reflecting, marshalling empirical research on the difficulties and constraints bearing upon empowerment to sharpen insights into the problematics of progressive practice, and nurture confidence and resilience among those inclined towards practical action. The second shifts the focus from thinking to doing, identifying options, possibilities and patterns of potentially viable intervention, especially from post-mortem studies of pioneering workplace initiatives and also community arts projects that support self-empowering activities among disadvantaged groups in the wider society. This dimension is explored in the second section of the book, along with the final aspect of critical practice, which relates to public policy and the shaping of the regulatory frameworks relating to work and management at the level of the state and the European Union.

Foreword to *Empowerment and Innovation*

This book aims to engage the interest of two constituencies. In career terms, the first operates at the sharp end of management and organization, in the practical world of affairs. This is an audience of prospective and practising managers, or, more specifically, people within this category who are favourably disposed towards employee empowerment, who articulate at least some commitment to the value of grassroots decision-taking, and who would do something positive to enact direct participation within their own situations. Although they represent the traditional target market for consultants and suppliers of prescriptive advice, these tend to be people who, through experience or involvement in management education, remain uneasy about the quality of the material that speaks directly to their concerns. Many of the readers in this category will, I'm sure, have encountered trite and unhelpful pronouncements and opportunistic interventions that draw a veil over the problems and issues that affect their practice. Some will have been disappointed or frustrated by 'how-to-do-it' techniques that are poorly grounded in the realities and dilemmas of organizational life. Collectively, this population is looking for more telling and potent management knowledge that can help them to make a difference in their working lives.

The people in our second constituency, namely critical social scientists and management commentators, provide the intellectual weight to support these everyday concerns, reinforcing the sense of inadequacy with prescriptive accounts of empowerment and participation. One of the most encouraging features of the past decade or so has been the dramatic expansion of work within the critical tradition of management studies that challenges the simplistic images and ideas traded in this area. As we shall see, social researchers are highly critical of a whole range of supposedly empowering initiatives, highlighting a contrast between rhetoric and substance, presenting rich empirical studies and offering a detailed analysis of contextualizing influences and constraints. The net result is a much stronger research base from which to explore the practical possibilities for empowerment. Yet this material is rarely

xix

absorbed into practitioner debates or followed through to agenda discussions that might assist front-line enthusiasts. Indeed, the findings of critical research regularly miss a practitioner audience, a situation that is largely attributable to the propensity of the research community to remain aloof.

Too many critical commentators unfortunately adopt an abstentionist position on practice, cutting their analyses short, stopping with the empirical results of their investigations, or demolishing guru prescriptions without considering the practical, organizational implications of their conclusions. Their work is loaded towards the early stages of what might usefully be called the full cycle of research. The major preoccupations, and indeed achievements, have been analytical and empirical, advancing our conceptual understanding of empowerment. Yet the momentum tends to stop at this point. The focus is almost exclusively on analysis and explanation, at the expense of following through to an explicit logic of practice. This dimension is conceded, by default, to consultants and prescriptive commentators who seem more interested or adept at engaging with practitioners, despite the negative reactions they often elicit. Even when attention is given to negative or unpalatable aspects of empowerment, the concern that critical writers demonstrate for staff on the receiving end is rarely matched by applied knowledge that can speak to those in the position, or with the inclination, to do something about it, to those who would become activists for change.

Some social scientists compound the access difficulty for managers by adopting a purist stance in their work, limiting their role to exploring ideas and articulating their sense of what ought to be in an ideal world, rather than addressing thorny issues of development. This is an understandable, if disappointing, position when so many research studies legitimately give rise to considerable pessimism about the obstacles to progress. For others, however, the flight from practical thinking is defensive and career-minded, rather than utopian.

Following the full research cycle from theoretical and investigative work to a consistent logic of practice is certainly fraught with difficulties. Generations of social scientists have issued warnings about the dangers of dual role compromises and the perils of dealing with practitioners. Eldridge (1981) provides a notable example with the call for researchers who would be relevant to beware. The gist of his argument is, quite rightly, that the challenge of being relevant often has strings attached. Recipients usually expect relevant research to be congenial rather than critical, useful on their own terms, otherwise it becomes unacceptable or threatening. This raises the spectre of conservatism that has long haunted the human relations tradition of management research, and which critical writers are determined to avoid. Hence, there are justifiable worries about 'managerialising the debate' (Thompson, 1986), or somehow encouraging the misappropriation of critical knowledge by enthusiasts for authoritarianism and tight labour control (Nord and Jermier, 1992).

Of course, the dangers of slippage from, or misappropriation of, progressive ideas are very real. However, it seems that there is also a thin line between caution and negativity. It can be easier and safer for critical commentators to rail against the prescriptive pronouncement of gurus and consultants, and to underscore the limited or tentative results of empowerment schemes, than extend their work to the challenge of managing and realizing change. Unhappily, social scientists can risk their research credentials in the realm of practice and open themselves to the charge of becoming ideologically unsound, possibilities that offer a powerful disincentive to applied work.

This is where we find the less excusable and debilitating side of critical management studies. Some contributions seem to equate the critical approach with an anti-management position, or at least their style can generate that perception among management readers. A deeply ingrained sense of 'them and us' feeds an oppositional stance in at least part of the critical literature, which aligns itself unambiguously with employee interests while presenting managers as the unquestioning and unitary agents of workplace misery. Mandel (1973) provides an obvious example, rejecting any link between contemporary management and progressive practice. His is not an abstentionist but a rejectionist position, saddling managers with an essential interest in labour control and dismissing empowerment as a means of concealing potential disagreements with staff.

Others produce negative assessments without such a rigidly servile image of managers. Hales (2000) provides a recent example, giving the impression, intentional or otherwise, that particular categories of middle and junior managers are against empowerment, or play calculating games with it to defend their own status and personal interests. This is theoretically positive insofar as it acknowledges the scope for managerial agency and choice, yet by reducing this to career politics and financial interests it reinforces the narrow, calculating and unhelpful image of management that survives within critical social research.

We are now at a point in history when people from a wide range of backgrounds, and with all sorts of personal values and beliefs, are employed under one management label or another. Some will have good reason to be worried about their jobs and to think defensively about their reactions to empowerment, especially where employers connect it with de-layering and downsizing policies. Yet management behaviour is not reducible to self-interest alone. For this category of humanity, as for any other, thoughts about personal advantage or disadvantage are cross cut by ethical considerations and various social values.

Contrary to the sentiments expressed by some critical writers, there are practising and aspiring managers who baulk at the traditions of tight labour control within modern organizations. There are managers who identify with critical writings and articulate a genuine concern for principles of fairness, justice and direct participation. Certainly, there are students in management education that would benefit from research that can lead to firmer views about how they can 'make a difference', how they can enact serious concerns and remain faithful to expressed values as they seek a living in management positions. More experienced hands can also be expected to benefit, empirical research indicating that personal concepts of self, integrity and morality continue to burn in managers throughout their careers, often adding a sense of struggle and dissatisfaction as they deal with everyday pressures and heartfelt contradictions (Watson, 1994).

Even if the suspicion remains that empowerment is somehow compromised or loaded towards employer interests, critical commentators could be more sensitive to the predicament of front-line managers who share a positive outlook. There could be more of an effort to acknowledge variability in the underlying values that move practitioners, and to relate this to a sense of management activism that might sustain progressive inclinations. This would enable the research community to reach beyond traditional debates and client groups, giving researchers the opportunity to apply their knowledge of organizational dilemmas and constraints, and to anticipate alternative possibilities, rather than occasionally wringing their hands about problems and poor experiences.

Initial pointers towards an applied research agenda have already been provided, albeit rather tentatively, by critical researchers who have taken employment in business school environments, and find that the issue has been forced for them as teachers of managers, especially on MBA and related programmes. Collins (2000) and Goulding and Currie (2000) provide examples of work that aims to package critical thinking and empirical research for a wider audience in management education, and to cultivate a more analytical and reflective practice. Using the phraseology adopted by Collins, this is 'critical-practical' in the sense of engaging with actors who may be committed to empowerment (Collins, 2000, p. 247) yet susceptible to technician thinking and the ill-conceived prescriptions of gurus and consultants.

As part of a broader attempt to inculcate the habits of critical scrutiny and promote active reflection, this line of development can be extremely useful, encouraging managers to 'stand back' from everyday pressures and question their attitudes, resources, activities and associations. However, it amounts to a partial and underdeveloped tendency, falling short of the effort needed to complete the full cycle of research.

In fact, some of the critical material that has emerged on reflective practice is disappointing, failing to match expressed aims with substantive content, and offering little more than a new spin on the old argument that 'there is nothing so practical as a good theory'. This is surely an accurate dictum when theoretical knowledge prompts an informed understanding of issues and an ability to interpret the problematics of empowerment, rendering practitioners less vulnerable to the toolkit views of consultants and the packaged accompaniments to passive management education. Yet the emphasis is still on a prior stage to action. What the researchers are aiming to provide is a sensitizing experience, equipping people with a greater ability to think and to play their own part in organizations as their awareness of conditions and constraints develops. The participants are then left to their own devices, to make their own sense of critical research and, more importantly, to find their own way of translating critical capabilities into a consistent practice. This is a truncated form of critical management studies.

Encouraging managers to reflect upon the principles and implications of their engagement with employees is only part of what is involved in pursuing the full cycle of critical research. Anticipating new possibilities and enlarging the collective stock of knowledge about alternative options is a neglected part of the agenda. Some of the most influential social scientists of the past half century, including Tom Burns (1967), C. Wright Mills (1973) and Richard Brown (1984), have argued along similar lines, that questioning, theorising and reflecting should be positively linked to the search for better ways of organizing and managing:

> Thus it seems to me that an essential part of our task is to question and to investigate alternatives – activities which may often be combined … few, if any, of us who try to find out and understand what work is like in our society will feel that there is no room for improvement; and exploring the conditions which make possible situations as they are is also, at least implicitly, to begin to establish how they might be different. (Brown, 1984, p. 317)

> The purpose of sociology is to achieve an understanding of social behaviour and social institutions which is different from that current among the people through whose conduct institutions exist, an understanding which is not merely different but new and better. The practice of sociology is criticism … It is the business of sociologists to conduct a critical debate with the public about its equipment of social institutions. (Burns, 1967, p. 366–7)

For these figures, it is a matter of professional responsibility that critical commentators enact the full research cycle and 'follow through' on the practicalities of progressive management. This means ranging beyond theoretical conventions, the rules of evidence and sensitive reflection, in this case relating critical reviews of empowerment to envisaging and programme building activities that have practical merit.

This book makes a deliberate attempt to apply critical research to the problematic of enacting and sustaining direct participation, and to the challenge of addressing managers who would give practical meaning to the concept of employee empowerment. It is written polemically, as well as academically, to stimulate creative thinking about the everyday meaning of principled and reflective management, and the prospects for channelling research on the 'working out' of participation schemes into applied knowledge that can inform a progressive practice in the 'here and now'. This is an attempt to frame possibilities for innovative management without slipping to unrealistic or utopian assumptions.

There is a significant degree of correspondence between this approach and transformative projects in engineering and computing innovation, where critiques of orthodox prescriptions and standard ways of organizing and managing development work have paved the way to innovative possibilities and very practical alternatives. Theorist-practitioners such as Cooley (1980) and Rosenbrock (1990), and computing scientists in the participatory design community (Greenbaum and Kyng, 1991), have made a point of 'getting their hands dirty', of contemplating, devising, enacting, testing and evaluating new possibilities. Echoing the sentiments of Burns and Brown, they conceive of their role as not merely adding to the stock of available knowledge, but as challenging conventional ideas and finding ways to increase the congruence between empowering values and everyday job performance.

Drawing inspiration from this material, as well as telling episodes from empowerment initiatives in other contexts, critical research will be connected to three levels of practical engagement. The first concentrates on the linkage to scrutinizing, thinking and reflecting, building upon the emerging tendency to cultivate analytical and interpretive capabilities through critical management studies. However, it will add focus and specificity to established images of 'critical-practical' knowledge (Collins, 2000) by mapping essential characteristics and qualities that can enhance reflective thinking about empowerment. These will be summarized in the penultimate chapter, although from the earliest stages empirical research will be harnessed to flag some of the issues, difficulties and dilemmas bearing upon practical initiatives, so that enthusiasts are better equipped to apply judgemental and interpretive abilities in favour of empowerment in their own settings.

Shifting the emphasis from thinking to doing, the second level of practice considers engaging and enacting activities, recalling Pateman's (1970) attention to participatory competence and the learned capacity to overcome obstacles and inhibitions. Recognizing the managerial challenge of aligning principles and ambitions with situated learning and sustainable collaboration, down to earth guidance about what helps and hinders will be drawn from the case material assembled through the early chapters, and by introducing insights from research on community theatre. The latter is instructive because community theatre practitioners are also de facto managers. Their role is to help members of the public to engage in the creative process of producing involving drama or delivering theatre that connects with local issues and speaks to local concerns. This means co-ordinating and enabling participants from a wide range of situations and predicaments (including young offenders, retired people, disabled and handicapped groups and residents of housing estates, among many others) to reach their full potential and express their views in a telling and effective manner. The precariousness of empowerment can be very obvious in this context, hence practitioners tend to have a heightened sense of the intimacy between sensitive reflection and management activism. Their experience in moving between these dimensions, together with their accumulated knowledge of creative possibilities for engagement, have much wider applicability, bringing options for negotiating progress and sustaining empowerment more sharply into focus.

Finally, attention turns to public policy and questions about the regulatory framework within which voluntary commitments to empowerment are articulated. State and supra-state initiatives will be evaluated in terms of their enabling or constraining effects on local attempts to enact empowerment. The effectiveness of the relevant social provisions of the European Union will be a prominent consideration, though in pursuing the full cycle of research the analysis will extend into the developmental aspects of building and refining framework initiatives that are conducive to progressive management at the grassroots.

Acknowledgements

The arguments presented in this book have been with me for some years now, and have been rehearsed at various workshops and conferences, in classrooms with students, and also informally, in cafe and bar room 'sessions' with friends and colleagues. So many people have influenced my thinking and offered encouragement to complete the book that I am unable to list them, or thank them all as I would like.

Many of the students on my honours, MSc and MBA classes at the University of Glasgow were kind enough to share their critical reactions to an earlier publication, *Empowerment and Innovation*. This, together with the enthusiasm and quality of our classroom debates, helped me to sharpen the presentation and, hopefully, render my explanations and arguments more accessible with this contribution.

Special thanks go to my colleague, Fiona Wilson, who reviewed parts of the manuscript and offered extremely helpful and candid feedback. Fiona is always available for a chat and to talk through ideas. We've shared both serious and humorous moments discussing the direction of academic research and employment, and these have been invaluable for 'keeping the faith'.

My interest in academic activism and conviction that critical research should have more to say to critical practitioners, to workers and managers at the sharp end of modernization, is rooted in friendships and community ties that date back many years. My life beyond university employment keeps my work grounded and sensitive to the situation of those around me. I am extremely grateful to our 'close circle' for their friendship and the insights and experiences they share.

During recent years, my research links to practitioner communities have widened via workshops and development meetings across Scotland and parts of Ireland with managers, workers and trade unionists in engineering, the arts, health care, design and distribution. Working with this network to review modernizing projects, and anticipate, negotiate and hear reactions to empowering interventions, has influenced my thinking and writing enormously, and I would offer my sincere thanks to all concerned.

Finally, I would like to acknowledge the patience, tolerance and support of my family, Heather, Sean and Leigh. Thankfully, they introduced a keen sense of perspective whenever the writing of this book threatened to disrupt their lives. Leigh and Heather also spent many hours reading and checking the manuscript, highlighting areas that required attention, and translating my often cryptic and colourful language into more accessible phraseology.

Martin Beirne
December 2012

1. Perspectives on empowerment and progressive change at work

Employee empowerment is one of the most widely touted and potentially potent concepts in modern management. Some writers have suggested that the 1990s marked the beginning of an empowerment era (Gandz, 1990; Hardy and Leiba-O'Sullivan, 1998; Appelbaum et al., 1999). The inference here is that a substantial proportion of management practitioners, as well as consultants and prescriptive 'how-to-do-management' commentators, now appreciate the value of 'humanizing organizations' (Notter and Grant, 2011) so that employees have more of an independent influence on job-related activities and a greater say in decision-making processes that affect the nature and impact of their employment (Littrell, 2007; Wooddell, 2009; Fernandez and Moldogaziev, 2011). The achievements of empowering managers and liberated employees have certainly been much-discussed over the past two decades, occupying a large promotional literature (Tracy, 1990; Foy, 1994; Caudron, 1995; Ward, 1996; Blanchard et al., 1999; Fracaro, 2006) and becoming part of the staple diet of management development courses and business school leadership programmes. Empowering staff is often presented as a 'key management competence', and a reliable means of achieving commercial success in the turbulent global markets that characterize the early twenty-first century (Carter, 2009; Men, 2011).

The business case for empowerment relies upon the actual or potential responsiveness and innovativeness of front-line employees, who are ostensibly capable of far greater and more lucrative contributions to organizational performance than established 'command and control' styles of management are able to release (Fracaro, 2006). Enthusiasts typically present a critique of directive and hierarchical approaches to controlling employees and limiting their discretion, arguing that these are anachronistic in fast-moving and complex competitive environments (Foy, 1994; Khan, 1997; Roth, 1997; Notter and Grant, 2011). The competitive challenges of thriving in global markets and harnessing rapidly changing technologies ostensibly put a premium on responsiveness, flexibility and imagination throughout organizations, qualities that are stifled rather than cultivated by rigid job structures and a regimented

1

demarcation of tasks and responsibilities. From here, empowerment is a matter of harnessing employee energy and expertise, of acknowledging the potential in untapped human resources, and the folly of restricting access to these by following outmoded practices in a changing world.

A great deal of attention has been given to psychological empowerment, and to cognitive processes that link employee experiences and perceptions about their work situation with expressed commitment and expended effort (Thomas and Velthouse, 1990; Appelbaum et al., 1999; Spreitzer and Doneson, 2008; Kazlauskaite et al., 2012). The consensus among researchers in this area is that employees who *feel* empowered, who believe that there is genuine scope for them to apply judgement and discretion in their work, have higher levels of intrinsic motivation and a more developed capacity for concentration and resilience than would otherwise be the case (Spreitzer, 1995; Spreitzer and Doneson, 2008). In short, employees with a positive sense of empowerment can be expected to work harder.

Promoting 'smarter working' with structural empowerment is also part of the business case, however. The emphasis here is on delegated authority and the adjustment of job structures and hierarchical relations so that employees have the flexibility and resources to act on their own initiative. The underpinning logic is that employees have more detailed insights into the nature of their work than supervisors and managers, and are often better placed to recognize weaknesses, rectify problems and identify opportunities (Fracaro, 2006). Experienced front-line workers are in a prime position to appreciate the intricacies of client relations, for example, and to 'surprise-and-delight customers' (Spreitzer and Doneson, 2008) with rapid responses to particular needs and the prompt correction of service failures if they have discretion to act on their own cognisance, rather than wait for supervisory intervention (Fernandez and Moldogaziev, 2011).

The local insight that workers acquire about their jobs, the tacit knowledge and accumulated experience that is routinely brought to the challenges of keeping equipment running, parts flowing and production moving, is also considered to be a wellspring of novel ideas, a stimulus to innovation and a cost-effective means of enhancing product and process development (Carter, 2009; Morrell and Wilkinson, 2002; Wooddell, 2009). For enthusiasts, empowerment offers a route to knowledge and to levels of co-operative, responsive and innovative behaviour that cannot be accessed by issuing orders or releasing management directives. It triggers voluntary contributions that take employees beyond job requirements to higher and more lucrative levels of performance.

With global economic pressures and intense competition in the markets for most goods and commercial services through the turn of the millennium, this view attracted considerable interest (Huq, 2010; Harris et al., 2011). The forces that delivered the Great Recession (Vaitilingam, 2011), or what some writers have labelled the Great Stagnation (Cowan, 2011), also had an amplifying effect on the business case for empowerment. The banking and broader financial crises that followed the 'subprime' mortgage scandal in the United States from 2007 depressed global demand and restricted business investment in the most sustained and serious economic downturn since the Great Depression of the 1930s (Vaitilingam, 2011). In this context, arguments about the linkage between empowerment and economic growth were highly attractive. There was a notional acceptance of the value of employee resilience in turbulent markets, and wide recognition that any willingness 'to go the extra mile' to serve available customers could help to enhance company reputation and results (Carter, 2009). Workplace innovation also became something of a rallying call for organizational rejuvenation, as tight resources prompted a greater reliance on local insights, initiative and creativity as a source of new opportunities and ways of competing (Harris et al., 2011). During the Great Recession, the business case for empowering workers resonated with the challenges of the time. Calls for more effective management were frequently associated with the liberation of front-line contributions and employee-reliant change.

To judge by the promotional literature, this is a message with universal relevance. It is not simply an approach to crisis management or temporary 'solution of last resort'. The core arguments have been applied to an extensive list of business sectors and organizations, and against contrasting contextual conditions. Empowerment initiatives have now been reported in areas as diverse as construction (Greasley et al., 2005), leisure and hospitality (D'Annunzio-Green and Macandrew, 1999; Hales, 2000; Klidas et al., 2007; Kazlauskaite et al., 2012), manufacturing (Collins, 1999; Vidal, 2007), pharmaceuticals (Collins, 1998), distribution (Cunningham and Hyman, 1999; Beirne, 2011), retailing and financial services (Holden, 1999; Wooddell, 2009). The prescription also transcends national boundaries.

Very little research has actually focused on how different cultures and societies interpret and respond to employee empowerment. However, received wisdom in the promotional press suggests that empowering workers anywhere in the world delivers benefits (Bhatnagar, 2005; Littrell, 2007; Carter, 2009; Men, 2011). The business case for empowering workers to generate improvements in job satisfaction and industrial relations, as well as customer and supplier relationships, has even been applied to some of most rapidly growing economies of recent years, including Brazil, China and India (Bhatnagar, 2005).

Brazil is the home country of Ricardo Semler, one of the most celebrated exponents of empowering management of the last 30 years (Semler, 1989, 1993). His family-owned machinery manufacturing company, Semco, has been applauded for operating with progressive forms of autonomous group working, and for demonstrating the commercial value of self-managing work units to others in South America and beyond (Morrell and Wilkinson, 2002). With reports of labour unrest in China and media investigations into the social and longer-term economic costs of exploitative management practices in the supply chains of major Western corporations (Barboza, 2010), empowerment has attracted attention as a cost-effective way of improving 'internal relationship management' in Chinese production facilities (Men, 2011). Adverse employee reactions to regimented control, narrow and monotonous job structures and low wages at contract manufacturers, such as Foxconn, and at Honda and Toyota parts factories, have raised concerns about delays, disruptions and staff turnover (Jacobs, 2010), enlivening discussions about appropriate management behaviour and conducive conditions for raising performance via greater discretion, autonomy, interest and job satisfaction (Littrell, 2007).

Empowerment has also been a recurring theme in attempts to reform public sector management in countries around the world. Some of the most confident endorsements have been issued in the United States, Australia, France and Britain in connection with projects aimed at reducing the cost and improving the delivery of public services (Wooddell, 2007; Fernandez and Moldogaziev, 2011). In this context, considerable weight is attached to 'cutting red tape' and challenging bureaucratic instincts so that client, rather than provider, interests are prioritized. Empowerment is presented as a means of freeing employees from cumbersome sets of rules and regulations so that they have greater scope to evaluate client needs and changing circumstances, and more of an inclination to behave humanely as they come to recognize that they are themselves treated as thoughtful and considerate people, rather than cogs in expensive bureaucratic machines (Fernandez and Moldogaziev, 2011).

In Britain, this logic has informed empowerment initiatives in the benefits agencies (Foster and Hoggett, 1999), the revenue and customs service (HMRC), and especially the National Health Service (Beirne, 1999; Lewis and Urmston, 2000; Edmonstone, 2000; Kuokkanen and Leino-Kilpi, 2001; Hyde et al., 2005). The Great Recession also added impetus to the empowerment of public sector workers, or at least to political interest in this as a way of raising productivity and securing spending cuts. By 2010 and through 2011, economists and politicians were focusing their attention on the state of the public finances more than stabilizing the banking system, stimulating demand or assisting economic recovery (Vaitilingam, 2011). Concerns about debt default had moved from mortgage holders to governments, especially in the Euro area, prompting austerity budgets and calls for radical thinking about the provision of public services.

Cuts in public sector spending in Britain are scheduled to continue until 2016, though in the absence of any reduction in the demand for services (Vaitilingam, 2011). Against this background, in the public as in the commercial sphere, visions of organizational health and effectiveness have been tied to slimmer and flatter structures, and smarter and more responsive employee contributions. To judge by the expressed interest and the sheer number of practical initiatives that carry the label, empowerment represents an attractive proposition. Enthusiasts assert that the future prosperity of the public as well as the commercial sector hinges on the enabling qualities of empowering managers and resulting commitment of liberated workers. The approach and confidence of those who extol the virtues of empowerment has attracted significant critical reaction, however.

Some commentators find it difficult to detect anything other than glib and fashionable phraseology, suggesting that the term has been so often and easily reproduced in the 'solutions business' and by purveyors of universal models of management that it has been trivialized, and even emptied of any reasonable meaning (Clutterbuck, 1998; Collins, 1998, 2000). Case evidence finds support for this view inside organizations, among groups of workers and managers who consider empowerment to be little more than flowery rhetoric that senior figures apply loosely to all manner of change initiatives in an effort to make them palatable (McCabe, 2000; Edwards and Collinson, 2002; Beirne, 2011). From here, the language of empowerment is faddish, clichéd and off-putting. It has become so common in business presentations, and such a typical ingredient of prescriptive management, that it represents a barrier to progressive change, inhibiting dialogue and frustrating efforts to identify realistic opportunities for improving work situations.

Others find the prescribed nature of the business case, and the emphasis placed on the top-down shaping of employee opportunities for influence, to be distasteful and patronizing (Hardy and Leiba-O'Sullivan, 1998; Lewis and Urmston, 2000). Empowerment is often portrayed in the promotional literature as something that senior managers do for, or to, their workers. Enlightened and benevolent figures in upper management are cast as 'the source of empowerment' (Fracaro, 2006, p. 4), delegating responsibilities down through the hierarchy (Carter, 2009; Fernandez and Moldogaziev, 2011). For critical writers, this misses the point. The meaning of empowerment reaches beyond delegation and permitted or demarcated discretion to independent influence (Edwards and Collinson, 2002; Morrell and Wilkinson, 2002). It signals a challenge to decision-making prerogatives and the privileging of rank and hierarchical approval, suggesting a more equitable distribution of decision-making authority.

These reactions have prompted some recasting of vocabulary and, in Britain, at least a partial displacement of the empowerment rhetoric. Employee engagement has emerged as the phrase of choice for many policy-makers, lobbyists and researchers (Purcell, 2010; ACAS, 2011), becoming a popular alternative to empowerment after it was headlined in the MacLeod Report to the Labour government in 2009 (MacLeod and Clarke, 2009). The underpinning arguments are essentially the same as those rehearsed in the business case for empowerment, that employee insight and cooperation are central to the success of work organizations in turbulent times (Purcell, 2010; Harris et al., 2011). In the foreword and in press releases welcoming the report, then Business Secretary, Lord Mandelson, offered an endorsement that could readily be accepted by business enthusiasts for empowerment: 'only organizations that truly engage and inspire their employees produce world class levels of innovation, productivity and performance' (MacLeod and Clarke, 2009, p. 1). There is an important difference in focus and ambition, however.

The literature on engagement currently conveys a greater concern for employee views and experiences at work, suggesting something more than an instrumental interest in 'leveraging' greater value from local insights and understandings. There are regular references to fair treatment and employee wellbeing and to the importance of establishing a respect agenda that can support improvements in job design and deliver benefits for staff, including a better quality of working life (Macleod and Clarke, 2009, p. 81; Purcell, 2010; ACAS, 2011). A humanist dimension is evident, with emphasis placed on cultivating skills and talent, and then providing an outlet for these with enriching jobs that encourage sustained voluntary contributions. Management inclinations and abilities to move in this direction, or even act seriously to expand employee input and decision-making, are also questioned rather than taken for granted. Indeed, management negativity is identified as a barrier to effective engagement, along with the poverty of enabling skill sets within management communities in Britain (MacLeod and Clarke, 2009, p. 69).

This last point cuts to the core of critical concerns about employee empowerment, and reflects a lingering unease with evident management shaping, constraining and limiting activity. There is an abundance of empirical evidence to show that empowerment is typically a matter of dialogue and verbiage rather than substance (Edwards and Collinson, 2002; Podro, 2011), and that the rhetoric is usually a wrapping for more conventional management thinking about forced or controlled workplace modernization (Harley et al., 2005). Headline references to 'smoke and mirrors' (Morrell and Wilkinson, 2002) and 'the emperor's new clothes' (Argyris, 1998) directly challenge the glowing endorsements in the prescriptive literature, and signal the consensual view among academic researchers that management-initiated empowerment schemes are typically less than truly empowering (Harley, 1999; Lewis and Urmston, 2000; Edwards and Collinson, 2002; Spreitzer and Doneson, 2008).

In practice, management teams frequently connect empowerment to more calculating and technically focused modernizing methodologies such as lean manufacturing, process re-engineering or 'kaizen' quality monitoring, either as a gloss to discourage employee resistance and stimulate cooperation or as a consequence of competing management values and contradictory behaviour (Noon et al., 2000; Vidal, 2007; Beirne, 2011). The results attributed to this, by researchers investigating initiatives in developing as well as stagnating economies (Zhang and Wu, 2004; Littrell, 2007; Men, 2011), include mounting scepticism and a growing recognition that impoverished notions of empowerment are frequently applied in practice.

In light of this evidence, some academics have developed dismissive and rejectionist positions that leave the avoidance stance of the engagement literature looking tame (Kizilos, 1990; Parker, 1993). A prominent stream of critical analysis argues that empowerment has a dark side which reflects narrow management interests in containing or curtailing independent employee decision-making (McKenna, 1990; Hardy and Liba-O'Sulivan, 1998). From here, empowerment is subject to manipulative management tendencies. It involves an inversion of reasonable meaning and an attempt to reinforce standard corporate values of consensual control and hierarchical direction where these may otherwise be challenged or found wanting (Willmott, 1993; Barker, 1993; O'Connor, 1995). Empowering initiatives are considered to have a disempowering effect or intent, encouraging employees to internalize the rhetoric of collective predicament in tough times, and normalizing modest experiences with autonomy so that they become accepting rather than questioning, busy rather than upset about the nature and extent of their contributions:

It is tempting to conclude that many companies are attracted to a fantasy version of empowerment and simultaneously repelled by the reality. How lovely to have energetic, dedicated workers who always seize the initiative (but only when 'appropriate'), who enjoy taking risks (but never risky ones), who volunteer their ideas (but only brilliant ones), who solve problems on their own (but make no mistakes), who aren't afraid to speak their minds (but never ruffle any feathers), who always give their best to the company (but ask no unpleasant questions about what the company is giving back). How nice it would be, in short, to empower workers without actually giving them any power. (Kizilos, 1990, p. 56)

This critical literature provides an important corrective to the benign imagery and the unrestrained optimism of promotional business accounts, indicating that the language of empowerment can be deceptive and that practical initiatives are subject to moulding and manipulating inclinations. Whether actual management activity is so completely or consistently calculating and disempowering is open to question, however. Existing evidence indicates that empowerment schemes are usually short on employee influence and loaded with superficial, insincere and overplayed rhetoric, not that they are inherently negative or that the meanings attached to them are invariably disingenuous.

Vidal (2007) introduces a useful distinction between nominal and substantive empowerment, offering practical examples of wider employee decision-making and increased autonomy, albeit on a modest, temporary or problematic basis. Edwards and Collinson (2002) also acknowledge employee gains in terms of relaxed controls and opportunities to exercise discretion, making similar points about the overall limits on worker autonomy, though adding that these are widely recognized, promoting scepticism and criticism on the part of workers, rather than demonstrating their gullibility. The corollary is that small-scale changes do not in themselves indicate that employees are misled by empowerment, or that management objectives are uniform and outcomes 'fixed'.

Of course, managers connect empowerment to performance considerations and ideas about organizational efficiency and effectiveness. Yet their behaviour is often pragmatic and uncoordinated, rather than dominated by an ideology of labour control. Available evidence about managerial reactions to top-down, executive-driven empowerment programmes reveals a range of variable, sectional and distancing behaviour, much of it attributable to junior- and middle-management fears about the intensification, monitoring or loss of their own jobs as a result of leadership preoccupations with cost-cutting and rationalization (Hales, 2000; Edwards and Collinson, 2002; Hassard et al., 2009; Beirne, 2011). Case research also points to a realm of principled management activity, highlighting value-based interventions by managers who favour empowerment and challenge the calculating approaches of other colleagues, usually at a personal and informal level (Holt, 2006; Barry et al., 2001; Watson and Watson, 1999). Some managers apparently consider manipulative management to be more trouble than it is worth, and so adopt relaxed or responsive attitudes to the progress of empowerment projects (Vidal, 2007). Others find it distasteful or inconsistent with their own sense of what empowering management involves, and so act to moderate the effects of spin and insincerity by demonstrating participative and supportive behaviour (Barry et al., 2001; Beirne, 2011).

Contrasting orientations and reactions to empowerment are also discernible on the employee side. Again, the dual classification of disempowering managers and passive, easily misled workers presented in some critical accounts does not stand up to scrutiny. Favourable, hostile, cynical and indifferent views have all been recorded (McCabe, 2000), with particular populations of workers moving between these different interpretations as empowerment projects develop (Beirne, 2011). Measured expressions of support have collided with instances of opposition and resistance, reflecting competing and contradictory evaluations of particular management initiatives, and this does not exhaust the repertoire of employee behaviour on empowerment. Independent self-empowering interventions have also been identified, on a work group basis (Fincham, 1989) and through collective action in trades unions (Ramsay, 1980; Beirne, 2011), as subsequent sections and chapters will demonstrate.

Contemporary accounts have tended to neglect self-empowering behaviour, although this was central to early thinking about the nature and practical significance of empowerment. Certainly, the roots of the concept are much richer than promotional business material, the engagement literature and dismissive critical views generally acknowledge. Empowerment is not synonymous with the business case for devolved responsibility and employee autonomy, nor reducible to popular ideas about more effective, permissive and less hierarchical management. Some of the earliest references connect it with notions of freedom, human dignity, self-help and self-determination, often positioning these within wider debates about citizenship and democracy (Huq, 2010).

Some authors trace the origins of empowerment to social projects that helped handicapped and disabled people to assert themselves and exert an independent influence on their situations (Heller, 1999, 2003). For others, they derive principally from the civil rights and feminist movements of the 1960s and '70s, and encapsulate the priorities and capabilities of disadvantaged groups pursuing their own interests as they, rather than others, deem appropriate (Fenton-O'Creevy, 1995; Spreitzer and Done-son, 2008). A further community of writers, mainly political commentators and activists, locate empowerment within long-running attempts to strengthen participatory democracy (Blumberg, 1968; Pateman, 1970), basically by targeting popular perceptions about the neglect of grassroots opinion and claiming space for greater citizen involvement as an antidote to indifference and negativity. With persistently high levels of political apathy, low voting patterns and cynicism about politicians and politics in Britain, the United States and elsewhere, this movement has captured significant interest (Bachrach and Botwinick, 1992; Johnson, 2006). Openly acknowledging and formally extending employee influence in the running of work organizations is believed to have wider political import-ance, cultivating social responsibility and harnessing relevant insights and abilities to the development of civil society. From here, employee empowerment is a viable means of enhancing both organizational and political citizenship, ensuring that a richer pool of talent and expertise is applied to charity work, school boards, tribunal systems, trade and consumer associations, and government oversight committees, for example.

These conceptualizations and approaches are distinguished by a strong emphasis on grassroots and bottom-up, rather than top-down or management-driven, empowerment. They prioritize independent thinking and influencing as a basis for constructive dialogue, active participation, mutual decision-taking and coherent collective behaviour, albeit across a diverse range of issues and activities. The focus, however, is on people 'doing things for themselves', forming and expressing their own views and reaching agreements about appropriate and effective ways of work-ing together to achieve valued objectives. This contrasts markedly with the prescriptive business view which urges leaders and managers to acquire empowerment, assign responsibilities, permit creativity, define boundaries of discretionary working, and take ownership of empowering processes (Fracaro, 2006; Tracy, 1990; Foy, 1994). As noted above, contemporary critical accounts rail against approved or official empow-erment schemes that encapsulate these priorities, precisely because they countermand independent influence and curtail grassroots initiative. There are surprisingly few links to the richer traditions of self-empowerment in this reaction, however.

Instead, the avoidance and dismissive positions seem to give up on empowerment. The alternative and rich history forged through social and political activism is set aside as the language and practical shaping of empowerment is conceded to advocates of the business 'model'. Propo-nents of engagement move on to a new vocabulary, while the dismissive tendency deflects attention from interventions and outcomes that flow directly from the efforts of employees. This is unnecessary and unhelpful. As others have argued (notably Morrell and Wilkinson, 2002), there is little to be gained from inventing new terms to replace empowerment, or relinquishing links to alternative traditions that give it historical and practical significance. It is important not to be swayed by unpalatable spin and prescriptive rhetoric or 'to try to exorcise the spirit of something which may improve the employment relationship and employment practice' (Morrell and Wilkinson, 2002, p. 120).

Empowerment is contested, rather than subject to proprietary rights or any dominating prescriptive reconstruction (Cunningham and Hyman, 1999). Despite its current approval rating in the business and management literature, empowerment is not conceptually confined to matters of internal functioning or employee performance. Nor is it restricted to the economics of employment and global competitiveness. Encapsulating democratic interests and concerns for social justice, it has wider significance as symbolic language for progressive management, as a way of encouraging personal growth and autonomy, as socially responsible corporate behaviour and as a route to wider political maturity.

Of course, these concerns reach well beyond the initial preoccupations of management writers, opening controversial issues, including the defence of managerial prerogatives and the legitimacy of collective decision-making on key areas of business activity. Despite the thrust of business-focused endorsements, the essence of what is considered to be empowerment varies significantly, in terms of the aims and ambitions that are attached to the topic and the conceptual underpinnings that produce contrasting evaluations of progress and practice. It is vital to acknowledge this level of complexity, not only to understand the reactions and tensions that can be generated by different pronouncements, but also to pursue a sensitive and consistent view of programmes and initiatives that claim to offer improvements of one sort or another.

CHALLENGING THE OLD ORTHODOXY?

The various meanings and ambitions that are attached to empowerment command attention, and often approval, because they seem to be at odds with the predominant principles of twentieth-century management and industrial organization. Enthusiasts from business and critical perspectives share a basic distaste for management orthodoxy and for traditional organizational structures that ostensibly weigh heavily on people, stifling their energy and enthusiasm and retarding human development, economically, socially or politically. This debilitating legacy is commonly associated with the ideology and apparatus of scientific management and the influence of Fordism in setting the terms on which jobs are usually designed and employee relations typically conducted (Morrell and Wilkinson, 2002; Huq, 2010).

The tendency over the past century has been for managers to take their cues from authoritarian ideas about good practice, operating with the assumption that workers are basically unreliable, troublesome or recalcitrant, requiring close supervision and disciplinary control to ensure any sort of consistent performance. These ideas were legitimized by Frederick Taylor with his pronouncements on scientific management (Taylor, 1911), and subsequently by Henry Ford who gave focus and force to their application with assembly line production methods (Ford and Crowther, 1926). Though originally developed at a time of expanding markets during the late nineteenth and early twentieth centuries, when the reorganization of work on the shop floor was considered to be a priority, the key to expanding output and satisfying demand, Taylorism and Fordism became pillars of orthodoxy, setting parameters for job design and for the conduct of labour relations through subsequent competitive conditions.

For Taylor and Ford, the fundamentals of management and organization turned on the core problem of labour control. This was taken to be the most pressing business challenge of the epoch, and Taylor offered a view that appealed to many of his contemporaries. Workers were deliberately pursuing their own sectional interests, exploiting their crucial knowledge of production processes and engaging in 'systematic soldiering' to inflate wages by restricting output, thereby damaging profitability, especially under conditions of buoyant demand. His solution was to wrest control from the shop floor, to capture essential knowledge from communities of workers and systematically disempower them by separating conception from execution, disconnecting the thinking and 'doing' aspects of work. Management specialists would take over the conceptual dimension, planning and organizing very detailed, non-discretionary and narrowly defined tasks that were to be the sole province of workers, with supervisors and overseers monitoring adherence and enforcing higher rates of productivity.

While Taylor applied his ideas to institutionalize control through tighter job structures in the US steel industry, it was Ford's mechanized regimentation and pacing of task performance that established hierarchical management and anti-employee involvement as mainstream features of organizational life (Wilson and McKinlay, 2010). The assembly line became the engine of mass production as Ford's ideas about the simplification of car making and the replacement of craft workers with cheaper sources of labour were taken up to service mass markets in other areas (Littler, 1985; Noon and Blyton, 1997). Consequently, the distinction between 'them and us', the 'two sides of industry', sharpened as the twentieth century progressed. Empowerment was conceptually reserved for management grades, at the expense of discretionary working on the shop floor and with knowledge that was previously concentrated in the minds of employees.

Despite the dramatic increases in output and productivity under Taylorist and Fordist regimes, and the corresponding distribution of goods and services to a wider population of consumers, there has always been an undercurrent of concern about the dehumanizing impact on staff. The pressures of machine pacing and the difficulties of coping with narrow, tedious and repetitive jobs have taken a serious toll on the health and wellbeing of generations of workers, as numerous reports and humanistic critiques have demonstrated over the years (Sward, 1948; Beynon, 1973; Littler, 1985; Ciulla, 2000). They have also prompted responses and reactions that have been played out against a shifting backdrop of economic conditions, often demonstrating the limitations of tight control systems and adversarial labour relations.

Ford himself discovered that elaborate authoritarian structures can be counterproductive when buoyant labour markets enable people to 'vote with their feet', to find alternative employment and an escape from what they regard as unsatisfactory jobs. From the earliest stages of mass production, Ford and his followers in the car industry and beyond experienced recurring problems with labour turnover, absenteeism and conflict that mirrored the distinctive phases of the business cycle (Ford and Crowther, 1926; Littler, 1985). These often prompted an apparent softening of the regime and the provision of financial and other incentives to retain people in Taylorized jobs, including in Ford's case dramatic wage rises and socialization programmes that aimed to induce a sense of commitment and duty to his company, especially among immigrant workers (Noon and Blyton, 1997).

Periods of high unemployment have typically been associated with the resurgence of authoritarian preoccupations, however, as in the late 1970s and early '80s when recession effectively halted a movement to improve working conditions and reduce labour market problems (Kelly, 1985; Payne and Keep, 2003). Many employers took this opportunity to restore command and control tactics, imposing wage cuts, extending working hours and intensifying job performance with little thought to the consequences for staff (Ciulla, 2000). Against the backdrop of unemployment and amid fears about job loss, they felt able to force through changes that would have been considered unacceptable or costly just a few years earlier.

Looking back on this particular period, many commentators are struck by the arrogance and myopia demonstrated by such employers. Influential management writers, including Tom Peters and Rosabeth Kanter, have pointed to the longer-term costs to companies that attempted to profit from economic coercion (D'Annunzio-Green and Macandrew, 1999). Their approach was not only insensitive; it signalled an insularity and failure to appreciate the changing nature of competition at a time when productivity was becoming less important as a source of business advantage than quality, responsiveness and flexibility. As markets became more turbulent, and manufacturers from the Pacific Rim captured ground from their Western counterparts by offering reliable and attractive products, Taylorized jobs and command structures looked increasingly anachronistic. Souring relations with disaffected workers seemed reckless. These people were central to the challenge of producing viable commodities for difficult markets. Yet the legacy of Taylorism and Fordism was stifling their capacity to care about what they produced or to seek improvements in products and processes by their own initiative. The lesson drawn, and still promulgated through the Great Recession, is that the reversal of orthodoxy is essential to future competitive success (Peters and Waterman, 1982; Kanter, 1984; D'Annunzio-Green and Macandrew, 1999; Fernandez and Moldogaziev, 2011). Employee empowerment rather than disempowerment is the key to business advantage, requiring the rejection of adversarial tendencies and the promotion of more humane and effective alternatives to Taylorism and Fordism.

Judgements about the scale and difficulty of this project differ significantly, however. Some envisage a fundamental break with the past, a paradigm shift from authoritarianism to empowerment as competitive imperatives effectively overturn orthodox instincts and preoccupations (Womack et al., 1990; Kenney and Florida, 1993; Foy 1994). The logic of survival ostensibly forces the issue for employers, requiring them to adjust to the new reality or run their businesses into the sand. Prescriptive writers and consultants often deploy this imagery to justify their own role as enablers, helping managers to make sense of the changing environment, and renounce 'the boss' concept as they coach their employees into more conducive forms of co-operative working (Johnson and Redmond, 1998; Khan, 1997; Carter, 2009).

Though widely rehearsed, this vision imputes an unwarranted degree of rationality to employee empowerment (Edwards and Collinson, 2002). It becomes the inevitable and technical consequence of enlightenment, rather than a highly charged, potentially fraught and problematic process. The rhetoric of imperatives rigidifies the connection between markets and labour management, deflecting attention from intervening factors and portraying managers and workers as ciphers that passively respond to broader economic exchanges.

This was demonstrated to compelling effect on British television in 1995. Some powerful programming that initially set out to exemplify the technical and prescriptive approach and to mobilize support for empowerment, inadvertently exposed the limitations of an over-rationalized view. Enthusiast and facilitator, Sid Joynson, was followed into six organizations by a BBC camera crew that expected to capture exemplary footage of empowering practices that were not only in tune with competitive requirements but capable of inspiring practitioners in other contexts. Instead, in the first episode, they revealed the shock and disbelief of a considerate and well-meaning consultant who was forced to confront some unpalatable and unanticipated realities (O'Reilly, 1995).

After two days of working with shop floor staff at the Ipswich factory of manufacturer Videoprint, Sid listened to their presentations to the management team, fully expecting a positive reaction and a commitment to continue with empowerment in the future. This was the logical consequence of demonstrating the specific benefits that could be realized in this case, or so it was imagined. The workers, for their part, had warmed to the challenge of proposing improvements, overcoming some initial scepticism to clean the workspace, rewrite parts of the training manual to make it accessible to new recruits and boost productivity by cutting the time taken to put inlays into video boxes. Projecting an obvious sense of achievement, Sid and the workers paused to hear the appreciative comments of managers. They were to be disappointed.

The managers took their cues from the director, Brian Bonner, who triggered dramatic changes of mood and body language with his first response, 'I expected more'. Others then rounded on the proposals, announcing, for example, that staff already had a responsibility for cleaning and housekeeping. At this point, it became too much for the consultant to take: 'You've made me look an absolute, complete berk. They told me you would do this and I told them, "No they will not. They will come and support you", and look what you've done ... Can you feel what you're doing to them? Can you feel what you are doing to them?' More intense exchanges followed, peppered with personalized and abusive remarks, and prompting a walk out by most of the workers, who then turned to the cameras to express their anger and disgust at the events inside (BBC, 1995).

This was absorbing television. It departed from expectations and, in the process, exposed the shortcomings of the over-rationalized, technical-prescriptive approach to empowerment (Collins, 2000). While Sid enjoyed a significant measure of success with his employee workshops, he was ill-equipped to deal with problems that very obviously have a bearing upon attempts to change established patterns of management and organization. His sense of the competitive advantages to be gleaned from empowerment blinded him to the potential for conflict that lies within attempts to roll out or cascade exemplary developments. In common with consultant and guru accounts generally, Sid offered a discourse on empowerment that misrepresents the dynamics of employee relations, overstating managerial responsiveness and deflecting attention from the accumulated insights and experiences of working life. With so much of the prescriptive effort devoted to presenting success stories and exemplary snapshots that showcase empowerment as a business solution (Johnson and Redmond, 1998; Peters and Waterman, 1982; Robson, 1988), the messy complexities of workplace behaviour and the problematics of retaining momentum behind practical initiatives are left unattended. Sid's application of the prescriptive approach had simply been subjected to a more immediate and dramatic examination than most.

For social scientists, the Videoprint episode is far from exceptional, the only surprise being that the resulting footage draws such an effective contrast between 'reality television' and the usual demonstration effects of business media. Scholars have argued for some time that the guru movement is theoretically and methodologically weak, and so offers an insubstantial foundation for promotional activities (Burnes, 1998; Collins, 2000). In social-scientific terms, it trades in superficial imagery, without an adequate theoretical and empirically grounded understanding of everyday life in modern organizations, which is ironic given that contributors are usually celebrated for their industry ties and management connections (see Johnson and Redmond, 1998, for example). What it offers is spuriously practical, short on substance and long on exhortation, touching commonsense notions about what management should or may involve, but without conceding the complexity of workplace relations.

As the Videoprint episode demonstrates, empowerment is controversial rather than straightforward, contested and not the inevitable result of enlightenment. Regardless of the benefits that can be ascribed to it, tensions do not dissolve rapidly or automatically. Nor can they be treated as side issues that only inhibit progress in unhealthy organizations. The Videoprint experience cannot be explained away as an unusual or atypical case. Other prescriptive commentators have experienced similar problems with obstructionist behaviour (Ward, 1996) and 'thinly disguised contempt' (Nicholls, 1995), and share Sid's frustration and even propensity to castigate those with the urge to over-control their employees. However, the most telling similarities are to be found in their conceptualization and tendency towards a superficial appreciation of relevant issues. This is usually betrayed by the banality of the 'solution' to hostility or resistance, which typically involves positive reinforcement with staff development and the creation of a supportive climate via promotional slogans, posters and mission statements (see Chapter 6). For social scientists, adverse reactions are not so easily contained. Nor are they so readily susceptible to economic influences. In fact, they point to the significance of a remarkably stable set of attitudes and orientations that render the idea of a straightforward paradigm shift unrealistic. Some assessments are even more pessimistic, suggesting that intervening attitudes, values and beliefs effectively undermine progressive inclinations, ensuring continuity with the past and a recasting of empowerment as neo-Taylorism, as more of a variation than a departure (Adler, 1993, 1995).

LOCATING THE POWER IN EMPOWERMENT

For prescriptive commentators such as Peters, Kanter and Sid Joynson, managerial opposition to employee empowerment is irrational and unhealthy. From their standpoint, there is nothing to fear or to reasonably argue against. Empowerment serves the economic and social self-interests of modern professional managers, enhancing their ability to mobilize resources and secure organizational objectives. By giving workers a measure of decision-making power, managers are exploiting the knowledge and capabilities of staff more effectively, improving their own results, and consequently their professional and personal standing, at the same time. This explains Kanter's view that 'delegation does not mean abdication' (1979, p. 73). Empowerment is conceptualized as a positive-sum activity that adds to the overall stock of power in a double-win situation that favours workers and managers alike (Foy, 1994). Rational managers who allocate power to their subordinates will capture the attention of executives, shareholders and competitors, enlarging rather than depleting their own capacity for influence as their departments or work teams outperform those governed by more conventional, Tayloristic measures.

Despite the resources and activity levels invested in promoting this prescriptive logic, important theoretical questions remain unanswered. Is power really a resource that can be given or, for that matter, taken away? Should empowerment be regarded as something that is 'done' to marginalized workers by the more enlightened of corporate power-holders?

As indicated earlier, this conceptualization is rather curiously endorsed and rehearsed by some of the most vehement critics of the prescriptive and managerialist approach (Hardy and Leiba-O'Sullivan, 1998; Edwards, 2006). A significant number of social theorists accept that power is a resource in the hands of managers, and that their capacity for exerting influence is extended rather than damaged by empowering workers (Lukes, 1974, 2005). The basis for their criticism is to be found in the assessment of outcomes, as opposed to theoretical underpinnings. The positive-sum optimism of the enthusiasts is replaced with a zero-sum depiction of winners and losers, with managers expanding their power base at the expense of their employees.

From this angle, the managerial interest in empowerment has more to do with control than competitive concerns about quality, flexibility or market responsiveness. It serves an ideological purpose, concealing deep-rooted beliefs about the legitimacy of hierarchical authority, and making the extension and consolidation of managerial prerogatives seem more palatable to staff. The purpose of empowerment is not to give power to employees, but to take it away, to masquerade for greater managerial control over the nature and intensity of the work process (Hardy and Leiba-O'Sullivan, 1998; Harley, 1999; Yates et al., 2001). In effect, the heirs to the Taylorist tradition use empowerment as double-speak to sweeten manoeuvres that workers might otherwise resist, thereby consolidating established power relations and reducing the potential for any independent challenge to managerial decisions (Lukes, 1974, 2005).

It is ironic that such polarized judgements, attributing overwhelming collective gains and debilitating sectional costs to employee empowerment, should flow from similar conceptual underpinnings. The theoretical images that tie them together are more significant than the evaluations that divide them, however. The most obvious weakness is to be found in the common assumption that the acquisition and application of power is unambiguous, uncontested and non-problematic. This crucially ignores the significance of countervailing power and the impact of contested interests and struggles that characterize relationships between people.

Judgements about empowerment that flow from the aggregate models of positive or zero-sum are unreliable because, at root, they trade on a basic misunderstanding of the nature of power. As noted, both camps present it as a resource, a quantity (Collins, 2000) or capacity (Hindess, 1982) that can be expanded or deployed at will by self-interested managers. This conceptualization leaves no room for choice, interpretation or reaction, and assigns no weight to reflections and actions other than those of a controlling elite. This amounts to a restrictive approach, deflecting attention away from the processes of negotiation through which people exercise agency and demonstrate their own ability to act, react and interact with their working environment.

Contrary to the aggregation logic, power cannot be associated with fully predictable and inevitable results. Nor can it be reduced to a one-way process in which a unified group of managers act on 'subjects' either for good or ill. There is a strong tradition of social research that highlights the pertinence of human independence and resilience, demonstrating that people are generally very good at exerting influence over their own lives, without the mediating effect of managerial or other professional expertise (Sayles, 1958; Roy, 1969; Noon and Blyton, 1997; Edwards, 2006). There is already some research evidence to suggest that employees actively question and often challenge management-inspired empowerment schemes, compromising declared aims and occasionally derailing them in practice (McCabe, 2000; Beirne, 2011). Collins (1999) and Graham (1994) provide powerful examples of shop floor action against management teams that were demonstrably, or by their own admission, changing working arrangements under the banner of empowerment. These workers retained the ability to scrutinize and influence, taking steps to empower themselves in ways that thwarted management ambitions. In the Graham case, female employees were moved to rebel against management images of empowerment that demanded flexibility, including short-notice overtime working that complicated domestic and child-care arrangements without offering valued gains or compensations in return.

This highlights the importance of reciprocal interactions at the workplace and the potency of the psychological contract, the shifting sense of mutual obligations and exchanges that affects the conduct of employee relations. The message from this tradition of social science is that people have independent qualities, to a greater or lesser extent, exhibiting reflective capabilities and forms of expression, even in difficult situations (see Roy, 1973). No matter how imbalanced they may be in terms of resources, people are adept at reading and interpreting relationships through their own priorities and preferences, and of responding in a fashion that affects their experience (Edwards, 2006; Beirne, 2008). Hence actors in subordinate positions are never wholly subservient or compliant. Force does not, of necessity, bring submission. Managerial authority and rationality may fail to inspire. Employees may be impervious to incentives or moral exhortations. These insights effectively challenge the proposition that managers can exercise power, give it or take it away, in the fashion that aggregate accounts of positive or zero-sum suggest.

The realm of independent reflection and subjective action points to a more ambiguous and ambivalent set of relationships between people at work than is typically acknowledged in promotional and dismissive accounts of empowerment. The corollary is that empowerment specifically, and management decision-making more generally, cannot be seen as having a straightforward, top-down impact on outcomes. A more sophisticated conceptualization is required to capture the complexity of reciprocal interactions, and the mediating influence of interpretations, choices, values and beliefs. A more plausible and conceptually robust view is that power is not a resource but a relational phenomenon, not a quantity or capacity but a variable quality of the interdependent relationships between people:

> Yet power is not a substance to be chopped up and weighed out in discrete lumps, like dough on a pastryboard. It is a characteristic of the relationships between individuals, groups and classes, as well as being the object of tension within and between them. (Schuller, 1985, p. 32)

In truth, power has no meaning outside of the dynamic relationships between people. It is embedded in their attitudes and actions towards each other, emerging from the exchanges between them rather than distributed as a property of some rather than others. Power in this sense is interactive, relational and networked, arising from mutual interdependencies and therefore subject to ongoing struggles and negotiations. Every manifestation of power is liable to change through the ebb and flow of responses, challenges and influences as reciprocal encounters and exchanges unfold. Power relationships are all embracing but they are not overwhelming, determining or static. As people interact, they exhibit agency and experience constraint, not as equivalents but as a quality of fluid relationships that have an ever-present potential for reinterpretation and change.

Even in extreme moments or situations, when the lines of influence seem entirely clear, as between master and slave, for example, or in 'total institutions' where authority is applied in order to change the identities of inmates in prisons or mental hospitals (see Goffman, 1961), it can never be assumed that the 'poorer' relations are so completely subordinated that all scope for personal expression is removed or denied. Thinking and acting can find an outlet and muster influence to retain a sense of selfhood, from clandestine attempts to tarnish food or damage property through to overtly challenging activities such as escape or resistance. The patterns of reflecting and reciprocating may vary enormously between the disadvantaged in such situations, yet they impinge upon the interests and activities of the more prominent actors, exposing the conditionality of their position. The influence of one party can only be understood in terms of their relational interdependency with others.

Of course, human agency cannot easily be separated from the structure or contextual circumstances in which it occurs. The relationships between people are played out against a shifting backdrop of economic, technological and environmental conditions that affect cognitive and social processes. Yet these can be accommodated without accepting the fatalism of the dismissive critics of empowerment or the determinism of the promotional consultants and gurus. The apparently inexorable effects of marketplace and technology have in reality to be balanced against the self-mobilizing agency and relational activities of actors, recognizing both aspects, structure and agency, macro and micro, as mutual influences, each acting upon the other rather than operating according to straightforward causal principles. These interconnections between macro and micro factors produce fluctuating inequalities of power and degrees of flux and instability in the relationships between people that are mirrored in empowerment initiatives.

Historical studies of employee participation schemes have already demonstrated the significance of these inequalities and instabilities, and the struggles around them. Writing in the 1970s and 1980s, Harvie Ramsay established that periods of expanding interest and activity coincided with particular phases of the business cycle, specifically with buoyant economic conditions and tight labour markets (Ramsay, 1977, 1980). These conditions alter the terms of exchange and struggle between managers and employees, as tensions heighten and managerial authority is challenged more directly by organized labour and by the performance problems that arise from staff turnover, shortages and industrial unrest. In their efforts to contain grassroots behaviour under these circumstances, managers have turned in significant numbers to participation practices, seeing them as a means of appeasing workers and of 'regaining control by sharing it' (Fox, 1971). Increases in the incidence of participative management have not been matched historically by improvements in scope, substance and longevity, however.

The heightened interest in participation during these periods of expansion, at least until the 1980s (Ackers et al., 1992), must be seen as the product of particular conditions of struggle and relational influence where managers were responding to 'pressures from below'. They were not generally demonstrating a commitment to participation per se. Indeed, there is evidence that management-initiated schemes were informed by a widespread antipathy to any dilution of managerial prerogatives (Ramsay, 1980, 1985). The choices and decisions that extended participation were influenced by the self-empowering activities of workers and their trades unions, reflecting the difficulty of securing consent and sustaining established prerogatives within a context and through relationships that made this inherently problematic. Since their attachment to participation was largely opportunistic, these managers had few qualms about abandoning formal arrangements when the economic conditions and, by extension, the relational terms of exchange with workers changed.

This is essentially what Ramsay discovered. His research points to a cyclical pattern of participation, extending over approximately 100 years, with periods of advance followed by decline and decay, showing no discernible improvement in levels of joint decision-taking, or in any other substantive indicator of employee empowerment overall. On this evidence, the outcomes generated within these particular conditions of struggle and in the context of these specific inequalities of power favoured defensive managerial interests. Managers with a manipulative commitment to psychological rather than objective participation (Anthony, 1977), who were concerned with appearance rather than substance, were able to contain employee action and defend their prerogatives by way of transience and triviality. By their own priorities, they successfully struggled to keep joint influence within tight boundaries, restricting it to non-controversial issues and to the petty realm of decisions about 'tea-breaks and toilets', until the pressures on them dissipated and their accommodative exercises could be happily forgotten or allowed to deteriorate (Ramsay, 1980). A substantial history of disappointing outcomes does not signal a given, predictable or bitter future, however.

The important point here is that empowerment and participation schemes emerge and exist through particular conditions of exchange and struggle between interdependent people. They are not the quasi-independent creations of an autonomous and powerful group of managers, as resource models of power suggest (Edwards, 2006; Beirne, 2008). Their features and effects are not directly within the hands of any particular interest group or party. The managers from history that Ramsay, Fox and others regard as opponents of meaningful empowerment were successful in pursuing their objectives not because they possessed power or were able to wield it unambiguously. The reason, in fact, is that they creatively and purposefully pursued patterns of action and interaction that secured differential gains under conditions and through exchanges that were only in part subject to their influence. The outcomes were conditional, not just on economic factors but also on the opposing practices, interpretations and responses of others, which in these cases were less perceptive, imaginative and effective.

The corollary is that empowerment must be taken seriously as a precarious project, embodying fluctuating instabilities and inequalities of power as definite practices, exchanges and struggles unfold under particular conditions. Any assessment of the potential for employee empowerment, or of claims about its transformative qualities, must be based upon a detailed examination of the interpretations, interdependencies and conditions affecting the exchanges between real people in specific situations. Judgements need to be empirically based, allowing for contradictions and slippage from the interests of any particular group, enthusiasts or opponents, who in any case are unable to predetermine outcomes or escape from conditions of struggle.

This relational approach, together with the available historical evidence, may warrant a high degree of caution, even scepticism, about the prospects for sustaining or generalizing any developments towards employee empowerment, yet it locates progress firmly within the realms of reflective practice. Advancing empowerment becomes an imaginative and purposeful matter of acting, engaging and struggling under dynamic conditions. It calls for an informed activism, and has little to do with patrician endowments or guru recipes. Nor can it be dismissed as an exercise in futility, fighting against determinate forces that will always win out in the end. In relational terms, there are no determinate forces, and it is simply meaningless to conceive of terminal points of struggle from which outcomes are assured. Although conditions change, the reciprocal interdependencies between people and the exchanges, negotiations and struggles that flow from these are part and parcel of life, and hence of any activity that involves cooperation, participation or empowerment.

Within the current recessionary climate, there are few signs of the distinctive factors that stimulated the peaks of interest in participation over the past century. The triggers to Ramsay's cycles of participation have been effectively removed by recessionary episodes, the weakening of organized labour and the effects of globalization (Ackers et al., 1992; Ramsay, 1993). Yet, as indicated earlier when discussing the impact of the Great Recession, struggles around participation and empowerment are alive and kicking. They are not necessarily of the same order, or even conducted so vociferously along the same axes of interest, but they are just as significant in terms of outcomes and understanding as those elucidated by Ramsay.

Some pointers towards crucial struggles under current conditions can be found in managerial reactions to downsizing and de-layering, and attendant fears about diminishing status and job loss. Available evidence suggests that calculative interests have informed many contemporary attempts at empowerment, not so much to harness the knowledge and skills of employees as to cut the costs of management and supervision (Marchington et al., 1992; Denham et al., 1997; Beirne, 2011). Through some telling case research, and by contrast with the conventional distinction between managers and workers, Hales (2000) reveals divisions of interest within management, and corresponding struggles, that deliver conflict rather than participative decision-making:

> the interpretation of empowerment which senior managers enthusiastically promote is rather different from the one which junior managers reluctantly accept ... empowerment programmes are as much about the putative reorganisation of junior managers' work as any substantive increase in worker autonomy. (Hales, 2000, p. 501)

Like Ramsay, Hales detects some ideological positioning around empowerment, although his contention is that senior managers are using it not to manufacture employee consent but to justify the dilution and replacement of supervisory and junior management positions. The destabilizing effect of the struggles between these managers becomes clear as Hales develops a relational appreciation of the way that junior managers read their situation, perceiving empowerment to be a significant threat and reciprocating out of a sense of injustice by 'engineering failure' and manoeuvring combinations of language and practice to defend their own interests.

Unfortunately, in his own analysis, Hales tends to slip away from the relational position, signposting important developments yet privileging this axis of reciprocity and struggle over others. Broader concerns and indeed actors, including employees themselves, fall out of focus as managerial protectionism and calculating self-interest come to dominate patterns of thinking and acting around empowerment. This amounts to an oversimplification that takes Hales to the point of reproducing the inadequacies of a dismissive zero-sum analysis, downgrading agency and relational dynamics through the blanket treatment of sectional interests and affiliations. On this analysis, empowerment is lost in the singular struggle between fearful, oppositional junior managers and manipulative, cost-saving executives.

Connecting empowerment to the expression of local grievances is valuable analytically and should help to lever open, rather than actually foreclose, serious analysis of relevant struggles and exchanges. While calculative attempts to defend managerial interests can now be expected to affect the conduct of employee empowerment, there is no reason to privilege them theoretically or to regard them as decisive, or even materially based. It will be clear from some of the studies cited earlier that junior managers are neither alone nor united in opposing calculative and restrictive views of empowerment. Nor do they have a monopoly on the worries and grievances that are associated with practical initiatives. It is inadequate even to consider that they operate within a fully shared frame of reference that puts personal and sectional advantage above other considerations, or rules out any serious or principled engagement with employees to pursue collaborative decision-making.

Whatever the contrasts between actors, be they managers or workers, attitudes cannot be assumed nor behaviour reduced to a wholly calculative assessment of material or positional interests. Personal sense-making or 'reflection-in-action' (Schon, 1983) reaches beyond matters of material advantage or disadvantage, attaching wider issues of principle to interpretations and struggles, with individuals forming associations and active alliances that express moral and ethical judgements (Watson and Watson, 1999; Barry et al., 2001; Holt, 2006). This raises the prospect of multiple axes and cross-cutting issues of struggle that are beyond the scope of a rigid positional or material analysis, and which call for a more open and consistently relational view of alliances as well as fractures, commitments as well as contests, principles as much as grievances, and enablers as well as constraints on the progress of empowerment.

This book aims for a more inclusive understanding of the complex mix of interests, interpretations, and struggles that surround employee empowerment, situating them within the particular conditions of their development so that outcomes can be evaluated realistically and tactically, with an eye to future prospects and in the absence of reflex judgements, wishful thinking or unwarranted pessimism. As noted at the outset, the purpose of the book is to connect theory, evidence and practice, enlarging our awareness of what constitutes an adequate analysis, of what needs to be taken into account to make sense of relevant processes, and to translate this into applied knowledge that can assist or support progressive programmes. The next step is to develop the relational approach, to follow through the logic of our theoretical position and take a more detailed look at the values and practices of the agents and parties associated with empowerment, the exchanges and struggles between them and the sort of contextual conditions in which particular outcomes are produced. This will take us through some of the most telling, novel and innovative tendencies of recent times, reviewing available evidence and tracking developments, instabilities and fluctuating inequalities of power through landmark projects in teamworking, user-participation in technological change, employee share ownership and financial participation, gender equality and the empowerment of women at work and attempts to manage cultural change in favour of empowerment. The final section will then offer a view on the overall impact and lessons to be drawn from the recurring interest in empowerment and participation schemes, thereafter broaching questions of practice, activism and regulatory structuring.

PART I

Contemporary developments

2. Progressive teamworking: disputes, promise and practicalities

Teamworking initiatives have been associated with employee empowerment for a large number of years, especially in operational matters where groups of people acquire formal responsibility for specific aspects of production or the delivery of particular services. The durable appeal of the topic conceals a number of distinct themes and possibilities, however, from collective monitoring of workflow, quality and health and safety issues to multi-skilling, work restructuring and the reversal of hierarchy. Contrasting perspectives and varieties of interest are distinguished by the broad range of labels that are commonly prefixed to the term, including self-managing, self-directing, high-performance, autonomous and semi-autonomous, on-line and off-line teams.

Many of the contemporary conceptualizations of progressive or alternative teams have a lineage that dates back to the middle decades of the twentieth century (Benders et al., 2006). Their roots can be traced to the pioneering work of consultants associated with the Tavistock Institute of Human Relations in London (Trist and Murray, 1993) and the Quality of Working Life movement, an international network connecting innovators in the Scandinavian countries, Britain, Australia, the United States and elsewhere (Davis and Taylor, 1972; Emery and Thorsrud, 1976; Mumford and Cooper, 1979). Offended by the restrictions on work under Taylorist and Fordist regimes, this community presented a moral and social vision of autonomous groups operating with a degree of freedom from management directives, and with the discretion and variety that could deliver a meaningful, enriching and productive experience. This was ostensibly in tune with the aspirations of a better-educated workforce and an expanding population of socially responsible managers, although the campaign for autonomous teams ranged beyond humanitarianism to the challenge of making the most of available technology.

As the theoretical justification for job reform developed – through socio-technical systems thinking, and with attention to influential ideas about cellular production (Mitrofanov, 1966) – the focus widened from individual needs and opportunities for enrichment (Herzberg, 1968) to collective responsibility for whole sections, or logically coherent portions, of work. By emphasizing the interdependence of social and technical dimensions of organization, pioneers such as Trist (Trist and Bamforth, 1951; Trist et al., 1963) and Miller and Rice (1967) connected the psychological and relational aspects of work design explicitly and purposefully to the specification and application of equipment. This extended the reach of the Quality of Working Life movement, generating a greater awareness of choices and possibilities and a propensity to challenge established images of 'given', constraining and limiting technology (Trist and Murray, 1993). It also promoted participation and empowerment, theoretically by considering the impact of systems and machinery from the standpoint of employees at the sharp end of them, and practically by supporting a relative shift from imposed 'solutions' to collective responsibility for the management, and occasionally design, of work in particular industries and companies (Benders, et al., 2006; Beirne, 2008).

The British coal industry was at the forefront of early Tavistock initiatives on the reversal of Fordist hierarchies and divisions of labour, demonstrating the commercial viability of multi-skilled, self-selecting, organizing and regulating teams as a counterweight to production and industrial relations problems (Trist and Bamforth, 1951; Trist et al., 1963). The iconic status of Volvo's team-based car manufacturing plants at Kalmar and Uddevalla in Sweden may have been even more significant, adding impetus to the debate on humanistic teamworking and providing a practical edge, as subsequent sections will reveal. Certainly, when these facilities were operating (from the 1970s and late '80s respectively), enthusiasts had a useful means of demonstrating the practicalities of their approach. Any doubts or management scepticism about idealized or impractical humanism could be challenged with inspirational case material from the far side of the North Sea.

Yet progress towards this vision of practical teamworking has often been compromised. The reform movement has suffered serious setbacks during times of recession and corporate instability, confronting frequent back-pedalling and fluctuating patterns of managerial responsiveness. In truth, business interest has often been stimulated by narrow concerns for settled staffing and consistent job performance under buoyant labour market conditions, when problems with absenteeism, recruitment and retention captured managerial attention. Against the backdrop of unemployment, or whenever depressed economic activity relegated these issues to the margins of management decision-making, the reform movement faltered, however. As indicated in the Foreword, interest waned, and advocates of the humanistic approach lost ground (see also Kelly, 1985 and Littler, 1985).

Economic trends over the past two decades have produced further complications, providing scope for competing conceptualizations that dilute the reformer's message. With the product market priorities of flexible, fast and quality-assured work dominating management discourse, a more commercially minded group of commentators and consultants has taken up the case for teamworking, mixing and matching ideas and language, though with very different impulses and orientations. A more assertive approach is discernible, attempting to engineer or re-engineer teamworking on a top-down basis. This has been nurtured by a plethora of 'how-to-do-it' guidebooks and packaged methodologies, many of them generated through the consultancy business in the United States (Peters, 1987; Humphries, 1998; Lencioni, 2002; Castiglione, 2007; Clemons and Kroth, 2011; see also Buchanan, 2000). References to high-performance and self-directed teamworking signal the main thrust in at least part of this literature. Yet discussion of common themes such as multi-skilling, knowledge-sharing and 'front to back' responsibility for core processes conceals ideological differences, even by comparison with 'social engineers' at the Tavistock Institute, who were themselves criticized for trying to shape or determine employee empowerment and experience, albeit benevolently (Loveridge, 1980).

This contrast between distinctive communities of activists, well-intentioned and commercially focused, variously aiming to drive practical teamworking from above the level of the workforce, is essential to an informed understanding of the exchanges between prescriptive and promotional commentators. Although prominent, and invariably setting the agenda for managerial explorations of the topic (in management development and MBA courses, for example), these top-down scenarios typically fail to capture the dynamics of teamworking, however.

CHALLENGING THE STATUS QUO

Employees often appear as the passive subjects of teamworking initiatives, as recipients who can be expected to welcome or benefit from the interventions of more senior others (Beirne, 2008). Prescriptive accounts tend to accentuate the gains for staff and the positive contribution of innovators who are delivering something that is innately good and constructive, boosting morale, eroding divisions and demarcations, and cultivating a sense of common purpose (Semler, 1993; Humphries, 1998; Clemons and Kroth, 2011). An idyllic image of corporate peace and collaborative working towards unitary aims is regularly traded as the antidote to workplace tension, disaffection and the damaging conflict associated with Fordism (Womack et al., 1990; Oakland, 1996, 2004; Owen, 2009).

Critical accounts by social scientists have repeatedly challenged this upbeat presentation, detecting a harder edge to managerial advocacy, and even a harshness that makes references to benevolent interventions seem perverse (Vallas, 2003a, b; Harley et al., 2005). An influential counter-current suggests that teamworking involves more of a calculating drive to subordinate workers and to reorganize and reassert managerial controls over them, intensifying performance more subtly and to a level unmatched by autocracy and direct supervision (Parker and Slaughter, 1988; Barker, 1993; Geary, 1993; Pollert, 1996; Upadhya, 2009). From here, references to devolved decision-making amount to a smokescreen for more stressful and manipulative ideological controls that reduce the likelihood of damaging conflict and resistance of the sort provoked by Fordist and other noticeably oppressive systems. With teamworking, any unpalatable or difficult experiences can be attributed to peer pressure or intra-group dynamics, allowing managers to deflect attention from 'them and us realities' and recast themselves as helpers and supporters of co-operative, committed and loyal staff.

While correcting for promotional mythology, much of this literature delivers an alternative package of overstatements and 'certainties' that polarize debate while reproducing some of the inadequacies apparent in managerial interpretations. At one level, there has been a tendency to apply overly idealistic judgements, benchmarking practical initiatives against implicit principles and success criteria that devalue modest, hesitant or potential benefits, even those that seem to find favour with participants on the ground. Idealized images of craft skills and independent working patterns lie behind some of these negative judgements, as Wright and Edwards (1998) and Vallas (2003a, b) observe. Yet craft traditions are so remote from the starting point and the local ambitions tied into practical teamworking that implicit or explicit references to them are prejudicial. It is simply unfair and unreasonable to evaluate self-management or devolved decision-making against a craft-like ability to shape work arrangements and outcomes. Indeed, the corollary of this inclination is to apply standards that can never realistically be achieved or pursued through the everyday situations that confront most modern employees, producing a reflex tendency towards negativity (Geary, 1995), and to a curious moral and analytical detachment, given the critical commitment to grassroots interests.

Contradictory tendencies are also discernible in the reification of ideological control and manipulation in much of the critical literature (Vallas, 2003; Beirne, 2008). The potency attributed to the ideology of teams, equating them unproblematically (and often unambiguously) with intensification and corporate conformity, contributes to the mystification of team-based management, reproducing the top-down prescriptive image of executives or senior managers as the central and most capable actors in practical situations. Ironically, employee criticism is often taken as the indicator that promotional rhetoric does not match reality, and that the game is deliberately and effectively 'rigged' by corporate bosses. Abuses have been found in the familiar tactics of containment, triviality and dumping, with additional, though very focused, operational responsibilities earmarked for group decision-making, frequently through 'off-line' deliberations so that 'on-line' working is intensified and 'stressed' within existing pay rates (Parker and Slaughter, 1988; Barker, 1993; Upadhya, 2009).

While employee revelations about this side of teamworking are telling and often powerful, accounts that relate them to dismissive or rejectionist positions or reduce them to a means of unmasking managerial manipulation (Barker, 1993; Geary, 1995; Danford, 1997) are unhelpful. Sharp-end views are only partially considered, and with a skewed sense of agency that presents workers as interpreters rather than actors, commentators on managerial manoeuvring whose critical pronouncements can be translated into a confident case against teamworking.

By contrast with this representation, historical and qualitative studies of established initiatives reveal that workers discern advantages as well as limitations, frequently connecting these to developmental arguments, forms of activism and effective intervention (Wright and Edwards, 1998; Buchanan, 2000; Vallas, 2003). In fact, employee reports provide a sobering counterweight to the spin mentality, positive *and* negative, that informs so much of the discussion around teamworking. Participant evaluations are often more measured and cautious, entertaining the possibility of favourable outcomes rather than dismissing initiatives out of hand, yet correcting for exaggerated claims and promotional rhetoric (Foster and Hoggett, 1999).

The frustrations of the past typically inform employee judgements about continuities as well as departures, extensions and variations in their work experience, along with opportunities and potential improvements that merit open-minded, though carefully qualified, support. Case evidence points to a welcome reduction in supervisory interference, directive management and Tayloristic controls in some situations, with employees reporting a greater propensity for managers to engage with them as responsible adults, rather than treating them as 'numbers', brainless automata or immature 'school kids' (Wright and Edwards, 1998; Findlay et al., 2000). There are also regular references to job enhancement, with participants expressing their appreciation for even a modicum of variety or discretionary activity, where previously they suffered the deadening experience of narrow tasks and mind-numbing repetition. Although, from a distance, the scale of the reported changes can seem quite modest – adjusting equipment in the absence of line engineers (Findlay et al., 2000), calling on maintenance or support staff without supervisory approval (Wright and Edwards, 1998), switching tasks with others in the team or acting on personal initiative to help them – the impact locally is often profound, delivering meaningful and welcome gains (Vallas, 2003). From the standpoint of the team member, lofty judgements about the overall sameness or debilitating tokenism of devolved decision-making and controlled teamishness can be churlish. Working life is more bearable, and even for some people enjoyable, as they learn to take advantage of adjustments in their situation.

Narratives from the sharp end that give some credence to teamworking sit uncomfortably with much of the established literature because they signal an independence of view and capacity for reflection that is not widely acknowledged. They defy available over-generalizations, and at the same time present a challenge to critical and managerialist accounts of a coherent and consistent restructuring of work around teams. To hear the views of employees on an historical basis, their experiences are not driven autonomously from the top by prudent, calculating or well-intentioned executives and consultants. They are not passive spectators, hapless victims or even worthy beneficiaries of the interventions of more senior others. Employees themselves are purposeful actors, shaping, as well as sensing, significant and often worthwhile outcomes (Beirne, 2008).

Buchanan (2000) provides a compelling demonstration of this in a review of the early Tavistock episodes. Castigating acolytes (specifically Mumford and Hendricks, 1996) for mythologizing the contribution of Trist, Bamforth and other consultants, he explains how the 'composite' coal-getting teams that effectively established the reputation of the Tavistock Institute actually emerged from the initiatives of miners themselves. They were not invented by Tavistock innovators, but rather acknowledged, appreciated and publicized for their significance during the course of diligent research.

As they investigated the problems associated with mechanized, long-wall coal mining in 1940s Britain, Trist and his colleagues discovered that workers had devised their own response to adverse conditions that made it dangerous to operate extended seams. Celebrating developments at one mine, they detailed the advantages of the 'Manley Innovation', explaining how miners at this pit resorted to team-based coal cutting, using their own knowledge to work flexibly, allocating and rotating tasks as necessary, while developing their skills and collective expertise at the same time. Despite persistent management efforts to reduce costs by enforcing long-wall methods, the Manley miners defended their team practices, eventually negotiating an agreement that formalized the composite approach of multi-skilled, self-selecting groups with collective responsibility for the full work cycle. This was a pivotal episode in the Tavistock story, although standard (including textbook) accounts give little or no credit to the intuitive and creative contributions of the Manley miners (Benders et al., 2006).

Fortunately, critical empirical studies reinforce the point of Buchanan's reinterpretation, providing confirmation that worker self-activity has an important bearing upon the nature and outcomes of practical teamworking (Vallas, 2003). McKinlay and Taylor (1996) provide a powerful example from case research at an electronics plant. Workers at this site were alert to team talk and tactics, seeing through the hoopla that managers attached to their initiatives, and even turning them to some collective advantage. The most obvious indicator was that staff deliberately and skilfully undermined an individualized appraisal system, using team targets and performance figures to defend members who were singled out for management criticism.

On this evidence, work teams are not self-evidently the source of management solutions. Nor are workers easily transformed into compliant and passive team members. The nature and outcomes of practical teamworking are contested. Participants are active, and their self-activity holds out the promise of potential benefits. This is not to deny the costs and negative consequences reported by the critics, for teamworking can certainly take its toll. The point is to put negotiation, struggle and intervention at the centre of analysis, as explained in the previous chapter.

Team members are 'close to the action', and can be expected, as reflective agents, to be acutely aware of what helps and hinders, of the unfolding features of a team initiative that variously improve, complicate or damage their situation at work. To judge by available case reports (Wright and Edwards, 1998; Foster and Hoggett, 1999; Findlay et al., 2000; Pedersen and Lewis, 2012), very few participants offer unequivocal or strident judgements one way or another, negative or positive. Many are attuned to the mixed blessings of change, and are genuinely torn in their evaluations. In fact, a range of opinion is discernible, with varying emphases and contrasting judgements as people assign relative weight to more or less favourable aspects in a manner that reflects their background, outlook and orientation.

In one of the most sensitive and discriminating discussions of work-force opinion, McCabe (2000) claims space for considered views that are simply ignored in the polarized accounts of dismissive and managerialist commentators. These are apparent in shopfloor reactions to teamworking at a British car company, which he elaborates under the labels 'bewitched', 'bothered' and 'bewildered'. Those in the first category accentuated the positive aspects of teamworking, mainly from an acute sense of personal disadvantage under previous arrangements. Team initiatives released them from some of the restrictions and drudgery of Taylorized jobs, so they embraced them as the basis for a more meaningful and even lucrative experience. Jonah was one of the most vocal respondents in this group, detecting an opportunity to develop and demonstrate his capabilities, to get ahead and perhaps aim for promotion: 'The frustration of a lifetime was channelled into teamworking and, therefore, it was viewed as his saviour' (McCabe, 2000, p. 210).

Others were more cautious, even negative in their assessments, quali-fying Jonah's sense of improvement or criticizing his gullibility. Employ-ees who were 'bothered' by teamworking took exception to the spin in management pronouncements and official commentaries. This was a bugbear that either took the shine off worthwhile improvements or served to camouflage less palatable tendencies. The more forceful critics saw an attempt to veil stressful change with hollow posturing and patronizing gestures. More tolerant opinion conceded the potential for improvements, though sought to puncture official claims. All of the respondents in this category were attuned to the stresses and strains of teamworking, and could demonstrate the impact of 'sloping shoulder syndrome' (Foster and Hoggett, 1999) as their groups assumed additional roles and responsibili-ties, and became more accountable for performance improvements.

McCabe's final group of respondents showed no apparent sense of novelty or impact in the transition to teamworking, and seemed to be puzzled by the fuss that it generated. By contrast with those who were 'bewitched' and 'bothered', 'bewildered' employees found little to com-mend or condemn it, sensing only background noise to accompany the main experiences of their working lives. There was little to suggest that they were moved or motivated, cynical or hostile. Teamworking left them cold. This is consistent with broader evidence, both on employee indifference to change programmes at work (Ogbonna and Wilkinson, 1990) and on the failure of culture-moulding interventions that target 'hearts and minds' (Ichniowski et al., 1996). In fact, these studies point to additional categories of response that extend McCabe's classification, bringing in those who are offended rather than 'bothered', for example, and including those who 'go through the motions', become resigned or exhibit 'deep acting' rather than express encouragement, approval or compliance.

By acknowledging a variety of employee interpretations and reactions, the studies reported here exhibit a sensitivity and respect for otherness that contrasts markedly with the popular discourse on teamworking. They recognize that team initiatives are embedded within distinctive social, organizational and historical contexts, and so develop in a fashion that ranges beyond the scope of technical or prescriptive definitions. Individual interpretations and responses are filtered through their reflective sense of self, of earlier life experiences and future expectations, and are not therefore reducible to a uniform set of cause and effect relationships (Martin and Fryer, 1975; Storey and Sisson, 1993).

People do not react in the same way; hence teamworking is a diverse phenomenon that covers a complex mix of practices, processes, experiences, reactions and potentialities. It is charged and fraught, problematical and contested, political rather than unitary, often magnifying differences between participants and raising tensions on the shop floor. A destabilizing effect is discernible, especially when opposing views trigger a clash and subsequent deterioration in sociability. This can be across managerial boundaries or among workers themselves. McCabe's case company provides an example of the latter, as Jonah's enthusiasm for teamworking prompted feelings of embarrassment in others that could spill over into resentment and bitterness, particularly when managers called him from the workspace to impress customers and outsiders.

Exchanges at this level of involvement compete with rhetorical accounts of teamworking, undermining the certainties of rigid analyses, whether positive or negative, and demonstrating the political nature of outcomes and evaluations. By calling attention to agency and negotiation, struggles and interventions, they also raise the intriguing possibility of nurturing alternative and innovative forms of practice that challenge narrow and constraining conceptualizations within organizations (Beirne, 2008). In light of this evidence and by these insights, contextualizing knowledge can be applied to influence the fortunes of teamworking, to identify promising and damaging circumstances and recognize patterns of progressive struggling that build resilience and enhance the collective capacity to secure benefits and limit costs.

POLITICS AND CONTRADICTIONS

Progressive images of teamworking are often presented in a very
confident and assured manner, as if proponents occupy some unassailable
intellectual and moral high ground. This was certainly the case through
much of the 1970s and '80s, when reformers were claiming relevance on
the strength of powerful demonstration experiments, especially at Volvo
where there seemed to be evidence of viable humanistic manufacturing to
confound sceptical or critical opinion (Mumford, 1979; Mumford and
Hendricks, 1996). In 1989, when Volvo brought its most advanced
team-based facility on-line at Uddevalla in Sweden, the plant manager
claimed triumphantly: 'this isn't just new production technology. It is the
death of the assembly line.' (Berggren, 1995, p. 278; Granath, 1998)

Uddevalla marked a watershed for enthusiasts, operationalizing parallel
whole-car assembly in the key strategic sector that had established linear,
short-cycle task execution as the norm for productive working. This was
poetic justice, a vindication for alternative thinking at the heartland of
Fordism. The innovations at this site incorporated inventory and materials
handling, tooling and engineering design, payment and grading arrangements, as well as the social organization of work. Here, apparently, was
an integrated facility with a consistent set of arrangements that allowed
teamworking to flourish.

Material handlers worked collaboratively to organize the distribution of
car kits to parallel assembly stations or 'docks' that delivered an
independent full-build programme covering various model types and
specifications. This meant that 40 teams of approximately ten workers
each dealt with between 1300 and 1700 components, all of them
delivered in a package by computer guided 'taxis'. Cars were built from
the ground up, with completion times ranging from 1.5 to 3.5 hours.
Enabling equipment was devised and installed to facilitate collaborative
working, including tilting and revolving platforms to support the emerging vehicles and flexible hand tools that could be adjusted to the
physical characteristics of the workers. Team members managed task
allocation, quality control and testing, as well as problem-solving and
dock maintenance. They even contributed to the annual round of product
and process engineering, specifying suitable assembly methods and
tooling adjustments to accommodate model upgrades. Pay was related to
knowledge and hence group flexibility, individuals qualifying for the top
rate when they could demonstrate 'whole-car competence', a grading that
required 16 months experience and the demonstrable ability to complete
a test car in 20 hours with no more than four minor defects.

With such an innovative and dramatic departure from traditional forms of car making, the confidence attached to the reform agenda during this period is perhaps understandable. However, it was severely, and all too rapidly, dented when Volvo closed Uddevalla in 1993. This was the first of several 'off–on' periods of operating at Uddevalla, which became the production base for two subsequent partnership agreements that delivered the Volvo C70 series of cars, first with Tom Walkinshaw Racing (as Autonova) from 1995, and then with Pininfarina between 2005 and 2013. The 1993 closure had the most dramatic effect, however, prompting many howls of disappointment and disapproval as the company dissociated itself from the 'noble experiment in humanistic manufacturing' (quoted by Berggren, 1992, p. 239). At that stage, production was transferred to a more conventional assembly plant near Gothenburg, confirming that Volvo, like many other organizations, is torn between competing management principles and tendencies (Vallas, 2003; Vidal, 2007; Beirne, 2011). As the company confronted mounting difficulties through the recessionary years of the early 1990s, more traditional management ideas and values held sway. With depressed markets, plummeting sales and excess capacity testing management decision-making, conservative forces and conventional business thinking took hold, reducing Uddevalla to the status of a dispensable satellite plant, a costly blot on the accounts that could be sacrificed to restore the general health of the organization.

Some sections of the business media immediately jumped to the conclusion that humanistic teamworking is uneconomical (Wickens, 1993). Closure was equated with failure, providing proof that work reform is 'a dead horse' (a phrase that James Womack applied to Uddevalla in a New York Times report on 7 July 1991). Sources of competitive advantage were now to be found in Japan rather than Sweden, specifically in the organizational apparatus of lean production with its sequential, interlocking assembly teams, intensive yet fragmented working patterns and off-line 'improvement' meetings (Womack et al., 1990; Conti and Warner, 1993). This was the logical successor to the traditional assembly line, a less challenging format for those versed in Fordism and ideologically opposed to Uddevalla. From this standpoint, the distractions of work reform could finally be left behind, discarded as an outmoded deviation from superior developments in linear teamworking, or what Wickens (1993) described as controlled Taylorism.

Of course, such a sweeping dismissal triggered fierce reactions from researchers within the work humanization community (Berggren, 1992, 1995; Sandberg, 1993, 1995; Granath, 1998), and not without justification. As indicated in the Foreword, tolerant opinion, expressed over the past decade and more, generally agrees that the closure decision cannot be reduced to a test of humanistic manufacturing (Adler and Cole, 1993). There was simply too much going on within the company.

Internal politicking and manoeuvring proved crucial, as stakeholders at the various plants – managers, workers and unions – struggled for position, jobs and influence. The existing structure of the company favoured the traditionalists at Gothenburg, who could link the market and manufacturing capacity issue to the unhindered and uninterrupted operation of broader engineering and product design facilities, which were also located at this traditional centre of operations. If Uddevalla was treated merely as a remote and under-utilized assembly operation, for products that were losing market share, then it could easily be considered redundant. Senior management changes made this a more likely interpretation, as, for example, the sitting chief executive who was associated with Uddevalla gave way to another with no personal ties to the plant. Again, if reduced to a capacity and convenience matter, closure could seem rational, a feeling that was likely to be magnified at the senior levels when the more powerful unions at Gothenburg mobilized to save local jobs at the expense of satellite plants (Berggren, 1992).

In reality, politics informed the closure of Uddevalla. It could not be attributed to the systematic appraisal of contrasting production methods, or to any conclusions about the relative viability of dock assembly in the developing car market. Indeed, enthusiasts have argued with conviction that Uddevalla was closed despite its commercial viability, in a display of myopic business thinking that patently ignored significant indicators of future advantage (Sandberg, 1993, 1995). In one of the most rigorous and thoroughly researched ripostes, Berggren (1992, 1995) contradicts the negative claims about Uddevalla, revealing crucial productivity, quality and flexibility improvements over the lifetime of the plant.

Assembly time per unit was cut by 50 per cent, giving Uddevalla an edge over Gothenburg on the work hours necessary to complete each car by November 1992, the month in which closure was announced. Berggren's figures on this are supported by earlier data from Sandberg (1993), refuting the argument by Womack, Jones and Roos that dock assembly is relatively inefficient. Uddevalla was also ahead on quality and flexibility, factors that are widely associated with competitive advantage in the car industry, though with little apparent impact on Volvo decision-making.

Within a year of operation, Uddevalla's quality rating was on a par with Gothenburg, the internal index giving it a higher points score from 1991 onwards. Management figures show that model upgrades were accommodated more efficiently, with cost and productivity savings of between 25 and 50 per cent over the more conventional facility. Uddevalla was also more effective in linking production to customer demand, altering the balance between stock and ordered cars, the latter increasing from 20 to 70 per cent of total output by November 1992. The corresponding figure at Gothenburg was 35 per cent, most of the output here incurring storage and occasionally discount costs with a time lag before value was realized in the depressed markets of the early 1990s. According to Berggren's interview data, and by his collation of internal documentation, Uddevalla was acknowledged to be Volvo's internal benchmark on market responsiveness and customer satisfaction when the closure was announced. There was also a sense (expressed at least by local managers) that significant improvements and potential gains had yet to be tapped. This accounts for much of the frustration generated by the closure, and also the persistent argument that it represents an economic loss.

During the intervening years, numerous practitioners, managers and workers, have shown considerable sensitivity to the association of teamworking with quality, flexibility and market responsiveness. Major companies have replaced assembly lines with variants of dock manufacturing at sites throughout the world, justifying the change with essentially the same points that Berggren and Sandberg registered about Uddevalla and the car market. Enthusiasts for change have also confronted similar difficulties and political struggles.

As noted in the Foreword, American domestic appliance manufacturer, Maytag, reorganized factories in Iowa and Tennessee during the 1990s for the stationary, whole-product assembly of top-end washing machines and dishwashers. Against a background of intense competition, the expressed purpose was to align production with customer orders, rather than build to internal forecasts or to replenish stock. Cellular teams, as they were labelled in this case, had the flexibility to complete any model in their particular product range, at any point in their working day, improving capacity utilization by responding directly to the orders submitted by sales departments. The Tennessee dishwasher facility was credited with improving quality by 55 per cent, cutting work in progress by 60 per cent, increasing capacity by 50 per cent and releasing 43 000 square feet of factory space (*The Economist*, 2001). After Whirlpool acquired Maytag in 2006, this logic and the accumulated evidence about the value attached to participative teamworking, was rejected. Rationalistic thinking predominated, and the innovative plants were closed, with production relocated to lower wage, non-union, conventional assembly plants in Ohio and Mexico (Uchitelle, 2007; Hewett, 2008).

A similar, though longer lasting, example of alternative working occurred at Sony in 2002. The focus here was on camcorder manufacturing, with the reversal of an established strategy of low-cost mass production centred on Chinese assembly lines. In this case, the company redirected investment towards cellular working in Japan.

Towards the end of the 1990s, it became clear to Sony executives that existing manufacturing strategies were dramatically out of line with patterns of demand, especially in the American marketplace where newer and more innovative camcorders quickly captured attention, and where internet sales put a premium on rapid delivery. Competing on price with cheaper, low-margin, yet relatively dated models was proving ineffective and costly. The move to stationary cell-based working with multi-skilled teams of employees, made it easier for Sony to adjust production and respond to fluctuating demand, cutting the inventory and discounting costs associated with mass-produced models at the same time (*The Financial Times*, 2003).

With the production arrangements worked out for the R8 sports car, Audi supported the notion that flexible group-based manufacturing has continuing merit in the car industry, at least for their top-end, high-value products. The R8 production space in the Neckarsulm plant in Germany is reminiscent of Volvo's early approach to dock assembly at Kalmar in Sweden (Sandberg, 1995; Granath, 1998), with a linear production flow through 14 distinct assembly stations. Car bodies are mounted on height-adjustable frames to ameliorate the discomfort associated with 'under-up' work on the car, reproducing the 'lifting and tilting' flexibility of the guided vehicles that moved through the docks at Kalmar. With the R8, however, cars are wheeled from one bay to another, reinforcing the hand-crafted image presented in Audi marketing, although this is mainly a matter of skilled job performance within the assembly stations.

Only one of these makes use of robot technology, applying six of them for windscreen installation. The other areas provide access to flexible equipment to support extended tasks, which are themselves completed by highly qualified workers on 30-minute task cycles. Employees need to be able to respond to whatever job requirements are associated with the equipment list or 'customized book' that accompanies each vehicle. Parts 'shoppers' are responsible for ensuring that each group has the equipment it needs to complete the work for whichever variant of the R8 reaches their station in every 30-minute production slot. The skill-based flexibility of this approach is credited by Audi managers and engineers as an indispensible feature of their operation, enabling the company to deliver the levels of quality and responsiveness required by the market for 'premium' vehicles (Audi, 2007a). Available employee reports also suggest that it beats the performance of traditional job structures in social as well as economic terms, providing genuine opportunities for skill development, discretionary working and job satisfaction (Audi, 2007b).

Sony and Audi are among the most prominent organizations that in recent times have associated themselves with the pioneering traditions of autonomous or decentralized group working. There are many others, large and small, public and private, manufacturing companies and service providers, from the English company, Griggs, using 'pod production' to create Dr Marten shoes (BBC, 2002), to health care teams in the NHS (Beirne, 1999; Royal College of Nursing, 2007; Squires, 2009). The demise of Volvo's Uddevalla and Maytag's Newton and Jackson plants did not signal the end of parallel assembly, or demonstrate the folly of workplace restructuring as Wickens and others anticipated. However, prescriptive and managerialist preoccupations with outcomes, and the confident yet mechanical association of competitive advantage with effective, sustainable teamworking, lingers on (Clemons and Kroth, 2011). Much of the continuing interest is founded upon the assumption that conditioning pressures, the evident forces of consumerism, competition and devolution, are pushing unambiguously in the same direction (Owen, 2009). The clearest lesson from the Volvo and Maytag episodes is that this sort of economic determinism is misplaced. Conducive forces do not deliver automatic improvements at the workplace, or trigger internally consistent and coherent restructuring programmes.

By demonstrating that a good case does not guarantee success, the closure of Uddevalla injected a welcome measure of sobriety to the work reform movement. Patently, parallel teamworking is not all things to all people. It is difficult rather than straightforward, socially constructed rather than dictated by commercial or technological requirements. In stark contrast to initially upbeat and later romantic accounts, Berggren's post-mortem studies of the Uddevalla experience provide a 'warts and all' insight into the complexities of establishing and sustaining principled teamworking. He resists any inclination to gloss over difficult episodes or ignore setbacks and complications, reaching beyond the familiar decontextualized descriptions of novel team structures to offer penetrating insights and pertinent lessons.

One of his key findings is that contradictory tendencies inhibited progress through the first two years or so, as traditional management policies, standards and administrative structures coexisted with the innovative shop floor arrangements. As a consequence of this, work teams were supplied with procedures and methods documentation that was informed by the Gothenburg operation. Conventional management thinkers, who were housed in a detached office block away from the assembly docks, were adhering to a logic that was at odds with the team structure. Personnel at the innovative parts of the plant were actively resisting these conservative influences, often ignoring contradictory guidelines yet struggling to develop parallel assembly without conducive support systems or a consistent network of central services. Adler and Cole (1993) provide corroboration for this with evidence gathered during a visit in 1991. In fact, they condemned the management approach at that stage, describing it as abandonment rather than empowerment.

Berggren adds an extra dimension, however, charting subsequent attempts to align wider organizational structures and management processes with the assembly operation. By this means, he captures something of the dynamics of practical teamworking, conceptualizing it as an uneven, contradictory and emergent phenomenon, rather than a coherent, highly integrated and decisive break with the past. He acknowledges that innovation is inherently problematical, generating tensions, contradictions and struggles to address them. This reality is confirmed by other detailed case investigations, especially in the public sector.

Using comparative data on work restructuring within the Benefits Agency (a British government welfare service), Foster and Hoggett (1999) offer a critical appreciation of inherent contradictions in the management of change that unsettled staff and destabilized teamwork initiatives. Employees at the three sites investigated for this study broadly welcomed restructuring, at least at the outset. They were critical of status divisions, demarcation lines and the continuing influence of insular civil service bureaucracy. Teamwork offered an escape from the restrictions of the past, an antidote to 'them and us' tensions that characterized their exchanges with managers and claimants alike. More critical views hardened as the new initiatives developed, however.

Employees increasingly questioned the consistency of management behaviour, notably on appraisal and reward policies that were not suitably aligned to the new collective working arrangements. As a legacy of government preoccupations with public sector productivity during the 1980s, managers were operating a very mechanical approach to staff appraisal, measuring the performance of individuals by their velocity of throughput, by the volume and rate at which they processed benefit claims. This was coupled with annual appraisal interviews that were conducted by line managers, who were required to rank each worker on a five-point scale. Despite some adjustments to accommodate multidisciplinary team activities, basically the introduction of guidelines for the collective assessment of individual contributions, workers were still being evaluated by supervisors who operated in isolation and had little or no technical knowledge about the mix of benefits and skills involved. Some workers likened the whole appraisal and reward system to factory piece rate schemes that are out of touch with the professed interest in devolved and responsive decision-making.

On this evidence, competing management priorities were pulling staff, and indeed the Benefits Agency itself, in different directions. Attempts to secure collective working and develop shared responsibilities were undermined by inappropriate appraisal and reward programmes that drained morale. This is consistent with other evidence about the disarticulation of work reform and human resource management (Vallas, 2003; Beirne, 2011). Buchanan and Preston (1992) and Wright and Edwards (1998) have documented the damaging impact of inflexible pay and grading systems that cut against the grain of multi-skilled, cross-functional work arrangements on the shop floor. Conducive human resource policies and practices are not the automatic accompaniment to devolved teamworking, though in their absence support can diminish and effectiveness decline.

Similar results have been attributed to interactional constraints within (as well as between) functional areas (Beirne, 2011). Indeed, intra-functional contradictions tend to have a more immediate impact than cross-boundary effects, creating flashpoints and sparking disputes that can rapidly derail welcome initiatives. The health care sector provides an obvious example. During a study of nursing empowerment in a paediatric hospital (Beirne, 1999), it was discovered that territorialism and non-correspondence in the management of everyday pressures on labour allocation quickly disrupted a project that devolved some clinical and ward management responsibilities to teams of registered, associate and assistant nurses.

Echoing the typical business case for reform, the logic here was to increase flexibility and responsiveness, to cut patient waiting times and improve the quality of care by challenging traditional demarcation lines and altering the balance of skills between health care professionals. The role and influence of nursing staff was to be enhanced. Two wards were reorganized to allow semi-autonomous groups of nurses to cater for a dedicated portfolio of patients and their families, assessing needs at the bedside, developing detailed care plans and co-ordinating contact with doctors and other professionals. Unfortunately, in practice, there was significant slippage from these principles as nurses and line managers endeavoured, by their own priorities, to cope with the throughput of patients and 'get things done'.

The unanticipated interventions of Service Managers had the most dramatic and lasting effect. These were the managers who tailored available resources across the hospital to patient demand, and the majority were interpreting their role in a fashion that brought them directly into conflict with the nurses. Responding to staffing shortages on a daily basis, what they regarded as a more pressing need than team-based care, these managers would pluck nurses out of their wards to cover work in other parts of the surgical directorate. They were also moving patients, boarding them out to make space for new admissions and to contain costs through weekend ward closure. This often occurred at night while the patients were sleeping. Children would waken in another ward, removed from their designated nursing team. The continuity of care was disrupted as nurses lost their patients, and with them the opportunity to apply the core principles behind the new initiative. Staff reactions were marked by frustration, disappointment and eventually cynicism as the logic of a specified caseload was replaced by a 'care as best you can' approach. Front-line workers in this case, as in the Benefits Agency, lost faith in the reform agenda as one set of management priorities undermined the realization of another.

These studies have an authenticity and realism that cannot be found in static descriptions or typologies of teamwork, or in ideological treatments, be they of left or right, prescription or denial, glorification, mystification or rejection. They offer an insight into the dynamics of work reorganization, contextualizing the connections between structure and agency while magnifying processes that impinge upon the deployment and development of teamwork initiatives. They alert us to variable and evolving interpretations and provide a means of understanding the tensions that often surround practical episodes. The corollary is that teamwork survives as a potentially progressive phenomenon. It is not something that is unduly restrictive or stifling per se. However, its practical application often embodies inconsistencies, confusions and contradictions, which is why arrangements frequently sour as projects unfold.

For Berggren, this realization permits learning and innovation. It highlights the importance of recognizing and tackling constraints, of adjusting the focus of reform from initially specifying to actively sustaining work humanization. His own interpretation of the Uddevalla experience culminates in a discussion of managerial adjustments and alterations through 1992. It is ostensibly from this period, the final six months or so of parallel assembly, that the most significant lessons are to be drawn.

By the summer of 1992, senior managers had acknowledged the need for consistent support systems and were introducing organizational arrangements that apparently suited the production concept. These were designed to be the logical extension of dock assembly, projecting outwards from the team structure in a way that challenged established ways of doing things while at the same time anticipating a more sensitive and 'reflective' approach to innovation. Radical decentralization was a key part of this, reducing the hierarchy to just two tiers, plant and shop (assembly and materials handling) managers, with the latter installed in Uddevalla's principal governing committee in order to emphasize the centrality of team production. A novel leadership development pro-gramme was also launched, incorporating a requirement for managerial, professional and technical staff to serve some manufacturing time with the assembly teams. This was considered to be a useful way of fostering understanding and cooperation, qualities that were to be enhanced by relocating all managers and senior administrators to space alongside the assembly docks. Innovative measures were also initiated to ensure that product development became a more interactive process. In fact, partici-pative working between industrial engineers and workers had reached the point where they were jointly setting requirements for designers in light of tooling and other technical capabilities, and then rearranging the workspace and available equipment to manufacture cars with the latest specifications.

By reporting these developments and exploring the problematics of alignment at Uddevalla, Berggren provides a valuable corrective to the early optimism and much of the naïvety associated with the work reform movement. Having said that, it is important not to overstate managerial achievements or romanticize the shift to 'reflective production' within Volvo during this period. The chequered history of closure and episodic re-opening in this case, and of short run initiatives in others (including Maytag), demonstrates the precariousness of practical teamworking, regardless of any economic or social advantages that can be achieved over rationalistic work designs.

3. Technology and user empowerment

The search for alternative and progressive forms of organization has been heavily influenced by reflections upon the nature and role of work technology. Since the Tavistock mining studies (Trist and Bamforth, 1951; Trist et al., 1963), researchers have been acutely aware that there are choices to be made about the organization of human activity around a given technology (Benders et al., 2006). Rejecting the fatalistic argument that technology strictly determines the conduct and experience of work, enthusiasts have claimed space for humanization, even around Fordist technologies, as the previous chapter indicated. By the late 1970s, however, this sense of choice and capacity for influence had developed to include the design and shaping of the technology itself, as opposed to job (re)design after the fact of its creation.

Socio-technical systems theorists were again at the forefront of research and activism. Indeed, it is possible to discern a second wave of interest in the principles of socio-technical design as debates around the development and deployment of computer and communications technology progressed through the 1980s (Beirne and Ramsay, 1988). With the growing realization that organizations faced problems in harnessing the most sophisticated technology, critical accounts of rationalistic tendencies and influences on the workplace resurfaced (Mowshowitz, 1980; Briefs et al., 1983). Perceptive authors realized that organizational problems were constraining technological innovation, and that this offered new opportunities, access to a new area, and a means of taking the reform message to an important category of professional actors, technologists and computing scientists (Mumford, 1983, 2003).

Following the established traditions of the reform movement, critical scrutiny provided the initial leverage to promote change. The target this time was applied science and the orthodox principles of computing design, rather than the authoritarian preoccupations of managers or legacy of Taylorism on the shop floor. By conventional accounts, the process of creating computer-based work technology proceeds through a series of detached and socially neutral techniques that deliver clarity, precision and a technically proficient operating system. The official history of the discipline is that progress has been achieved through the application of engineering principles and standards that have institutionalized control in a complex, demanding and labour intensive activity that was previously vulnerable to errors and shortfalls in productivity and performance relative to expectations. Consequently, the common conceptualization is of a self-contained, monolithically expert and rational discipline that thrives independently of the organizational context in which the technology is eventually used (Cooley, 1980; Rosenbrock, 1990).

The management of computing development itself is typically informed by two closely connected manifestations of engineering rationality that perpetuate this image of technically dominated or technocentric design: an adherence to formal methodologies based on mathematical and logical processing techniques, and a step-wise progression through the precisely defined stages of a project life cycle. Although various brands of methodology now vie for attention, the vast majority share common characteristics and a familial tendency to lay down very precise protocols, tools and procedures for structuring the development process. The central organizing vision is of a linear track through isolated compartments of work, allied to a sequential delineation of the activities that designers are expected to follow. Occasionally, the image presented is of a cascading waterfall of discrete project segments that proceed through some variant of requirements specification, outline and then detailed design, testing and implementation, with fine-tuning, maintenance and documentation incorporated at the end (Beirne et al., 1998b).

For social science commentators, the similarities with Taylorism are compelling (Mumford, 1983, 2003). Common roots and characteristics are discernible in the drive to divide, standardize and formally specify the boundary lines between associated work tasks (Benders et al., 2006). This, in turn, reveals a corresponding commitment to top-down co-ordination and control, and to the concentration of decision-making authority among 'objective' experts, social actors who supposedly have an advantage over other stakeholders by virtue of their independent ability to create ordered systems and deliver rational outcomes. This most revealing of genealogical preoccupations translates into the systematic marginalization of alternative interests and sources of expertise, notably workers under Taylorism and the users of technology under computing orthodoxy (Greenbaum and Kyng, 1991; Beirne et al., 1998b).

Yet the parallels with Taylorism continue to hold through the reactions and controversies that have been triggered by rationalistic computing development. Since the 1980s, the pages of computing and systems management journals have been peppered with articles lamenting the limited returns on investment, persistent problems with 'usability' and high levels of frustration associated with technologies that have been created by conventional methods. There are numerous illustrations of technically interesting and sophisticated systems that failed to match their operating specifications, falling dramatically short of what people in the receiving organizations envisaged, wanted or expected (Wagner and Piccoli, 2007; Subramanyam et al., 2010). Some have been spectacular, such as those widely reported in Britain at the Stock Exchange, customs and ambulance services and at the Performing Rights Society in the 1990s (BBC, 1994; Flowers, 1996). There is also an abundance of anecdotal evidence from workers and managers who bemoan the fact that remote and over-rationalized creations have little or no correspondence with the realities of their situation, and require costly amendments and organizational adaptations to secure even basic levels of performance. From this grassroots position, rationalistic computing seems vulnerable to the same basic criticism that was, and still is, levelled at the Taylorist management of labour, namely, that it is more trouble than it is worth (Mumford, 1983, 2003; Greenbaum and Kyng, 1991; Bossen et al., 2012).

For traditionalists, of course, rationalism can be defended if disappointing outcomes are attributable to departures or deviations from the prescribed approach. Some custodians of 'good practice' have argued that systematic methods are not adequately followed by computing practitioners, that developers are not demonstrating the take-up of a 'mature' approach, and that rationalism should now be aligned with national and transnational quality assurance regimes to encourage compliance (Wilson et al., 1996). This view is canvassed against a strong current of alternative opinion, however. Instead of criticizing developers for pursuing a lax or less than systemic approach, influential commentators are actively challenging received wisdom and registering doubts about the adequacy of the computing orthodoxy itself (Curtis et al., 1988; Greenbaum and Kyng, 1991; Bansler and Bodker, 1992; Kanstrup, 2012).

The central argument here is that the established ideal of highly structured, top-down development is just too simplistic and remote from the everyday pressures of organizational innovation, relying on abstract and over-rationalized images that are at odds with realities on the ground. The immediate context of 'live' computing projects and the target environments for their applications display a level of complexity and subtlety that is beyond rationalistic models. The reason, ultimately, is that they lack an informed understanding of important socio-economic factors that affect how the process unfolds. These are beyond the reach of formal modelling and data capturing tools that privilege the more accessible, obvious and official aspects of management and organizational behaviour. As the post-mortem analyses of systems failures reveal, informal exchanges and activities that rely on tacit skills and abilities, especially under exceptional as opposed to routine circumstances, remain out of focus. Moreover, the consensus of critical opinion is that this is unlikely to change so long as the perceptions of workers and other organizational members connect the mechanical application of standard tools with the cult of the expert and the imposition of 'designer' computing 'solutions', regardless of local views and concerns (Mumford, 1983, 2003).

The corollary is that increasingly strident or strictly enforced rationalism will obstruct rather than promote the more effective application of work technology. The problems of failure and frustration will be exacerbated as the constraining influence of technocentric design fosters distrust and resistance, manifest in a reluctance to provide reliable information, a refusal to adapt to new systems, and possibly even attempts to sabotage attendant processes or outcomes. The message that comes across here is that the successful development of work technology is contingent not only upon the technical science of computing, but also upon a grounded understanding of human orientations and behaviour within and between organizations (Berner, 2008; Notter and Grant, 2011).

This is not in itself a novel argument, but rather a variation on long standing themes in the computing literature. The charge that rationalists are out of touch and that their methodologies are ill-conceived has been rehearsed over five decades. During the 1960s and '70s, penetrating critiques by authors such as Boguslaw (1965) and Weizenbaum (1976) stimulated debates about the poverty of abstract systems thinking that relegates sections of humanity to the status of machine substitutes, that promotes a concern for 'non-people' rather than developing human roles and relationships through technological innovation. From here, technologists have no effective means of engaging with people who have relevant work or business knowledge because they reject their input ideologically, and exclude them by design. The corresponding call for root-and-branch change, for a more open and inclusive approach that anchors technology to the interests and knowledge of those on the receiving end, left many practitioners unmoved until relatively recently, until the facts of failure and frustration became so glaringly obvious. Now there are signs that client communities and user groups have sufficient confidence to express their concerns about emerging technologies, and to challenge the internal logic of engineering rationality. User groups are certainly more vocal about the limitations of computing orthodoxy and the litany of empty promises associated with its application (Beirne et al., 1998a; Greenbaum and Kyng, 1991). There is also evidence that user managers are acting purposefully to influence the economics of systems development, rather than passively accepting rationalistic prescriptions and the attendant costs of adhering to more rigidly defined methodologies (Beirne et al., 1998b; Guidon and Curtis, 1988; Bansler and Bodker, 1993; Wagner and Piccoli, 2007; Notter and Grant, 2011).

Commercial systems builders are confronting this in the marketplace, reporting that clients are pressing them to contain costs and provide a responsive service, requirements that sit uneasily with rationalistic drives to benchmark their performance against tighter engineering standards and process controls. Responding to the commercial context in which they operate, some front-line developers, notably those working for small- to medium-sized systems providers, are negotiating their way around formal methods that are felt to be hampering their efforts. Their clients are effectively forcing their hand, asserting managerial influence and restricting the levels of delegated control available to computing 'experts' (Beirne et al., 1998b). Bad experiences and the reported failures of the past are conditioning the contractual and everyday exchanges between users and technologists, with those on the receiving end squeezing costs and completion dates while demanding systems that are functional on their own terms, that add value to their business or operation rather than by reference to some technical and externally generated success criteria.

For developers working against these pressures, the economics of innovation put a premium on applied knowledge, on their ability to relate technical skills to an understanding of the receiving organizations and how they, in fact, can make the most of available technology (Wagner and Piccoli, 2007). Cultivating local knowledge and the status of a trusted partner is the key to repeat business and a solid reputation for these technologists. Knowing their clients and relating technology visibly and directly to their business contexts is more important than adhering to an engineering rulebook that sets predefined procedures in stone and monitors compliance according to engineering rather than business priorities (Beirne et al., 1998b). Departures from rationalism and the traditional life cycle become sensible instead of dangerous, entrepreneurial more than deviant, promoting success by tailoring the process to client concerns and avoiding the imposition of costly controls that are viewed with suspicion (on documenting progress or altering specifications beyond the initial steps, for example). By this evidence and these interpretations (Beirne et al., 1998b; Guidon and Curtis, 1988; Bansler and Bodker, 1993; Harding and Gilbert, 1993), engineering and organizational responses to the technology problem are far from congruent. On a broadening front, and certainly at the level of practice, the wisdom of the traditional experts, the custodians of rationalism, is questioned rather than taken for granted.

These points about the human and commercial blind spots in orthodox thinking puncture the illusion of rational design, viz., that effective technology is created by objective outsiders who are untainted by workplace preoccupations and local interests, and who promote ordered progress by virtue of their technical expertise. Patently, work technology does not develop in isolation from human and commercial considerations. Nor for that matter does rationalism since it incorporates a particular ideological treatment of people and organization, as previously mentioned. The application of computing to the workplace has been flawed, compromised and expensive, calling doubt upon even the most ardent defence of rationalism. This reality, or rather the widespread acceptance of it, provides a powerful impetus for change.

An established body of researchers and practitioners now accept that systems development is an integrative activity that depends entirely upon the synthesis of particular socio-economic and technical processes and relationships (Beirne et al., 1998b; Howcroft and Wilson, 2003). Openness and cooperation have emerged as developmental themes, as essential attributes for understanding and developing this rich mix of ingredients to the point where technology actually (rather than hypothetically) adds value to work or to business (Wagner and Piccoli, 2007). More inclusive forms of knowledge-sharing and joint decision-making are advocated to straddle the gap between technologists and user communities in terms of their respective skills, insights and experience. User involvement and participative systems design, topics that have figured prominently in the research literature since the 1970s, are attracting greater attention (Howcroft and Wilson, 2003; Kanstrup, 2012). The net result is that theorists and practitioners from a range of different backgrounds, and with computing, management and social science affiliations, are actively conceptualizing systems development in more novel and innovative ways than hitherto. This does not signal an emerging consensus, however.

The contention that systems development should be less exclusive, more open and heavily reliant upon local knowledge is rehearsed by theorists and practitioners with very different ideas and prescriptions (Beirne and Ramsay, 1988, 1992). Some articulate a view that is striking for its continuity with the orthodoxy rather than any departure from it. Users are to be courted through amendments to rationalistic practice that focus narrowly on the challenge of extracting relevant information and generating consent for designer systems when they arrive in the workplace (Benders et al., 2006; Wagner and Piccoli, 2007; Harris and Weistroffer, 2009). This is most obvious in discussions of knowledge elicitation, prototyping and overcoming resistance in packaged outlines of structured practices and formal methodologies (Yeates et al., 1994;

Blum, 1996). Established prerogatives and procedures are not considered to be problematical per se, requiring only the passive involvement of users where professional technologists deem it necessary to combat systems 'noise' or to attend to 'human factors', phraseology that usefully signals the continuing influence and limited intent of traditional thinking.

This response either rejects or fails to grasp the full significance of critical commentary, attaching a minimal, instrumental value to user input. Proponents are preoccupied with the legitimacy of design decisions and the success of their applications, rather than the advantages or disadvantages for users. The validity of such involvement is judged according to the development conditions prevailing for particular projects (Heinbokel et al., 1996; Subramanyam et al., 2010). Hence the importance ascribed to user roles varies with the type of system being introduced. Where effective installation is considered to be dependent upon the voluntary use of the technology, as in the application of management decision support systems, for instance, involvement is put at a premium. Conversely, if design teams can be shown to contain all the expertise required, if specifications can be clearly defined, or if the product is likely to be invisible or unimportant to users then involvement is considered unnecessary.

This is a calculative approach that maintains the divisions and top-down feel of orthodox engineering. Adherents assume, on rationalistic grounds, that computing professionals have a legitimate role to manage and control the contributions of users. While conceding that user input is potentially significant and that design is not exclusively a technical exercise, the inference is that effectiveness will be compromised if existing conventions and demarcations are challenged rather than amended. Again the implication is that users lack the necessary expertise to make an independent contribution. Indeed, they appear in these representations not as purposeful human beings with interests and preferences, but as resources or components that can be used advantageously to improve design decisions and widen the range of options open to technologists.

Following this line, a substantial body of research has focused on the classification of conditional variables that influence the success of involvement episodes. This suggests that the impact of involvement on resistance and utilization, and in generating information, varies with the types of user involved, the phases of development during which it is practised, and the nature of the communication processes that are brought into play. Correspondingly, guidelines on good practice have emerged that encourage designers to assess the status of users according to their knowledge or influence, and to vet candidates for involvement on whether they are likely to divulge information or promote the acceptance and effective use of systems when installed. Restricting the scope of involvement to particular stages of the traditional life cycle is also considered to be prudent. Recommendations typically centre on requirements analysis and implementation, where additional 'tools' are needed to capture data or overcome resistance to change (Wong and Tate, 1994; Wagner and Piccoli, 2007; Harris and Weistroffer, 2009; Subramanyam et al., 2010).

By these methods, user involvement is reduced to an early warning mechanism that can let designers test out their assumptions about work situations, and head off any difficulties prior to costly disruptions. Users are conceptualized merely as intervening factors that can be dispossessed of their intrinsic knowledge and encouraged to conform to the technology process by the application of formal techniques and 'logic'. Interestingly, the question of whether users will accept involvement on these terms, or even use the process to pursue other objectives, is rarely asked. Involvement is assumed to be a concession that users cannot refuse, or a mechanism that can operate effectively where user managers demand compliance.

TOWARDS A RADICAL AGENDA

The cold calculation that informs this variant of rationalism is anathema to writers and activists versed in the participative traditions of workplace reform. From their standpoint, the advance of work technology is a social and ethical project, and not just a technical exercise. Analyses in this vein support social as well as performance goals, presenting the case for involvement not only on pragmatic grounds as an indispensable functional requirement for sound design, but also as a fair and morally justifiable course of action. Principles are at stake for this community, and the key one is that technology should be developed and modified to satisfy user interests and requirements, not the other way around.

Attempts to operationalize this alternative vision have been heavily influenced by socio-technical design ideals (Benders et al., 2006). Enid Mumford is the most celebrated pioneer of what is now called socio-technical systems development, an approach that presents involvement not as a communication exercise but as a legitimate right and end in itself (Mumford, 1983, 1996, 2003). Mumford and her colleagues aim to increase the potential for self-determination, rather than capture data or minimize possible resistance (Hirschheim and Klein, 1994). Drawing upon earlier generations of job-centred socio-technical theory, they blend ethical and effectiveness arguments to challenge instrumental thinking and encourage user communities to take control of the technology process.

From here passive involvement is unacceptably manipulative, and so transparent that users are unlikely to volunteer their insights, expertise and commitment on a sustained basis. What is missing is the recognition that design relates not to technical systems that have behavioural consequences, but to extensive social systems that have a technical dimension. The process of remedial activity is therefore much larger and more complex than is commonly envisaged by those who argue for restricted and constrained user involvement. Designers have to locate the technical features of new systems within a surrounding organizational framework of priorities, roles and relationships that cannot be fully appreciated by the application of passive procedures through the early stages of development when users may be unsure about their requirements and the possibilities for satisfying them. Designers must also incorporate socio-psychological phenomena if resistance is to be reduced, giving user views on work experience and job satisfaction equal credence alongside technical issues and constraints. By contrast with calculating involvement, socio-technical approaches call for a dual 'fit' between users and their 'needs' on one hand and technologies and organizational structures on the other.

The corollary is that involvement per se is not enough. Users must have an active role, with genuine decision-making influence. Mumford's ETHICS methodology, an acronym for Effective Technical and Human Implementation of Computer Systems, is the most widely publicized and applied means of pursuing this (Mumford, 2003). As an alternative to prescriptive orthodoxy (Hirschheim and Klein, 1994), it offers what purports to be a toolkit for enacting consensus forms of user-driven, even democratic, design. Hierarchy is de-emphasized as larger numbers of stakeholders are brought into the process and given formal opportunities to influence outcomes in a concrete way. A novel mix of analytical tools is available as part of the package to elicit user views and promote a shared understanding of issues and options, including a diagramming technique to focus discussion on workflow and layout, and diagnostic questionnaires to relate personal needs and expectations to organizational priorities and technical possibilities. These provide the means of situating Quality of Working Life concerns for interesting and rewarding work at the centre of computing projects, and for retaining an everyday focus on the joint optimization of technical resources and human effort.

Various options for structuring participation are also identified, signalling a pragmatic concern to make progress even under difficult situations that require compromise. Mumford herself proposes three categories of participation, ranging from least to most desirable (Mumford, 1980, 1981, 2003). At the conservative end of her spectrum is Consultative Design, which locates decision-making predominantly with the traditional sources of technical expertise. Users are entitled to give 'evidence' through formal procedures like interviews or questionnaires, by offering information directly, and by subjecting the final pool of knowledge to cross-examination. Representative Design gives user communities a more positive or forceful role through a formal structural mechanism such as a steering committee, or by a process of secondment where certain users sit on design teams. Representatives are chosen by various means, including appointment by managers (Mumford and Henshall, 1979) or by a ballot of users for candidates nominated either by managers or the users themselves. The formal influence of these representatives can vary from simply providing input and reporting progress to channelling user decisions on whether design options should be modified or vetoed.

Consensus Design is the most ambitions format identified by Mumford, and the one that she personally favours for its democratic characteristics. This aims to give entire users communities the opportunity to influence decisions directly and throughout the development process. The machinery is still representative, which can be a source of confusion, though at this level there are two groups, again a steering committee and a design team, the latter including elected members and operating with a brief to develop viable options and final arrangements. The steering group consists of user managers and representatives of trades unions and other interests (such as nursing or medical personnel), and carries responsibility for setting basic objectives and constraints, for monitoring progress and ensuring that decisions are consistent with broader policies and strategic priorities.

Through four decades of practice across a range of settings, and in major organizations such as Rolls Royce, KLM, Dutch Telecom, Tetley Walker, DEC and ICI, this socio-technical approach has captured interest and approval. Enthusiasts have commended its 'emancipatory' intent and ability to deliver 'authentic' participation (Hirschheim and Klein, 1994). Others remain cautious, even sceptical, however. Hasty and unrestrained judgements can have an unsettling rather than a reassuring effect, suggesting that proponents are out of touch, or insensitive to everyday challenges and constraints. While the discussion around ETHICS and socio-technical design has played an important role in claiming space for user-participation (rather than merely involvement), it may have exercised researchers more than practitioners, with little overall effect on the conduct of systems development (Howcroft and Wilson, 2003).

Moreover, it trades so heavily on positive imagery and convivial possibilities that the challenges of enacting and sustaining direct participation in the technology processes are given insufficient attention.

Writers allied to the Scandinavian traditions of workplace reform have reached beyond a wider sense of unease to register some of the most telling concerns about the socio-technical approach (Ehn, 1988; Bjerknes et al., 1987). Central to this is the charge that it lacks a critical edge, theoretically and practically, that it represents a conservative influence and is therefore ill-equipped to deliver authentic participation. It is considered to be tame, to pursue harmony and consensus with little obvious grasp of real-world tensions and conflicting interests, making it a soft target for cynical managers or other professionals who would co-opt, manipulate or abuse the process (Bjerknes et al., 1987). The potential for drift and for the watering down of any progressive intent is highlighted, along with the danger of slippage downwards through Mumford's hierarchy of participation to the point where front-line users detect little more than constrained or curtailed involvement.

These critics articulate the case for a more politicized, less vulnerable and resilient approach to participative design. Although various shades of opinion inform Scandinavian commentary, and there is no single, precisely defined approach, adherents share a common antipathy for managerialism and the corporate shaping of technology. They act as advocates for user rights and align themselves explicitly with trades unions, third party organizations that carry favour for their independent ability to safeguard user interests, on the technology front as elsewhere. Consequently, their underlying conceptualization connects technology to thorny issues of workplace control and the defence of established prerogatives that socio-technical accounts tend to miss or avoid. Their references to democracy and emancipation are therefore sharper, considered rather than bland, and developed with a greater apparent feel for the problematics of advancing participative design.

The socio-technical emphasis on consensus, harmony and mutually beneficial innovation (Brown, 1967) is thrown into relief by the attention given to politics, conflict and tensions, and their resonance with the felt realities of participation on the ground, as often expressed by practitioners and users themselves (Beirne et al., 1998a; Clement, 1994). The commentaries offered by Mumford and her colleagues seem aloof and sanitized by comparison, lacking the analytical wherewithal to accommodate relevant issues or counteract inhibiting tendencies. Despite their common professed commitment to democratizing the technology process and humanizing work, these traditions are at odds with each other theoretically and practically, with one denying that the other is fit for purpose. While they share a basic distaste for mechanical and restricted user involvement, the Scandinavian researchers fear that socio-technical approaches degenerate to this in applied content. Hence, they present a very different framework and vocabulary of practice.

To differentiate their own work from socio-technical interventions, Ehn and Kyng developed the collective resource approach (Bjerknes et al., 1987; Ehn, 1988). This, again, is an indicative blend of ideas and innovations from across the Scandinavian research community, rather than a unifying approach. It speaks to the wider interest in mobilizing trade unions in the technology process, drawing on a productive history of cross-boundary collaboration between researchers and union activists in Sweden, Denmark and Norway. This famously dates back to the mid-1970s and the DEMOS project, Democratic Planning and Control in Working Life: on Computers, Industrial Democracy and Trade Unions. 'Investigation groups' were established at a number of sites to bring workers and their unions together with a multidisciplinary research team to consider local problems and open horizons for developing technology and enhancing work experience. This was an initial, albeit rather tentative, move against the conventional logic of integrating users into the established patterns and priorities of systems analysis and implementation, exploring the potential for people to shape the nature of the technology they eventually use. Given its localized operation, it was felt to be largely reactive, an aspect that subsequent projects would tackle through a more explicit emphasis on specifying and creating skill enhancing and socially useful technologies.

Probably the most influential and frequently cited initiative in this regard was labelled UTOPIA, Training, Technology and Products from the Quality of Work Perspective. This was initiated at the beginning of the 1980s, and set out to deliver new and highly marketable computing tools for text and image processing to the graphics industry. The challenge for the collaborators was to find ways of harnessing technology that could develop the skills and experiential contribution of employees while improving the typographical quality of newspapers. Shop stewards and members of the Nordic Graphic Workers Union participated in a design group with computing scientists and practitioners from an independent systems supplier. This was to be an arena for mutual learning and collaborative influence, with contributors applying their professional expertise and political interests to produce novel and viable technology for the marketplace, for general rather than their own immediate use.

The results attracted international attention, and are widely acknowledged to be significant. Advances are recognized in terms of the accessibility and humanizing qualities of the resulting technology, and also in the pioneering methods devised for its creation (Bjerknes et al., 1987; Greenbaum and Kyng, 1991). The boundaries of systems development were extended by contributions that encouraged mutual learning. Organizational simulations, distinctive prototypes and design mock ups, even cardboard computers, enabled technologists to learn from the experiences of designated users, rather than formal systems descriptions. They were working not from abstractions but the situated actions of the people doing the work. Their interventions therefore had an authenticity that continues to draw respect in the literature (Blomberg et al., 1996; Howcroft and Wilson, 2003).

Of course, there were setbacks and difficulties that also figure in measured evaluations. The participating vendor eventually stopped producing the resulting system. Trade union politics magnified the tensions that can be generated by different levels of interest, commitment and activism, even within organizations that profess to be working towards common objectives through a shared ideology. Ehn (1988) candidly admits to the fragility of these episodes, a feature that others have identified when considering how they might translate to less supportive environments, to those without the conducive legal and historical labour relations traditions that characterize the Scandinavian countries.

What they contribute, nonetheless, is a rich basis for reflection and some novel ideas about the conduct of participative design. They help to flesh out Berggren's notion of reflective production, relating issues about the consistency of progressive practice to personal sense-making about values, reactions and patterns of engagement. Reflective technologists in other countries have responded to the principles of learning and designing 'by doing', by rooting analysis in local activities and understandings and creating space for user influence through 'situated design'. A particularly influential group emerged in the United States in the 1990s, preferring to talk about participatory or co-operative design, though bringing the Scandinavian work to a wider audience and sustaining the momentum behind more ambitious or radical formats (Blomberg et al., 1996; Bossen et al., 2012). This interest in the Scandinavian contributions even prompted a revision of ETHICS and the socio-technical approach.

Responding to the criticisms levelled at ETHICS, Hirschheim and Klein (1994) endeavoured to reformulate and reinvigorate it, to enhance its emancipatory potential. They acknowledge that the collective resource approach has made substantial progress in grounding development activities and promoting self-awareness through critical reflection about the context in which technology is actually used. ETHICS, they concede, is weak in this regard, although it could, in their view, be modified to develop these qualities in practitioners. Diary-keeping and electronic meeting systems are introduced as viable means of capturing and advertising ideas, recognizing views and conducting arguments, and generally building confidence and the capacity to engage with others. However, at the core of their contribution is the contention that ETHICS has distinctive qualities in itself that make it the most viable candidate for upgrading to achieve emancipatory goals.

Ostensibly, ETHICS has an advantage as a framework that can actively support self-determination and reduce the risks of passive or manipulative user-participation. While the Scandinavian interventions operate on a 'top-down' or 'outside-in' basis, the 'overwhelming emphasis on bottom-up (grassroots) participation' (p. 87) gives ETHICS an edge. This is a controversial argument that is far from secure in its attempt to answer the critics. It rests on the proposition that ETHICS has an essential integrity to its process, that it incorporates checks and balances, for example, that target negative influences and provide a compelling reason for stakeholders to collaborate in genuine and meaningful ways. Hirschheim and Klein attempt to extend and strengthen these elements to institutionalize critical reflection, mutual learning and collective influence via ETHICS. They add teamwork incentives, group decision support concepts and many of the ingredients of the collective resource approach to solidify the ETHICS methodology and secure its credentials as the most robust structure for organizing participation.

Strong claims are made to support this project, although in truth the authors deliver an affirmation of faith, asserting rather than demonstrating the suitability of the host methodology. For all the emphasis on critical reflection and local influence, ETHICS is endorsed by means of abstract arguments that reflect prevailing debates within the research community, again suggesting an insularity of outlook rather than a serious attempt to act on practitioner views. Hirschheim and Klein commend their work in terms of its responsiveness to critical opinion: 'the reformulation can be called critical insofar as the underlying philosophical principles have passed the critical scrutiny of the relevant informed community' (p. 99). Grassroots practitioners with experience on the receiving end of ETHICS interventions seem to be excluded from this community. Opinion from the sharp end is conspicuous by its absence, yet the folly of endorsing the framework without such a critical reference point is apparent from available studies of ETHICS in action.

Of the various episodes reported to vindicate this approach (Mumford and MacDonald, 1989; Mumford, 1996, 2003), one stands out in terms of the frequency and positive nature of its citation (Mumford and Henshall,

1979; Mumford, 1980, 1981, 1996, 2003; Land and Hirschheim, 1983). The host company was Rolls Royce. During the 1970s, Enid Mumford was invited to operationalize ETHICS at its Derby engine plant for the introduction of a supplier accounts system. This involved some 60 employees at the Purchase Invoice and Treasurers Departments, areas that were plagued by inefficiencies manifest in rapid staff turnover and significant delays in the payment of outstanding accounts. A design group of six clerical workers from the affected departments and two systems analysts from the management services division was established and charged with assessing efficiency and job satisfaction requirements, and for incorporating these in proposals for computer-based reorganiza- tion. At a higher level, a steering committee of middle and senior managers, plus a trade union official, operated to review progress and arbitrate on whether design decisions complied with company policy. After some seven months of working half a day per week, the design group produced three successive designs, submitting each in turn to the management group and to employees until a version was finally settled upon and implemented.

At face value, this is an encouraging example of what ETHICS can deliver. Indeed, Mumford repeatedly presents it as an unambiguous and fairly straightforward success story. The main text says as much in a bold and unqualified opening statement (Mumford and Henshall, 1979). Land and Hirschheim (1983) describe it as a good example of the 'rare democratic form of decision-making … [where] … all participants have an equal voice in the decision process' (p. 103). Closer inspection provides good reason to doubt this, however. Problems are discernible, both in the detail of the case and the manner of its reporting. Surpris- ingly, significant issues and constraints on the process are glossed over, revealing a lack of critical self-reflection. More importantly, there is little in Hirschheim and Klein's reformulation to signal that they are any more sensitive or better equipped to grant them serious attention.

First, the design objectives and outcomes seem to have been clearly predefined by senior figures. The 'Internal Consultant' on the project (and co-author of the main text) was the Systems Manager of the accounts section. Members of the design group, supposedly the hub of the process, were hand-picked by this individual in collaboration with the supervisor of the Purchase Invoice Department and the manager of the Treasurers Department. This was justified as a means of assembling a representative spread of contributors, rather than just a collection of the most popular members of staff. Yet the possible consequences of this, of selecting unpopular people, for example, or individuals who command little respect in the wider community, are not even considered. There is little sign of reflective management or sensitive engagement with the wider community on the composition and functioning of the design group.

Despite this conservative influence, the design group presented three options, ranging from job enrichment within the existing operational structure to multi-skilled teamworking for particular grades of staff and categories of activity. The more radical option, though preferred by the designers, was rejected by managers, and, after some pressure salesmanship, a watered-down version was accepted, which Henshall hoped would lead to his own preferred option in good time (Mumford and Henshall, 1979, p. 73). His favoured approach seemed to tie precise numbers of staff to each team and involve the attendant elimination of the established grading scheme, an option that was considered too revolutionary for higher grades to accept in the first instance. This is hardly surprising given the implied loss of status, and possibly also remuneration.

This apparent interest in revisiting or altering terms and conditions of employment as the participation process developed passes without any independent comment from Mumford, or from her supporters in the research community. Without any hint of irony, the Mumford and Henshall text reports that senior figures never imposed any constraints on the design group or intervened in a negative manner:

> The role of senior management through their membership of the Steering Group was both helpful and liberating. (Mumford and Henshal, 1979, p. 105)

> The Steering Group's advice enabled the Design Group to free itself from a too timid approach to the redesign of work. (Mumford and Henshall, 1979, p. 106)

> Without encouragement from the Steering Group, the Design Group might have been too conservative in its approach. (Mumford and Henshall, 1979, p. 27)

The apparent failure to detect any difficulties with this situation begs some fundamental questions about the putative safeguards and participative credentials of socio-technical practice. While the Scandinavian researchers would be looking for trade union involvement under these circumstances, the ETHICS accounts offer nothing at all under the heading 'union versions'.

In the Mumford and Henshall text, a book of 190 pages, the question of union involvement is dismissed with a few bland words of appreciation in the preface. This treatment may seem entirely justified, since union officials made only guest appearances and the lone representative on the steering committee was absent when Mumford and the managers decided how the project was to proceed (p. 18). Critical reflection offers another possibility, however. Union figures could have been reading the situation with a more acute sense of micro politics, running for cover at the thought of being embroiled in any challenge to approved grading systems.

The failure to recognize the difficulties with this case, and the persistence in presenting it as an exemplary episode, seriously undermines the case for an ETHICS-based activism. This is a matter of theory and conceptualization, of obscuring rather than illuminating the problematics of participation. No matter how skilfully constructed the methodology, or elegantly defended, theoretical sensitivity is required to target factors that inhibit progress, that are experienced as limiting or constraining at close quarters by those involved. It is not enough merely to condemn token participation, or to acknowledge the risks of manipulation without the social realism to recognize and tackle it in practice. Despite the references to critical reflection and broader social theory, there is nothing in the ETHICS package that permits an effective analysis of the impact that status differences, organizational hierarchies and established control systems can have upon the process. The interplay between organizational structures, cultures and the conduct of participation projects is conceptualized in abstract and unrealistically consensual terms. Hence, the judgement offered by the Scandinavian critics is well founded. To the extent that local worries and reported constraints remain out of focus, Hirschheim and Klein's reformulation fails to release ETHICS from its conservative influence.

STRUCTURES AND STRUGGLES

Alternative, less promotional survey and case material (Beirne and Ramsay, 1988, 1992; Beath and Orlikowski, 1994; Howcroft and Wilson, 2003) illustrates the typical obstacles and the degree of difficulty that confronts those who would seriously strive to achieve participative design. Constraints on the prospects for more open collaboration are located within established hierarchies, institutional settings and cultural contexts, including professional affiliations and the continuing influence of rationalistic frames of reference. The net result is a far less cheerful picture of the practice of user-participation to date, and of the patterns of intervention necessary to secure more progressive formats in the future.

Counteracting the attractive socio-technical image of unambiguous and relatively painless user empowerment, the findings from these studies reveal the importance of authority relations, the reproduction of hierarchy and the lingering defence of decision-making prerogatives by managerial grades from both operational and information systems spheres of influence. The outcome is that elaborate structures of participation operate to frame the exchanges between the various stakeholders in each technology process, affecting and often restricting their contributions.

Design projects in practice typically work on a separation of issues, distinguishing aspects that are worthy of user collaboration from others that are decidedly non-negotiable or non-participatory. This is reinforced by complex arrangements that fragment and formalize the process, incorporating users selectively according to protocols, prerogatives, and occasionally the whims of specialists and more senior others. Hence the discovery that user-participation is typically splintered by grade, status and stage of development, with only a very small proportion of available users experiencing any kind of sustained involvement in design activities (Beirne and Ramsay, 1988, 1992).

Considering the composition of user groups, survey data from the 1980s suggests that middle and senior managers have the closest involvement, contributing to 55 and 46 per cent of schemes, respectively (Beirne and Ramsay, 1988). Lower managerial and clerical staff experienced curtailed contact, the latter having an input to only 37 per cent of the schemes identified at that time. Involvement by secretarial and manual workers was a fleeting and minority activity, apparent in just 4 per cent of reported cases, and showing little sign of expansion according to more recent reports (Howcroft and Wilson, 2003). To make matters worse, there are peaks and troughs of participation for particular categories of user through the distinct phases of the technology process. Non-managerial white-collar workers are predominantly involved, if at all, in the work analysis, implementation and operational adjustment phases of any project. Shop floor workers are marginalized to an even greater extent, with far lower numbers involved though at similar points. This picture contrasts sharply with reported socio-technical episodes (Mumford, 2003; Benders et al., 2006), suggesting that participation is seriously restricted in practice, limiting the contribution that knowledgeable people can make.

These conclusions are bolstered by case study evidence that provides additional depth to supplement the profile information from available surveys (Beirne and Ramsay, 1992; Howcroft and Wilson, 2003). This fills out the detail of a typically fragmented and divided process, even among developers, the experts formally credited with driving and controlling progress. Although technologists and users are often treated as homogeneous groups, the case evidence reveals a differentiated pattern of multiple team involvement, with extensive filtering and tiering of user and expert contributions along conventional lines of authority.

Users, for their part, are selectively incorporated according to their position and status, rather than their knowledge per se. It is common to find a clustering of users from similar grades and levels in the employment ladder (Beirne and Ramsay, 1992). The time that each group devotes to development matters, the steps at which it occurs and the influence achieved depends very much upon the member's existing position within formal decision-making structures. Involvement therefore proceeds by way of an elaborate division of labour.

Senior executives form strategic planning teams that have high levels of discretion though short spans of participation, dealing mainly with the priorities and direction of each development. Beneath this level of strategic decision-making there are various management teams, ranging from quite senior standing committees responsible for steering, planning and budgeting decisions to junior advisory councils and work groups that are convened for a specific purpose at a particular stage of development. Computing professionals are involved in all of these, though again the hierarchy within the information systems or management services department has a bearing on the level of interaction with users. Senior computing professionals have formal responsibility for organizing and managing user contributions. Systems analysts and front-line computing workers deal mainly with lower managerial and shop floor users on ad hoc involvement committees that are assembled during each of the key stages mentioned above.

For junior managerial and shop floor staff, this structuring of their involvement delivers a restricted and controlled experience. Despite the heavy emphasis or 'spin' that project managers commonly put on user-participation, they are acutely aware that computing professionals are acting as gatekeepers on their input, 'picking their brains' during systems analysis or trying to head off resistance when it comes to implementation. They sense that their contribution is contained within narrow boundaries, and by the terms on which participation takes place (Beirne and Ramsay, 1992; Howcroft and Wilson, 2003; Bossen et al., 2012; Bratteteig and Wagner, 2012).

This evidence highlights the very partial progress of user-participation in practice, and the prevalence of shallow conceptions of user roles and authority. While proponents variously advocate engagement and emancipation, prevailing wisdom on how the process should be structured and managed effectively dilutes the experience, imposing familiar restrictions and conventions (Beath and Orlikowski, 1994). It seems that here, as elsewhere, participation is a resource that is used selectively by decision-makers to tackle particular problems in a manner that is consistent with their overall approach to employee relations. The lingering commitment to hierarchy, and to rationalistic management traditions generally within organizations, coincides with a strong professional attachment to technical divisions of labour, clear prerogatives and top-down design within the computing community (Harris and Weistroffer, 2009).

Senior systems and user managers are often quite happy to endorse this, offering candid comments about their orientation (Beirne and Ramsay, 1992; Beirne et al., 1998b; Subramanyam et al., 2010). Far from welcoming progressive or extensive participation, a high proportion of them (especially those managing large departments or working for major employers) see it as destabilizing, undermining the rigour of development practices and storing up employee relations problems for the future. Retaining a conventional engineering approach, they favour a minimum interaction model of involvement, targeting and monitoring user input through formal quality assurance arrangements. They also aim to tighten the control of technical staff, bringing them within more explicit hierarchical and bureaucratic management systems, and subjecting them to 'performance metrics' and monitoring tools that can differentiate fast from slow computing workers, for example. Sanctions have even been applied to developers who have overstepped their authority on user contact, with written warnings and reprimands issued to those who have acted on informal contact, making changes or correcting systems errors without going through approved channels (Beirne et al., 1998b).

This evidence magnifies the difficulties surrounding the participative development of work technologies. For all the laudable sentiments in the research literature, the usual practice of participation has little to do with empowering users or conceding any independent influence over development decisions. The good intentions and innovative interventions proposed by enthusiasts therefore need to be evaluated against real-world obstacles and constraints, including the capacity of conservative interests to defend or modify conventional practice. Realism should not be equated with determinate or inevitably debilitating outcomes, however. Rationalistic inclinations do not in themselves guarantee results, either on the imposition of process controls or the delivery of effective technology. Recalling the relational theory of power and political interaction from Chapter 1, it is also important to map out the space for struggle and progressive action, recognizing that rationalistic attempts to structure and control user-participation do not exhaust the possibilities or even attract universal approval among senior figures.

In common with broader accounts of unfettered managerial control over employees, images of passive involvement can obscure the contested nature of organizational relations. There is evidence that users 'see through' narrow conceptualizations, and are often very adept at creating space for themselves and contriving more positive roles, despite significant difficulties (Beirne et al., 1998a). Just as rationalistic strategies have met resistance from workers in other areas, so users and developers have acted against rationalistic computing design. There are examples of grassroots activity beneath the surface of structured methods, with bank staff and engineering workers taking the initiative to defeat monitoring functions, penetrate security screens and disable productivity controls (Salzman and Rosenthal, 1994). Perhaps more surprisingly, there is evidence of users acting to improve systems performance, intervening 'after the fact' of top-down design to make them workable.

Clement (1993, 1994) and Nardi and Miller (1991) explain how clerical workers are able to adapt generic software packages on an incremental basis to make them useful for their own work, establishing spreadsheet templates, constructing databases and devising word processing conventions. These workers extend development processes beyond formal 'sign offs' and completion arrangements, accomplishing de facto design tasks on their own terms.

One of the most striking examples of this informal, yet very direct, user influence was discovered at a Scottish further education college (Beirne et al., 1998a). Staff employed on short-term contracts to input data to a new, though seriously flawed, student records system redefined their job boundaries to include programming and development work, securing positive results which eluded in-house project managers and the contracted suppliers of the application software. Two users who had some computing training were particularly creative, experimenting with unfamiliar query languages and, through trial and error, devising a way of delivering useful reports to administrators, lecturers and senior managers. These de facto designers were motivated by a sense of disenchantment with the pressures they were confronting in their work, and which they eventually felt compelled to tackle by overstepping the terms of their employment contracts. They informally re-skilled themselves with the tacit backing of the college authorities after news spread about their effectiveness. While stressing that their activities were unofficial and 'on their own heads', senior figures turned a 'blind eye', even paying for them to attend training courses at a local university to refine their illicit skills.

This case provides an insight into the fundamental and sometimes subtle social processes that affect the development of work technology. In this respect, it counteracts the influence of over-rationalized prescriptions and formalized models of the technology process. Yet the informal interventions and concessions that characterized this episode occurred within a structural context. They were enacted within a managerial regime where enthusiasm for more direct control, and frustration at its elusiveness, were nonetheless readily apparent. There was a ceiling on managerial approval. This was informed partly by rationalistic leanings, but also by traditional orientations that are familiar from other work contexts. The divisions and demarcations in this case clearly reflected gender dynamics, a feature that exacerbated the constraints and contradictions in the process, generating tensions that eventually took their toll on some of the key people involved (Beirne et al., 1998a).

The data-entry workers here, as in many other information systems settings were female, their managers male. Eventually, the two key users found themselves in a more directive environment with male systems managers appointed above them. Although keen to develop their own roles, and initially confident that their proven creativity would be acknowledged through more secure terms of employment, senior managers seemed eager to forget about this user-driven reality, and to install a more conventionally 'safe' set of arrangements. Ultimately, they were uncomfortable with the achievements of their user designers, feeling obliged to restrict grassroots influence and even take decisions that adversely affected the employment situation of the shopfloor staff. The female systems workers in this case lost the advantages of their informal role in terms of skill development, job satisfaction and sense of achievement as their methods were officialized. They also experienced personal slights and difficulties in dealing with management as the new appointments and controls took effect, and the dilution of their own contribution was justified to them. This raises broader issues about the agenda for progressive management, extending the focus of critical reflection to include a richer mix of cultural and subcultural forces and prevailing patterns of socialization, as Chapter 6 will explain.

4. Financial participation

Financial participation has attracted considerable international interest as an innovation which complements participative decision-making through work teams and user-design groups (Jenkins and Poole, 1990; Poutsma, 2001; de Nijs and Poutsma, 2006; McCarthy et al., 2010; Nuttall, 2012). Indeed, it may be the next logical step, extending the influence of workers beyond task, technology and job-related decisions by ensuring that they have a stake in the ownership of their employing organizations, and with that some say in company governance and direction.

Much of the general literature on employee participation considers this level of financial interest to be part of an integrated approach, supporting and sustaining participative decision-making on everyday matters of job performance (Kalmi et al., 2005; Poutsma et al., 2006). There are warnings that participative group working may be ineffective or short-lived in the absence of an ownership dimension, especially if perform-ance improvements at the workplace feed through to higher profits or stock-market valuations that benefit wider interests without delivering reasonable financial returns to those who participated in their develop-ment (Levine and D'Andrea Tyson, 1990). Financial participation offers a means of addressing these concerns, presenting employees with formal arrangements that are capable of delivering financial returns over and above their regular wages, either through the distribution of free shares or profit-related payments, or by exercising options to acquire shares on favourable terms.

Profit sharing and employee share ownership are now regularly pre-sented as essential parts of a distinctive European approach to partici-pation, which covers every level of organizational decision-taking and combines direct shop floor influence with indirect or representative participation via trade unions:

> Direct participation at the workplace, representative forms of participation through works councils, trade union delegations, health and safety commit-tees, workers' involvement in company boards or supervisory councils and financial participation *all* have to be considered as part of an overall participative framework. (Gill and Krieger, 2000, p. 126)

From here, financial participation promotes inclusivity and social partnership at work, pulling the various stakeholders in employment – managers and workers, employers, investors and unions – together in more constructive, less adversarial relationships. It provides an economic justification for meaningful collaboration on the wider aspects of organizational life (Poutsma, 2001; D'Art and Turner, 2004). By this view, widening ownership and access to profits challenges narrow concentrations of wealth and influence, thereby counteracting historical tensions between traditional owners and investors on the one side and workers and their unions on the other (D'Art, 1992). Releasing shares and profits to workers who contribute to their creation represents a form of economic democracy (or at least a potential basis for achieving this), aligning stakeholder interests on matters of such fundamental importance – ownership and financial results – that participative decision-making, directly or indirectly, on the full range of issues that affect organizational performance, becomes more likely.

This is a controversial interpretation, encapsulating principles that contrast markedly with those expressed by other supporters of profit sharing and employee share ownership. Liberal and neo-liberal ideas are also important, attracting particular interest in political and policy-making circles in Britain and the United States (D'Art, 1992; Pendleton, 2005). From this value standpoint, the appeal of financial participation is very different, arising from market-focused concerns about the conduct of industrial relations rather than an interest in participative management. The distribution of shares and profits among populations of workers is endorsed, on principle, as a viable means of strengthening traditional ownership rights and prerogatives, and of resisting rather than achieving social partnership.

This view was highly influential in Britain during the 1980s, informing various Conservative government interventions that were fundamentally at odds with notions of representative participation. Against a background of industrial militancy and industrial relations disputes, the governments of Margaret Thatcher set out to cultivate an enterprise consciousness or culture that would make workers feel more like capitalists (Pendleton, 2005). The problems with adversarial 'them and us' relations at work were attributed to the orientations and activities of trade unionists, and the indirect or representative forms of participation that gave them a voice and capacity for disruption. Part of the Conservative response was to weaken the links between workers and unions and promote a greater identification with employers. Financial participation was attractive as a means of placing workers and employers on the same side, of establishing a 'people's capitalism' that would render trade unions, representative participation and talk of social partnership redundant. The privatization of state-controlled organizations, especially in the utilities industries, provided a channel for these objectives, proceeding with large-scale, preferential share release arrangements that favoured employees (Baddon et al., 1989; Hyman et al., 1989). The deregulation of the financial sector added further impetus to this realigning project, extending share-based financial participation during the 1990s (Chen et al., 2006; Dong et al., 2010). However, an important consequence of this development was that far greater benefits accrued to senior managers than workers, adding a new twist to political debates about the merits of employee share ownership in recent years.

As subsequent sections will demonstrate, financial participation has been associated with controversy and accusations of executive excess over the past two decades (Crystal, 1991; High Pay Commission, 2011; Caulkin, 2012). This is because preferential profit sharing and share option arrangements have had a vastly disproportionate impact on the remuneration packages of those at the highest levels of work organizations. Consequently, some politicians (BBC, 2012a; Lamb, 2012) and expert commentators (Nuttall, 2012) have recast employee financial participation as a vehicle for bringing executive attitudes and behaviour into line with those of their wider organizations. Their rhetoric still prioritizes a greater harmony of interests between the owners and controllers of economic resources and those who depend upon them for a livelihood. Curbing executive opportunism with share options and profit-sharing initiatives is a key consideration, however. Extending ownership rights and responsibilities to larger populations of workers ostensibly offers a viable means of challenging 'crony capitalism' and cultivating 'responsible capitalism' (BBC, 2012a). By this reasoning, it should also help to counteract any employee sense that financial participation attends to executive and elite interests, more so than their own or those of their work communities. Hence, in Britain, the debate on financial participation has moved on to consider proposals for introducing a legal right for workers to request shares in their companies (Lamb 2012; Nuttall, 2012) and to exert a restraining influence on executive remuneration (TUC, 2012).

TRENDS IN FINANCIAL PARTICIPATION

Political interests have played a crucial role in the development of financial participation. Governments of different political orientation have matched their ideological approval with a financial commitment, providing support in the form of tax relief granted to profit-sharing and share-ownership schemes that are formally approved by their tax authorities. Tax concessions, together with legislative interventions that establish employer obligations in this area, have delivered 'mass financial participation' in Britain, France and the United States (Pendleton, 2005), and strong growth in the Netherlands, Germany and other parts of the European Union over recent decades (Welz and Fernandez-Macias, 2008).

Four broad categories of approved financial participation account for this expansion: cash-based and deferred profit-sharing arrangements, share option schemes and share incentive plans. Various labels and titles have been applied to each of these over the years as different national governments have adjusted and refined their provisions. Their distinguishing features are widely recognized, however.

Under profit-sharing arrangements, the fixed wage of an employee is supplemented with some variable remuneration that is directly linked to company profits. This is the portion that may be subject to tax concessions in approved profit-sharing schemes. Access is the distinguishing feature between the cash-based and deferred variants. With the latter, the profit share is usually allocated to a fund or trust, which is then managed on behalf of the employee for a specified minimum period before the final entitlement is released. The allocation itself can be in cash or shares, although tax advantages can only be achieved if the amount is tied to the fund for the qualifying interval. Cash-based profit sharing involves a more immediate release of money drawn directly from declared profits.

Share option schemes grant participants the opportunity to purchase shares in their employing company at some future date, either at a discounted rate set at the point of joining or at the share price at that time. For employees, this usually involves a tax-efficient saving plan, where monthly contributions from after-tax pay are combined with bank interest on the deposits (and frequently a bonus payment for adhering to the contract) to create a lump sum that can then be used to exercise the option to acquire the shares. Limits are typically set on the monthly contributions, the discount on the option and the duration of the contract. However, if these are observed, any gains achieved from selling the shares and from interest accumulated with the savings plan are taxed at lower levels, if at all. In the case of executive share options, the exercise costs tend to be covered by company loans rather than savings plans. These are also provided on favourable terms, often with nominal interest rates and clearance for the loan to be repaid once the shares have been sold.

Share incentive plans cover the allocation of free shares to employees, either directly or through some approved 'matching' arrangement where employers provide extra shares as a bonus for employees who purchase their own, and pay for them via deductions from their pre-tax salary. Typically, one or two free shares are issued with every share purchased. Again, conditions apply, invariably to the total value of the shares that can be issued, purchased and matched each year, and the length of time they must be held before any tax advantages can be realized. If these requirements are satisfied, the income used to purchase shares, together with any dividend payments received and gains achieved through growth in value or subsequent sale, are liable to lower levels of taxation. Some elements can even be tax-free.

These basic categories of financial participation are now familiar to large numbers of workers in commercial enterprises, certainly across Europe and North America. Britain and France have recorded some of the highest levels of financial participation. Profit sharing is particularly significant in France, where legislative support dates back to the late 1950s (Welz and Fernandez-Macias, 2008). In Britain, share-based profit sharing gathered impetus towards the end of the 1970s, when a Labour government introduced tax concessions (Poutsma et al., 2006). Employee share ownership was subsequently encouraged by Conservative administrations through the 1980s, producing a dramatic increase in the number of share schemes operated by employers. This coincided with a shift away from collective bargaining over pay, which in itself reflected the decline of the traditional heartland industries of British trade unionism, including heavy engineering, coal mining and manufacturing (Pendleton, 2005; Marginson et al., 2007). The net result was that employers demonstrated a greater inclination to experiment with reward policies, adding fresh opportunities for workers to engage in financial participation.

The incidence of both profit sharing and employee share ownership more than doubled in Britain by the end of the 1980s (Pendleton, 2005), becoming an establishing feature of employment in the largest organizations. A 2008 study for the British revenue and customs service (HMRC) suggested that around 63 per cent of private sector companies were offering savings-based share options or share incentive schemes to all their employees (Kerr and Tait, 2008). The figure for those with 200 or more employees is consistently placed even higher, with some estimates suggesting that in excess of 80 per cent of the companies in this category have broadly based share-ownership plans in operation (Mathieu, 2012). Similar numbers have been produced for the large-firm sector in France, against a European Union average of 53.4 per cent (Mathieu, 2012).

The political institutions of the European Union have formally endorsed and actively supported financial participation since the early 1990s, and some significant growth has been recognized across the member states during the intervening years (Welz and Fernandez-Macias, 2008). Consequently, in terms of headline figures for the incidence of profit sharing and employee share ownership, and the number of employers making use of approved arrangements, financial participation is a significant international phenomenon. A sense of perspective and discriminating judgement is essential when aiming to draw conclusions from this, however, since very limited amounts of capital have actually been transferred to employee ownership, and the number of workers affected by these developments remains extremely low (Baddon et al., 1989; Pendleton, 2005).

Recent estimates suggest that employees across the European Union collectively own less than 3 per cent of their companies. In Britain, the figure is only 2.49 per cent (Mathieu, 2012). This is with a participation rate of around 50 per cent in France, though with less than one third of the occupied population in Britain, and on average across the European Union, taking advantage of approved share-ownership initiatives (Welz and Fernandez-Macias, 2008; Mathieu, 2012).

DÉJÀ VU WITH RHETORIC AND EVIDENCE: ANOTHER DEFICIT?

In theory, financial participation delivers significant benefits for individual participants and their wider organizational communities, including managers, executives and investors. The workers who sign up to profit-sharing and share-ownership plans are promised a direct financial return from any improvement in the economic health and development of their companies. Of course, this introduces an element of risk, since profits and the value of shares can fluctuate widely, falling as well as rising. There is some evidence that this is a source of worry for potential participants, although in practice a measure of protection is afforded by the tax concessions available with approved schemes, and also the matching shares in incentive plans, which help to offset any decline (Pendleton and Robinson, 2011). The discounts and favourable terms available with share options have a similar compensating potential, although the major safeguard with this arrangement is that the option can be declined rather than exercised if financially disadvantageous. Participants in savings-based share option plans can elect to withdraw their lump sum at the end of the qualifying period, and settle for the tax and interest gains instead of committing themselves to share ownership.

Of course, for enthusiasts, the attraction of financial participation is that it provides a co-operative basis for delivering economic gains (Lamb, 2012; Nuttall, 2012). Profit-sharing and employee share-ownership initiatives ostensibly encourage performance-oriented behaviour that tackles the sort of inefficiencies that sap value and threaten profitability. The clear expectation is that developments in these areas will strengthen the financial fortunes of companies, promoting confidence and reducing the risks attached to ownership and investment.

Enthusiasts insist that as part-owners, or because they draw additional income directly from profits, employees will develop an acute sensitivity to factors that affect the 'bottom line' (Nuttall, 2012). This is likely to manifest itself in a greater cost-awareness, more active engagement with revenue-earning activities, a reduction in 'them and us' attitudes, and possibly also wage restraint, or at least a collective concern for sobriety in relation to terms and conditions of employment (Poole, 1989; D'Art, 1992). By connecting employee interests directly with ownership and profitability, an enterprise consciousness is expected to emerge, along with a propensity towards 'good citizenship' (McCarthy et al., 2010; Pendleton and Robinson, 2011). Enthusiasts anticipate that share-owning employees will be more likely to 'put themselves out' for the company, to perform tasks other than those assigned to them, to assist co-workers and be more responsive with customers. They should develop a greater sense of the impact that shop floor behaviour has on the financial wellbeing of the organization, and so be more diligent about time-keeping, careful with materials and equipment, thoughtful about absenteeism, and focused on how they and their colleagues can enhance profitability (Kalmi et al., 2005). The cumulative effect, theoretically at least, is that financial participation will foster cohesion and a closer identity of interests between employers, managers and workers, replacing adversarial tensions in the workplace (Long, 2000).

Though outlined with considerable confidence in the promotional literature, these outcomes are far from certain, and have been elusive in practice. Advocates have struggled to convince people that employee-focused schemes are effectively resourced, and that they operate in a fair and balanced way. Reactions, on the shop floor and beyond, have been influenced by recurring 'fat-cat' salary scandals, and concerns expressed consistently since the early 1990s that profit sharing, share options and share incentives have fuelled executive excess at the expense of organizational cohesion (Crystal, 1991; High Pay Commission, 2011; Caulkin, 2012).

Executive remuneration packages now routinely include favourable profit and share acquisition arrangements (Chen et al., 2006; Dong et al., 2010). This is largely due to economic and political influences that were particularly significant during the 1980s. At that time, some prominent economists captured the attention of politicians, especially Conservatives in Britain and Republicans in the United States, arguing that the separation of ownership from control, from the everyday running of public companies, could undermine shareholder value, given the scope for leaders to pursue their own sectional interests (such as empire-building) instead of the best possible returns on investment (Dong et al., 2010; High Pay Commission, 2011; Caulkin, 2012). There were fears that this could damage the privatization project in Britain, which aimed to boost the performance of previously state-controlled organizations, notably in the utilities sector, by opening them to the entrepreneurialism and discipline of the marketplace. For this to happen, for market thinking to supplant sectional or bureaucratic instincts at the highest levels of business organizations, the interests of leaders had to be tied more closely to those of shareholders. Financial incentives were presented as the way forward, aligning executive compensation with returns to investors through an expansion of profit and share-based rewards, over and above core salary (Crystal, 1991; High Pay Commission, 2011).

The result has been a dramatic rise in boardroom pay since the 1980s, despite recessionary pressures and even the fluctuating corporate financial statements posted by some executives (Crystal, 1991; *The Sunday Telegraph*, 1993; BBC, 2012b). In the years following the Great Recession, executives were again criticized for being out of step with investors. Critics, including groups of shareholders, argued that too many leaders of major companies were preoccupied with financial short-termism and personal gain, at the expense of stability and longer-term value generation (*The Financial Times*, 2012; Caulkin, 2012; BBC 2012b). Executive financial participation in general, and share plans in particular, were associated with excessive risk taking, an absence of responsible corporate behaviour and even failure, especially in the banking sector (Chen et al., 2006; Dong et al., 2010; High Pay Commission, 2011).

Misalignment issues were also obvious to workers. As the income gap between executives and others widened, especially during extended periods of recessionary pay restraint for employees, it became very clear that those at the top were the major beneficiaries of financial participation. Some reports suggest that the ratio between average chief executive earnings and the median salary of a worker in the United States increased from 40 to 1 in 1980 to 325 to 1 in 2010 (Caulkin, 2012). The comparable figures for Britain, drawn from average FTSE data, suggest an increase from around 20 to 1 up to 150 to 1. Company specific information was assembled by the High Pay Commission (2011, p. 9), revealing the total earnings of lead executives in some of the largest listed companies as a multiple of the average pay of their employees. In Barclays, the chief executive earned 75 times more than their average worker in 2011, compared with a figure of 14.5 in 1979. With BP, the multiple was 63 in 2011, up from 16.5. The lead executive in the Lloyds Banking Group also reached an earnings figure that was 75 times higher than the average employee of the company in 2011, compared with a multiple of 13.6 in 1979. These increases were heavily influenced by favourable profit and share acquisition arrangements (High Pay Commission, 2011, pp. 41–43).

Available evidence indicates that employees are highly sensitive to inequalities in financial participation schemes, recognizing differences between their own arrangements and those for executives in terms of scale and capitalization, discounts, options and acquisition plans, and also the opportunities for reaping financial benefits (Baddon et al., 1989; O'Connell-Davidson and Nichols, 1991). A steady flow of information through newspapers and reports, typically linked to editorials and condemnations of executive excess, has magnified this disparity (*The Daily Record*, 2003; *The Financial Times*, 2004, 2012; BBC 2012b; Caulkin, 2012; High Pay Commission, 2011).

The most common complaint against share schemes, and financial participation arrangements more generally, is that they disrupt relations and fragment team behaviour, causing disappointment, disgruntlement and even resentment (Hyman et al., 1989; *The Herald*, 1996; Pendleton, 1995). Inflated remuneration packages that favour executives with share options and other bonuses that are out of line with company performance or realized during periods of 'downsizing' and 'cut backs' (Randle, 1997; *Scotland on Sunday*, 1999; Labour Research Department, 2002; Caulkin, 2012; High Pay Commission, 2011) have been sending signals about organizational values that are at odds with the underpinning logic set out by many advocates (Nuttal, 2012). They support images of sectionalism and elitism, rather than unity and cohesion, working against desirable behaviour such as collaboration and collective commitment by seeming to reward insular, instrumental and even greedy behaviour by those at the top.

Accusations of greed and hypocrisy have certainly been heard by researchers and reported in the media, with employees and managers criticizing what they regard as the 'do as I say and not as I do' subculture in some of Britain's major companies (*Scotland on Sunday*, 1999; *The Daily Record*, 1998; *The Financial Times*, 2004, 2012; BBC, 2012b). Not surprisingly, perceptions about unfair practice and the divisiveness of schemes that seem to be 'rigged' in favour of executives have undermined declarations about cohesion and collaboration, reinforcing rather than replacing 'them and us' attitudes:

> By aligning themselves with external shareholders, CEOs broke the link with their own employees. (Caulkin, 2012, p. 42)

> When executive rewards seem to go beyond what is linked to that executive's contribution to the success or welfare of the company, it damages public trust and contributes to an attitude that business leaders are 'in it for themselves'. (High Pay Commission, 2011, p. 10)

> The ideologically motivated experiment of using pay to align top managers exclusively with shareholders has also failed ... managers need to be reconnected (aligned, even) with their own employees and customers, who create the underlying value in companies, not shareholders. (Caulkin, 2012, p. 43)

THE EVIDENCE ON EMPLOYEE SCHEMES

When introducing employee-focused profit-sharing and share-ownership initiatives, managers have tended to prioritize organizational rather than employee benefits, echoing claims set out in the promotional literature (and summarized in the previous section). D'Art and Turner (2004) highlight three distinct categories of interest that have encouraged managers to act on financial participation for workers, suggesting that these inform 'sophisticated', 'cost–benefit' and 'unitary' approaches in practice.

The first concentrates on recruiting, developing and retaining talent, acting on the assumption that financial participation will appeal to people who are happy to have an element of their remuneration contingent upon overall organizational performance. These will be company-minded individuals who demonstrate the attachment, commitment and good citizenship anticipated in the literature. A second group of managers, those adopting the cost–benefit position, are more interested in demonstrable outcomes than intangible inputs, qualities or relations, and expect productivity gains or cost reductions to materialize from active commitment, for instance, with higher output and reductions in absenteeism and turnover. Unitary managers, by contrast, focus on industrial relations gains and the potential for financial participation to contain wages by removing elements of pay from the scope of collective bargaining and, as a corollary of that, weaken the ties between workers and trade unions.

Historically, some British employers have introduced financial partici-pation with the expressed intention of limiting wage demands (Poole, 1989) and restricting union influence (Hyman et al., 1989). However, accumulating evidence suggests that managerial objectives have shifted in line with contextual conditions and the decline of collective bargaining (Pendleton, 2005; Kalmi et al., 2005; Pendleton and Robinson, 2011). Sustaining employee commitment is now a more pressing concern, in Britain and beyond, especially in companies that are struggling to provide the traditional inducements to regular diligence and loyal service.

Competitive, recessionary and financial pressures have prompted many employers to loosen their attachment to job security, career advancement and generous pension provisions as viable means of eliciting long-term commitment and encouraging 'good citizenship' behaviour on the part of their employees. Some authors have argued that financial participation represents an alternative way of 'locking' workers into their organ-izations, or at least of incentivizing them to maintain a strong commit-ment to employers that invest in their training and development, rather than responding opportunistically to better job offers that come their way (Pendleton, 2005; Pendleton and Robinson, 2011). This suggests that the 'sophisticated' approach to cultivating loyalty and closer corporate ties via profit sharing and employee share ownership is of growing import-ance to managers, over and above any cost–benefit interests they have in realizing productivity gains or improving attendance. A couple of very obvious questions arise from this, however. Does financial participation deliver on these terms, and what does the evidence indicate about employee reactions?

Contrary to management objectives and the claims of enthusiasts (Nuttall, 2012), the balance of empirical evidence on employee attitudes and orientations associates financial participation more closely with negative or negligible effects than expressions of loyalty or a closer identity of interests. Very few studies report positive attitudinal changes, and in these rare instances the researchers tend to qualify their findings, adding cautionary notes and caveats (see, for example, Pendleton, 2005).

Some of the most detailed case research on this front was conducted in Britain and in Ireland. In one of the earliest investigations, Baddon et al. (1989) looked for differences between the attitudes and orientations of employees who were participating in profit-sharing and share-ownership plans and their workplace colleagues who were non-participants. From a survey of 350 companies and five case studies, they concluded that attitudes towards their employing organizations were broadly consistent. Attitudinal differences were marginal or barely dis-cernible, with participants and non-participants expressing similar views about their employment experiences and the state of labour-management relations within their organizations.

Instead of identifying with their employers, participants had formed their own views about financial participation, and were pursing personal rather than collective or corporate goals. The rhetoric that surrounded the introduction of the schemes failed to move them. Indeed, management claims and declared objectives were at odds with employee evaluations, which were modest and instrumental. Most of those participating in the schemes regarded them as the route to a welcome bonus, an easy way of acquiring some additional income. They were motivated by financial opportunism rather than expressions of attachment, commitment or ownership, and those gaining shares had no hesitation in disposing of them to finance family 'treats', such as holidays or special purchases. Financial calculations also governed the decisions of non-participants, lack of resources or an inability to afford the contributions being offered as the most common reasons for not taking part (Baddon et al., 1989; Hyman et al., 1989).

More recent studies add weight to these findings, suggesting that financial participation schemes have been characterized by a relatively stable pattern of tensions and limitations. Subsequent research by Pendleton (2005) and by Kerr and Tait (2008) reached similar conclusions about the divergence between management objectives and employee calculations. From their own survey data, these researchers agreed that the vast majority of participants – in excess of 90 per cent of those joining share-based schemes – limited their expectations to financial benefits, or what they regarded as windfall gains. They offered essentially the same reasons for participating as the earlier respondents, namely that they were in a position to afford the contributions and were keen to take advantage of favourable terms and 'easy money' (Baddon et al., 1989; Hyman et al., 1989; Kerr and Tait, 2008). Again, the major reason given for non-participation was financial hardship.

For Baddon and her colleagues, the corollary is that financial participation schemes are typically too conservative to produce anything other than an instrumental, self-interested response from workers. The amount of ownership that employers have been willing to concede, and the financial gains that employees have been able to achieve with share plans and profit-related payments, are simply too small to encourage more favourable attitudes or dispositions, certainly by comparison with executive schemes. Whether better resourced initiatives, with more substantial transfers, produce different results is open to debate, however.

Relevant studies here have produced contradictory findings. McCarthy et al. (2010) and Pendleton et al. (1998) investigated two of the largest ever employee share-ownership schemes, giving particular attention to their impact on employee attitudes and orientations. Both were associated with substantial privatization projects, one in the Irish telecommunications sector, the other in the British bus industry. From their investigation into the Irish case, McCarthy and his co-researchers concluded that the impact was decidedly limited. This initiative failed to deliver anticipated improvements in employee commitment and citizenship behaviour. While the analysis presented with this research is broadly consistent with the earlier work of Baddon and colleagues (Baddon et al., 1989; Hyman et al., 1989), it demonstrates that employee responses are influenced by wider perceptions and developments (including the notions of fairness and divisiveness discussed in the previous section), and are not simply a function of scale or the proportion of equity transferred to the workforce.

This last point is significant for understanding the contradictory results from the earlier bus company study by Pendleton et al. (1998). The researchers in this instance were altogether more confident that a major shift in ownership had generated significant attitudinal change in favour of the organization. However, they acknowledge that this was contingent upon complementary developments in participative decision-making, perhaps most significantly through the representative channels of established trade unionism (Pendleton, 2001, 2005). In other words, positive (as opposed to instrumental) responses were generated by substantial transfers of ownership *and* control, and were not attributable to the share-ownership scheme itself.

This is an important qualification, which draws attention back to the ideas identified at the beginning of this chapter about the complementarity of financial and other forms of employee participation. As previously explained, prominent advocates of empowerment and workplace innovation, most notably in Europe, have argued for an integrated approach that extends across the various facets of organizational decision-making through a combination of financial, direct and representative participation (Gill and Krieger, 2000). Ostensibly, these various forms need to be consistent with each other if the interests of different stakeholders are to be effectively aligned and more co-operative and constructive ties established within work organizations. In other words, meaningful change requires broad-ranging rather than narrowly focused developments in participation, or at least compatible and mutually reinforcing initiatives on a number of fronts (Gill and Krieger, 2000; Poutsma et al., 2006).

The bus company research conducted by Pendleton and his colleagues offers some corroborating evidence for this argument, although when considered together with the full range of empirical research on profit sharing and share ownership it also indicates how rare such complementarity is in practice. Financial participation schemes are typically very different, in terms of both resources and approach. As previously indicated, and noted by Pendleton in subsequent work (Pendleton, 2005), the profits and shares transferred to employees are usually very low. The links to other forms of participation are also underdeveloped or ignored (Kalmi et al., 2005; Poutsma et al., 2006).

An abundance of empirical evidence confirms that the bus case is exceptional rather than representative, and that the examples, objectives and responses uncovered by Baddon and her colleagues correspond more closely with the everyday realities of financial participation. The vast majority of managers and workers who have been surveyed or interviewed on this topic offer the impression of a self-contained aspect of employment that has little bearing upon the regular features of management, work and employee relations. Profit-sharing and share-ownership initiatives tend to be developed and introduced as 'added extras', independently of other forms of participation and on top of established job structures, management arrangements and patterns of employment. Although the anticipated gains for organizations that move in this direction are far from modest – conjuring up images of committed and loyal, company-minded workers – the marginal and additional character of financial participation works against any substantial change in practice, and is occasionally associated with deteriorating relations, notably when perceptions about unfair or tokenistic employee provisions take hold, say in connection with executive arrangements and reports of excess.

There is little in the available evidence to suggest that workers have developed more positive attitudes towards their employers as a result of financial participation, or that 'sophisticated' management thinking in this area has secured performance improvements. The view from the shop floor – among the participants in profit-sharing and share-ownership schemes as well as their colleagues who decide not to take part – is that relations remain much the same. For some, the abiding impression is still of 'us and them'. Financial participation is basically regarded as a gloss on mainstream management efforts to improve performance, and so has little impact on their diligence, attendance or attachment to work (Baddon et al., 1989; Hyman et al., 1989; O'Connell-Davidson and Nichols, 1991; D'Art and Turner, 2003; Kalmi et al., 2005; Welz and Fernandez-Macias, 2008; McCarthy et al., 2010; High Pay Commission, 2011; Caulkin, 2012).

5. Gender and empowerment

The most potent and compelling arguments for empowerment tend to address concerns about injustice and disadvantage, rather than matters of business, commerce or job performance. As Chapter 1 established, the consciousness-raising polemics of the civil rights and women's move-ments of the 1960s and '70s played an important role in encouraging people, in large numbers, to take empowerment seriously, and to reflect on underpinning principles and options for progressive intervention. Gender represents one of the most widely analysed and frequently discussed sources of privilege and disadvantage at work and in manage-ment, and has been at the centre of some heated debates and highly controversial thinking about employee empowerment.

International workplace and public policy studies have repeatedly and dramatically highlighted gender-based inequalities of opportunity and reward in companies and countries around the world, exposing significant earnings differentials between men and women, job segregation and limited career advancement for women, even where they represent a majority of the occupied population (Kanter, 1977; Purcell, 1990; Wajcman, 1998; Equality and Human Rights Commission, 2008; Alves-son and Billings, 2009; Broadbridge and Simpson, 2011; Scholarios and Taylor, 2011; Al-Ahmadi, 2011). Historically, female employment has centred on particular sectors and occupations, demonstrating inequalities in the distribution of work and also rewards and decision-making influence.

Service jobs have provided the highest levels of female participation, with clerical work, education, catering, cleaning and personal care accounting for the greatest concentrations of women in paid employment, though on a segregated basis, covering basic jobs and affording relatively few opportunities to reach responsible and well-paid positions. These are areas where the oft-cited 'glass ceiling' seems to inhibit advancement, where women dominate the workforce yet are under-represented at senior levels and proportionately unsuccessful in securing access to managerial posts and benefits (Broadbridge and Simpson, 2011). Lateral barriers or 'glass walls' have also had a containing effect on the breadth of women's employment, making it difficult for them to reach or prosper in other occupations (Weidenfeller, 2012). The success rate for women is much lower than that for men in joining and advancing through the legal and medical professions, for instance, and in science and engineering, transport, construction and manufacturing (Mills, 2002; Equality and Human Rights Commission, 2008).

This pattern of inequality has been remarkably persistent over time, despite regular fluctuations, with evident narrowing in some areas and periods offset by frequent back-sliding and retrogression (Kanter, 1977; Wajcman, 1998; Mills, 2002; Alvesson and Billing, 2009; Broadbridge and Simpson, 2011; Scholarios and Taylor, 2011). Yet for all that has been written about gender disadvantage and the marginalization of women in employment, some commentators have argued that this is not the issue it once was. There is a view, certainly in prescriptive management circles, that gendered privilege is 'a thing of the past' (Fondas, 1997), that the future of work and management looks good for women, and even that 'the future is female' (Holme, 2000; Davidson, 2007; Craven, 2009).

Women have been credited with distinctive qualities and capabilities that have latent economic value and the potential to secure a progressive feminization of work and management (Fondas, 1997; Weidenfeller, 2012). Media reports, especially since the Great Recession, have popularized the notion that there are innately feminine ways of working and managing which have found their time, which resonate with demands for socially responsible corporate behaviour and address the most pressing of contemporary business imperatives (Holme, 2000; Davidson, 2007; Craven, 2009). Women, it seems, are more responsive, empathetic and participative than men. There are suggestions that they are naturally inclined towards engaging and nurturing behaviour, pursuing profits and wider organizational objectives in a principled, collaborative and networked fashion, rather than issuing directives and resorting to autocratic control.

If the claims in these promotional reports are correct, women are also less inclined towards reckless risk taking and the self-centred, bonus-pursuing individualism that triggered so many of the difficulties experienced with the Great Recession. Given adverse public reaction to aggressive corporate behaviour, and prescriptive business models that prioritize leaner structures, flatter hierarchies, flexible teams and responsive service, women are ostensibly well-equipped for modern management and emerging forms of work organization, and have the mindset to fare much better than their male counterparts (Fondas, 1997; Davidson, 2007; Craven, 2009; Weidenfeller, 2012).

This feminization thesis is proving attractive, especially to the younger women of Generation Y, the children of the 1980s and early '90s, who evidently sense that there are now fewer constraints on work and career (Kelan et al., 2009). The celebration of femininity as an asset, as a distinct advantage in the emerging organizational landscape, may be encouraging young women to believe that they have choices and opportunities that were denied to earlier generations, to imagine that gender disadvantage was a problem for their parents and grandparents, though is less of an issue for their own employment.

Some writers are fearful that claims about the feminization of work and management will instil complacency, or worse, a denial of gender disadvantage and a naïve belief that market forces will eliminate the historical inequalities between men and women in employment (Broadbridge and Simpson, 2011). Available research and prominent debates in the media (Kantor, 2012; Medland, 2012) provide important counterweights to this, however.

Prominent authors have challenged the functionalist parts of the feminization thesis, the notion that corrective markets and business imperatives will deliver equality because feminine virtues are lucrative (Mills, 2002; Noon, 2010). The point that tends to be made here is that markets are far from perfect, and that progress since business prescriptions about responsive and flexible working first appeared has been slow and insecure. Even if there is a link between market forces and feminine qualities, this could be weak rather than strong, mediated instead of direct. Estimates based on the rate of change over the past decade suggest that equal pay could be 60 years away (Street, 2010), and that 70 years could pass before men and women are equally represented on the boards of the top one hundred British companies (Noon, 2010).

Other commentators target the essentialist position that men and women are fundamentally different, focusing particularly on the proposition that male and female managers adopt intrinsically different management styles (Wajcman, 1998; Ramsay and Scholarios, 2005). The balance of available academic research on this issue – including 'life cycle' studies that account for age and social status when examining attitudes and orientations, for example – indicates that the substantive differences between men and women at work are marginal (Ramsay and Scholarios, 2005; Alvesson and Billings, 2009; Medland, 2012). This evidence casts doubt on the argument that women occupy a separate realm of management, or adhere to a consistently different set of values and orientations. It also raises a question about the implications of accentuating difference. By some accounts, this could have a damaging effect in seeming to legitimize, rather than challenge, established divisions and inequalities (Mills, 2002).

Some of the most telling criticisms of feminization concentrate on the images of a nascent meritocracy that flow from accounts of market and business-driven equality, and the corresponding treatment of women who fail to secure the positions they pursue, or realize their ambitions and potential. Research confirms that merit-arguments are often used to conceal privilege and disadvantage and deflect attention from prejudicial views (Noon, 2010; Broadbridge and Simpson, 2011). The incidence of inequality in recruitment and promotion is clouded by justifying statements that focus on personal shortcomings, in terms of skills, experience or endeavour, for example. In other words, the disadvantage is covert, and applied with the added twist that those on the receiving end are somehow responsible for not meeting required standards.

In these circumstances, notions of meritocracy effectively re-frame inequality as a matter of personal choice or inability. Women who are unsuccessful with job and promotion applications have supposedly made the wrong choices, say, about developing their skill-set or acquiring relevant experience, or they lack the requisite talent. One of the key dangers that researchers associate with the feminization thesis is that it increases the pressure on women to succeed, and then opens them to criticism if equality is not achieved. The corollary is that women are more likely to be identified as the source of any disadvantage they experience.

This emerged as a key issue in recent media debates between women from different generations of the equality movement. During the summer of 2012, a *New York Times* report on reactions to feminization encouraged women to 'stop blaming themselves' and to be less susceptible to the 'higher-harder-faster school of female achievement'. A former American State Department official, Anne-Marie Slaughter, offered the following view:

> Women of my generation have clung to the feminist credo we were raised with ... because we were determined not to drop the flag for the next generation ... But when many members of the younger generation have stopped listening, it is time to talk ... Glibly repeating 'you can have it all' is simply airbrushing reality. (Kantor, 2012, p. A14)

From here, the future is not so assuredly female, and the feminization thesis itself is problematical and potentially damaging.

Of course, there is nothing in these critical views to deny that positive steps have been taken towards gender equality. Few observers doubt that the situation of women seeking employment, promotion and fair treatment at work has improved through the last half century, and there is no shortage of information about the key developments. Government policies in many countries now openly encourage female participation, and legislative interventions (including the 2010 Equality Act in Britain) make it easier to challenge gendered inequalities in pay, recruitment and promotion through the courts (Al-Ahmadi, 2011; Broadbridge and Simpson, 2011; Conley, 2012). There are many more women in the workforce, greater numbers progressing through higher education, and a larger proportion securing supervisory and managerial positions (Scott et al., 2010).

Economic and occupational restructuring, together with recessionary pressures at various points through the latter part of the twentieth century, altered the gender distribution of work fundamentally, certainly in Britain and the United States. De-industrialization and shifts in the economy towards the service sector favoured women more than men because they were under-represented in the areas most affected by economic decline, such as coal mining, shipbuilding and heavy engineering. Conversely, they were over-represented in the occupational categories that were generating the greatest opportunities for new employment during that period, in areas supporting call centre expansion, for instance (Kottke and Agars, 2005; Scholarios and Taylor, 2011). The irony here is that established patterns of job segregation ensured that men experienced greater unemployment, while the balance of workforce participation shifted significantly in favour of women.

It is possible to acknowledge this progress in employment rights and workforce participation for women without accepting that recent change is sufficient or secure. Indeed, there is reason to believe that the latest economic downturn, the Great Recession, has spoiled any optimism or confidence that could reasonably be attached to these developments. This recession and the cost-cutting and restructuring that it triggered have again altered the pattern of employment, though with more of an impact on women. Sectors with high female concentrations, including local government and health care, are at the forefront of those facing cutbacks, tight controls and austerity budgets. Funding constraints have limited progress towards pay equalization in the public sector in Britain, for example, with city councils in Birmingham, Newcastle, Glasgow, Aberdeen and London attracting media criticism for failing to eliminate earnings differentials between male and female employees performing the same categories of work (Poling, 2005; BBC, 2012c; Butler, 2012). Despite some very clear and widely reported breaches of employment legislation by these councils, representatives of the employers have repeatedly pointed to the financial burden attached to pay equality, arguing that this would impose unacceptable costs on local tax payers, and potentially damage the politicians who sanctioned such change in subsequent elections.

Other areas that have been associated with unhindered opportunities for women to progress in work and management have also failed to deliver positive outcomes. Call centres fall into this category, providing a major source of employment for women though with very restricted routes to high-quality work and to supervisory and managerial responsibilities. Recent research by Scholarios and Taylor (2011) indicates that men have a much better success rate in securing team leader and managerial appointments in this sector than women with the same educational qualifications, despite the preponderance of female workers. Following earlier studies, most notably by Belt (2002), these authors confirm that women are disproportionately segregated into routinized and highly regimented jobs that are subject to remote monitoring and stress-inducing targets. The opportunities for women to find an escape from this type of work into more responsible or varied roles are limited, and appear to be receding as the proportion with weaker educational qualifications increases. Rather than highlighting progressive developments, the findings from this research point to a sharpening of gender inequalities in call centre employment, with female workers increasingly 'trapped' in poor quality jobs while men secure access to most of the supervisory and managerial roles that are available.

The significance of gender at the highest levels of management hierarchies is also raising concerns about continuing, and indeed entrenched, inequality. Although some women have successfully broken through the glass ceiling, evidence suggests that their experience on the other side is far from palatable or fair. The ranks of senior management continue to be dominated by men, who tend to be better rewarded, less stressed and have more secure employment than their female counterparts (Alvesson and Billings, 2009; Vinnicombe et al., 2010). Most were also better supported, mentored and developed *en route* to the top.

Studies of women in major leadership roles reveal that gender inequality has an additional dimension, the glass cliff, which presents a more vulnerable and compromised work experience than that encountered by their male colleagues (Broadbridge and Simpson, 2011; Al-Ahmadi, 2011). Pioneering research conducted in the 1990s by Wajcman (1998) suggested that female executives felt obliged to suppress their femininity and learn to 'manage like a man', at no small cost to themselves. They were constrained by the male ethos and symbolism of the majority, and tended to respond by trying to comply with established expectations about how management should be conducted, even if this was at odds with their own sense of purpose. In other words, they were influenced, and even intimidated, by the stark reality of the male management cultures that they faced.

Though occasionally interpreted as lending support to the problematic, essentialist position on innate difference and gendered managerial styles, Wajcman's distinctive contribution was to demonstrate that women who succeed in a predominantly male management world do so by confronting additional pressures that can exact a heavy toll on their health and wellbeing. She was highly critical of essentialist arguments, recognizing that people respond to those around them, to subcultural norms and habitual thinking about consistent and effective behaviour. Subsequent studies have cast further light on the dilemmas experienced by women when they reach executive positions, demonstrating how ingrained notions and ways of acting and communicating in predominantly male management environments can produce cliff-edge anxieties among female entrants (Al-Ahmadi, 2011; Weidenfeller, 2012). On the one hand they often struggle to be taken seriously, and feel obliged to push for visible roles and responsibilities in which they can prove their abilities. On the other, they feel scrutinized and isolated, more exposed to criticism and challenge than the men around them, sensing that they can't afford to make a mistake. Accounts of the glass cliff capture feelings of vulnerability among women who are not reasonably integrated or accepted into leadership communities, who may be treated as outsiders or interlopers, and who recognize that they can be marginalized as 'the others' if their decisions prove to be less than successful.

Considering the weight of available evidence, it would be naïve to believe that the days of gendered inequality in employment are past or numbered. Female disadvantage remains a major issue in work and management. It is neither old-fashioned nor redundant. Of course there are success stories of women who have secured 'better' jobs and reached management, and even executive, positions. However, many more experience limiting 'dead end' jobs, and those who do find ways of shattering the various glass barriers often encounter additional, unanticipated forms of disadvantage. So what explains this lack of empowerment? How is this continuing gender inequality to be interpreted?

EXPLAINING GENDER INEQUALITY

The explanatory literature on gender inequality is marked by a tension between accounts that focus on choices and preferences, and others that concentrate on discrimination. With the former, personal choice has an important bearing upon the pattern of job segregation and underrepresentation (Kottke and Agars, 2005). The interests and inclinations of women are presented as crucial factors, influencing their decisions about education and skill development and leading them into particular categories of work. When asked, significant numbers of women, and indeed men, evidently rely on this sort of view, attributing experienced or acknowledged disadvantage to personal priorities or conscious decisions rather than barriers that are put in their way (Anderson et al., 2010; Street, 2010; Broadbridge and Simpson, 2011).

There may be a defensive element in reports of this nature, especially for women who have reached management positions and feel uncomfortable about stating publically that opportunities are stacked against them, preferring instead to project some positive influence over their own situation (Anderson et al., 2010; Broadbridge and Simpson, 2011). However, the implication is that some element of gender inequality is 'self-imposed' (Street, 2010, p. 66), that women are choosing to avoid certain jobs and take themselves out of the running for various senior appointments.

A prominent strand of 'supply-side' economics supports this contention. Human capital theory suggests that gender inequalities in work and management are the result, not of discrimination, but of the voluntary smaller investments that women make in their own training and development. They are the consequence of rational choices rather than imposed glass barriers. Women, or at least a substantial proportion of them, ostensibly elect to take part-time jobs, work flexible hours or interrupt their paid employment to accommodate concerns with home and family, and this affects their marketable capital (Becker, 1985; Metz and Tharenou, 2001). Their priorities and choices leave them short of the skills that are necessary to access the sectors in which they are under-represented, and to acquire the experience and accumulated service to advance to senior positions in those in which they predominate.

Although it seems to be in tune with some sections of popular opinion and the self-reported accounts of women who followed particular career paths (Anderson et al., 2010), this explanatory approach accords very little significance to constraints on choice, and has little to say about earnings differentials between men and women performing the same work. Alternative explanations that are less accepting of rational choice and articulated preferences, point to discrimination as the primary source of disadvantage. Feminist writers have been particularly effective in calling attention to deeply rooted masculine ideologies and cultures that introduce bias into organizational relations, bolstering male privilege while restricting and undermining female contributions (Walby, 1990; Korvajarvi, 1998; Charles, 2005). From this perspective, male interests, values and traditions are institutionalized and perpetuated through discriminatory structures and detrimental influences such as the 'old boy's network' and men's club cultures that promote insular thinking, the maintenance of gendered hierarchies at work, and the marginalization of women into subordinate service roles.

This literature connects the workplace to wider patterns of socialization through the family and the domestic sphere where patriarchal relations are deeply entrenched and highly influential in perpetuating gender inequality. Patriarchy refers to male domination and the consolidation of male power over women through family and kinship ties and traditions that present men as symbolic overlords, with women cast in lesser, subservient positions. In theory, masculine values and the power and status of men are secured and reproduced through domestic pressures and the division of family responsibilities, typically with men controlling the flow of money and major household decisions while women deal with cleaning, catering and child care, for instance. These patriarchal relations are then carried over to the sphere of employment, restricting women's access to senior, decision-making roles and confining them to economic versions of their unpaid home and family work. The masculine values and practices of the domestic world become the management and organizational priorities of the workplace. As a result of socialization in the home, authority and leadership are ideologically associated with men and male employment. Meanwhile, job segregation is sustained by patriarchal practices among workers and in representative bodies that reflect male opinion, including trade unions. Patriarchal notions about appropriate male and female employment are expressed in collective agreements and through appeals to 'custom and practice' that restrict access to training and affect the classification of skills and grading of jobs (Jenkins et al., 2002; Mills, 2002; Ramsay and Scholarios, 2005).

While underlining the significance of discrimination and correcting for simplistic notions that women are the source of their own disadvantage, this literature on patriarchy can deflect attention from women as thoughtful, resourceful people who are capable of reading and responding to the obstacles they face. It can encourage a preoccupation with passive victims who are controlled and subordinated, and who may even internalize patriarchal values and come to accept that gender inequality is 'normal' or acceptable. The danger of analytical slippage to a default position where women are essentially passive and exploited has been highlighted by Hakim, who warns of 'feminist fallacies' (1995) and calls for a more constructive, women-centred focus (2000, 2004).

Hakim argues that lifestyle considerations have an important bearing upon female attitudes towards employment, informing conscious decisions that should be respected. Focusing on the expression of personal preferences, she insists that blanket generalizations about women's priorities should be avoided. While some may be career-minded, the majority balance paid work with family and other interests, and so take an adaptive approach to employment, working in ways that are convenient, and possibly alter with the family life cycle. From here, the pattern of female employment, including intermittent and part-time working and presence in full-time jobs with fixed or non-standard hours, has been shaped by preferences and is not straightforwardly a matter of prejudice or patriarchy. Women have been choosing jobs that suit their interests. There is a voluntary element to the pattern, with women making conscious decisions about their employment on the basis of different work–lifestyle preferences. According to Hakim's preference theory, this voluntary element has growing explanatory significance, with contextual factors and institutional constraints becoming less important (2000, p. 275; 2004).

This is a controversial opinion that seems to overpower Hakim's correction for the feminist concentration on men and masculinity. She moves too far in the other direction, towards female agency and away from structural constraint, challenging male-centred thinking to the point of apparently discounting discriminatory tendencies. There are undoubtedly women who look beyond their own preferences to account for what happens to them at work and in the labour market. The female council workers mentioned in the previous section fall into this category. They earn less than men performing the same grade or classification of work, and even identical tasks (in janitorial jobs, for example). Their employers in Birmingham, Newcastle and Glasgow (among other city authorities) have acknowledged that this is the case (Poling, 2005; BBC, 2012c; Butler, 2012). Hence, these women are acutely aware that their experience at work is unfair. Their declared preference is for the disadvantage on pay to be eliminated. However, they also realize that this is beyond their immediate control, that progress towards equality is less than straightforward since their preference is at odds with prevailing contextual conditions, established pay structures and the strategic priorities of those who currently occupy key positions in council management hierarchies.

This demonstrates that gender inequality is not a single-factor phenomenon, and that long-running debates that set preferences and attitudes against structural constraints pose a false dichotomy. In fact, accounts that privilege one side or the other are not well supported by the available evidence, which suggests that personal and structural aspects intersect as mutual influences on job segregation, underrepresentation and pay differentials. Large-scale surveys (Ramsay and Scholarios, 2005) and qualitative case investigations (Scholarios and Taylor, 2011) confirm that convenience is an important consideration for many women in the labour market, and that part-time or fixed-hour positions are often sought as a means of balancing employment interests and requirements with those beyond the workplace, relating to home and family in particular. In-work opportunities to apply discretion, make the best use of their skills and abilities, gain responsibility and have interesting and rewarding experiences are no less important for women than these off-workplace preferences and priorities, however. Indeed, at this level, the differences between female and male orientations, preferences and ambitions are marginal (Ramsay and Scholarios, 2005).

These studies endorse Hakim's points about diversity and adaptive attempts to achieve an effective work–life balance. Yet they also promote an essential sensitivity to context and the structural conditioning of gendered experiences. By this evidence, women are undoubtedly making conscious decisions about their employment and commitment at the workplace, although these are pragmatic and constrained, as indeed they are for men. The constraints on women include open and tacit discriminatory practices by men, however, which are far more significant than preference theory can appreciate. Scholarios and Taylor (2011) uncovered some dramatic evidence of this in their call centre research. Women who were combining their work with major domestic responsibilities though were keen to move up the job ladder were prevented from doing so by supervisors on the basis of stereotypical assumptions.

These supervisors were preselecting men and women for developmental and training opportunities that would prepare them for promotion, or at least improve their chances of reaching the shortlist for promoted posts. The evidence indicated that men and women with similar qualifications, experience and career ambitions were treated differently, and that supervisors were restricting access on the basis of entrenched assumptions about domestic status and orientation to work. Domestic and household circumstances were considered to be relevant for decisions about women rather than men, and where these were obviously important to candidates for development, the supervisors equated this with limited potential and a lack of serious intent. Women who clearly had domestic responsibilities were automatically assumed to have their minds full of matters beyond work that would distract them from the demands of promoted positions, and so deliver a poor return on any investment in their training. Regardless of the commitment, ability and experience of the interested women, exclusionary practices were applied and they were confined to low status work as a result of crude male stereotyping. Their lack of progress was again interpreted realistically by the women in this situation, as it was for the female council workers. They were clear that this inequality was the result of socialized obstruction, and their preference was for the obstacles to be removed.

These theoretical points have important practical implications, informing various reactions to gender inequality and debates about the viability of empowering women. Preference theory seems to discourage any sort of practical activism in favour of equality, accepting that women are making conscious choices that satisfy their wider interests and commitments. Feminism, on the other hand, requires a fundamental assault on patriarchal values and the institutionalized practices that subordinate women. It also suggests that traditional means of protest and worker mobilization against inequality are closed to women. Trade unions, for example, are often regarded as part of the problem rather than the solution, as bastions of male power. The corollary is that other educational, legal and regulatory interventions are needed to re-shape attitudes and challenge patriarchal socialization and exclusionary practices. Integrated approaches, by contrast, leave room for purposeful action by people at the sharp end of inequality. They are more likely to acknowledge traditions of self-empowerment, to concede that structural constraints do not deliver passivity, and recognize more basic grassroots interventions where 'sisters may be doing things for themselves'.

ACTION, AT THE WORKPLACE AND BEYOND

The distinction between positive action and positive discrimination figures prominently in debates about how best to tackle gender inequality and empower women at work. Positive action is a generic term for supportive policies and developmental programmes that aim to help women compete more effectively with men, and redress their disadvantage in employment by securing a higher proportion of the positions that become available. Typically this begins with an employer or agency commitment to furthering equal opportunities (informed by ACAS or the Equality and Human Rights Commission, for instance), leading on to awareness raising initiatives, dedicated training and mentoring schemes for women, and also flexible employment practices.

Tailored measures that boost confidence and provide greater access to skills and experience are usually part of this, including job sharing and career breaks, dedicated recruitment and pre-selection events, and even open days, all to encourage female applicants in male dominated sectors. Positive action on career development is also covered, notably with female-only management courses that cater directly for the expressed requirements of women, ensuring that their concerns and issues are addressed directly and not overwhelmed or marginalized by the weight of male numbers in mixed events. To use a popular sporting analogy, the logic behind this package of measures is to 'level the playing field' for women and men, and improve the chances of them competing equally on merit.

Though often confused and conflated with positive action, positive discrimination is quite different, involving concerted attempts to tilt the playing field in favour of women and attain gender equality in a much tighter timescale. There are various forms of positive discrimination, although it is generally associated with 'quota' systems that require a set level of female representation in particular organizational categories or roles. For example, in Norway there is a much-quoted legal requirement for public limited companies and state enterprises to have women in at least 40 per cent of their boardroom positions (Noon, 2010; *Business Week*, 2011).

Arguments for positive discrimination have attracted some very negative reactions. Some critics insist that it undermines cherished principles of meritocracy. They fear that if gender becomes the most important criteria for differentiating between people in employment then less qualified women will inevitably be given preference over more qualified men, and organizational performance may suffer. For others, this amounts to 'reverse discrimination', and 'two wrongs don't make a right'. Discrimination of any sort is morally wrong, and this approach discriminates against men. These views are regularly rehearsed by groups such as the Chartered Institute of Personnel and Development in Britain, although they have prompted some robust counter-arguments and rebuttals in recent years.

Opponents, perhaps most notably Noon (2010), claim that appeals to the primacy of non-discrimination have a hollow ring when men have for so long accepted the benefits that glass barriers generate for them at the expense of women. For Noon, fair treatment for men is less of an issue than correcting the historical inequalities experienced by women, and positive discrimination is necessary to accelerate the pace of change and deliver equality as a matter of urgency rather than a drawn-out project that adds insult to injury. This view has been highly significant in British political circles since the late 1990s, ensuring that a moderate form of positive discrimination was included in the 2010 Equality Act.

The provisions of this Act allow employers to hire and promote women in preference to men whenever a tie-break situation arises, and a shortlisted group of men and women are equally qualified for available positions. In the event of a tie-break on job-specific qualifications, women can be lawfully appointed over men. The intention with this is to counteract any hidden or tacit endorsement of men in such situations, through the 'old boy' network, for instance, or from the sort of gender stereotyping that Scholarios and Taylor (2011) found in supervisory 'hunches' about women not fitting in or becoming pregnant and leaving. The Act calls for systematic and transparent differentiation based on recognized imbalances, rather than spurious or questionable assumptions. However, employers are not obliged to follow this convention. It is permissive rather than mandatory, meaning that it is not unlawful to recruit or promote a woman with qualifications equivalent to any male candidates. It is left to employers to decide whether they adhere to the provisions and favour women in a tie-break situation, and the legislation was presented as an extension of positive action and not a form of positive discrimination.

This reflects the sensitivities that surround positive discrimination, although many enthusiasts view the British Equality Act as a fudge or tame intervention (Noon, 2010). Since the process of acquiring skills, qualifications and experience is itself problematic for women, the voluntary tie-break provisions are considered to be largely irrelevant for many, to apply after the fact of their disadvantage, and to have little or no impact on the basic barriers to progress, such as prior assumptions about the suitability of women for training or impact of their domestic situation on the uptake of developmental opportunities (Scholarios and Taylor, 2011). From this standpoint, the tie-break provisions of the Act amount to an incremental adjustment at the margins of the problem of gender inequality, benefiting some women though failing many more. Rather than concentrating on the niceties of non-discrimination and equal treatment, progressive action is needed on the fundamental sources of disadvantage, and this ostensibly means treating women differently, granting them preferential status with stronger forms of positive discrimination (Noon, 2010).

These arguments are fuelled by frustration and disappointment at the lack of progress through four decades of equal opportunities legislation in Britain (from the Equal Pay Act of 1970 and the 1975 Sex Discrimination Act), and from an acute sense of the limitations of positive action programmes. There is broad-ranging evidence that the course of female empowerment at work has not followed a steady developmental trajectory, and that the rhetoric on positive action for equality conceals regular backsliding and prevarication (Mills, 2002).

Positive action initiatives are all too often half-hearted and contradictory. The call centre research conducted by Scholarios and Taylor (2011) provides some contemporary evidence of this. All of the organizations they studied expressed support for equal opportunities and had positive action measures in place, including training and development schemes, career breaks and job sharing. However, these seemingly enlightened management regimes also barred job sharers from becoming team leaders and, as previously explained, allowed their supervisors to pre-select men and women for development events on the basis of crude assumptions about their suitability. These practices undermined managerial claims about their sensitivity to gender equality, suggesting a token or rhetorical commitment rather than a considered and consistent approach.

Arguably, the most dramatic demonstration of the weakness and vulnerability of action programmes occurred in the United States, at the American Telephone and Telegraph Corporation (AT&T). Taking employment figures as an indicator of 'progress', Hacker (1990) discovered that three years after an equality action plan had been implemented 16 300 men had entered areas previously dominated by women, while 9400 women had gained access to traditional male preserves. The upshot was that 13 767 more men and 2200 fewer women were employed by the company. Hacker attributes this to changing technology within this industry, which eclipsed the action plan as women were encouraged to take on roles that were becoming redundant, learning to climb telegraph poles as new transmission systems reduced the need for them, for instance (Hacker, 1990, pp. 53–59).

These accounts are far from novel (Mills, 2002; Broadbridge and Simpson, 2011) and provide telling evidence of continuing disadvantage within the modern framework of positive action and equal opportunities legislation. This is why proponents of positive discrimination argue for more radical, less compromised interventions. Noon is among the most eloquent, drawing on some powerful imagery that American President Lyndon Johnson used to seek redress for racial discrimination. This is worth reproducing in full:

> Imagine a hundred yard dash in which one of the two runners has his legs shackled together. He has progressed 10 yards, while the unshackled runner has gone 50 yards. At that point the judges decide that the race is unfair. How do they rectify the situation? Do they merely remove the shackles and allow the race to proceed? Then they could say that equal opportunity now prevailed. But one of the runners would still be forty yards ahead of the other. Would it not be the better part of justice to allow the previously shackled runner to make up the forty yard gap; or to start the race all over again? (Quoted by Noon, 2010, p. 728)

For Noon, the priority is to make up the ground that women have lost in employment, and deal with the legacy of gender inequality seriously and urgently. Hence, he advocates positive discrimination as a necessary precondition for meaningful change, acknowledging that this requires more determined state intervention (Noon, 2010, p. 737). There is little likelihood of politicians in Britain openly agreeing with this or acting on Noon's advice any time soon. Other developments do signal a shift in the way that some employers are dealing with gender inequality, however, with 'third party' influences pushing them beyond their positive action comfort zone.

One of the most significant effects of the equality legislation has been to create space for campaign groups, activists and other agents to challenge discriminating employers, particularly on pay inequality. There is a growing literature on 'new actors' and new forms of activism on gender equality. Conley (2012) highlighted the efforts of the Fawcett Society, a campaigning charity on women's rights, in launching a legal challenge to a government budget in 2010 on the grounds that it had a disproportionately negative effect on women. This particular intervention was unsuccessful. However, another group, Action-4-Equality, has made a considerable difference on pay inequality, forcing local authorities across Britain to accept their legal responsibilities under the equality legislation, at the same time exposing some weaknesses and contradictions in trade union representation on this issue.

Action-4-Equality has encouraged thousands of female council workers to use the services of 'no-win-no-fee' lawyers to pursue compensation on their behalf (Poling, 2005). Tribunals have established, and the employers have conceded, that women in some areas of the British public sector have been illegally and systematically underpaid for many years, and are now eligible for substantial settlements that could have a major impact on local authority finances. Some estimates suggest that the costs to Glasgow and Aberdeen city councils could run to £200 million and £40 million respectively (Poling, 2005). This has prompted employers to negotiate their own compensation arrangements with the public sector trade unions, notably the GMB and UNISON. Though involving lump-sum payments that have been accepted by many women, those pursuing legal redress have been achieving around three times as much, with additional pension benefits and more rapid pay rises as part of their final settlement.

These disparities, and broader debates about the financial impact of pay equality in this sector, have triggered some acrimonious exchanges, many of them reminiscent of patriarchal arguments about the role of trade unions in perpetuating disadvantages imposed on women by management practices. Many critical comments have been recorded by women who feel that the unions have 'let them down', been colluding with the employers, and failing to represent the interests of all of their members (Poling, 2005; BBC, 2012c; Butler, 2012). Responding to this negativity, union representatives claim to have secured responsible compensation packages that avoid any job-threatening damage to local authority budgets. Alongside employer spokespeople, union officials have condemned the 'no-win-no-fee' lawyers as a mercenary, self-serving group with no long-term commitment to the health and wellbeing of the sector. Against this, the Action-4-Equality campaign claims to have moved the employers further and faster than the unions, demonstrating a far more serious commitment to reducing gendered pay inequality. While legal fees draw between 12 and 25 per cent of the final amount awarded to their clients, they insist that this 'third party' representation invariably delivers far more that any union-negotiated compensation package. To judge by the available feedback from women using this service, there is a broad measure of satisfaction with these 'new actors' on equality, and some genuine appreciation for their interventions and relative success in securing positive outcomes for low-paid female workers. Perhaps there are signals here about the sort of leverage that is necessary for progress on equality and the empowerment of women, and which is lacking with positive action.

6. Culture, management and innovation

While much of the interest in advancing employee empowerment has been channelled into technical arrangements – redefining job structures and changing skill content, layout and work space design – mixed reactions and tensions between rival interpretations have drawn attention to subjectivity and culture as crucial aspects of innovation. As previous chapters have established, front-line accounts of empowerment are pluralistic, covering a range of meanings and reflecting different readings, interests and orientations. Regardless of sector and setting, large numbers of people, managers and employees remain to be convinced about the merits and practicalities of empowerment. A sense of caution underpins even favourable evaluations, while negative judgements point to fragmented, temporary or contradictory outcomes. Reactions to the same scheme often range from measured approval to complaints from some 'empowered' staff that the experience reproduced rather than transformed their sense of inequality, injustice or disadvantage.

The stance that different people adopt has much to do with their underlying values and established ways of thinking, feeling and sense-making. Particular views and ways of reading and engaging with organizational events 'live on' through innovative episodes, filtering and influencing them as they unfold from a sense of the past. This means that structural interventions are mediated through habitual and traditional ways of living and coping with a dynamic world. For all the attention given to structures and the technical apparatus of empowerment, the fortunes of practical programmes are crucially dependent upon cultural and subcultural influences.

This chapter takes an in-depth look at culture and subjectivity, evaluating their significance for the empowerment project and considering how they simultaneously impinge upon, and develop from, patterns of innovation. In terms of the conceptual framework explained at the outset and developed through previous chapters, the point here is to accommodate cultural dimensions explicitly and effectively within a relational understanding of power, struggle and practice.

PRESCRIPTIONS FOR CULTURAL CHANGE

The mixed reactions of those affected by empowerment programmes are often difficult for prescriptive management theorists and consultants to take. For this group, they signify an unhealthy or wrong-headed fixation with outmoded values and the legacy of the past. There is a frustration, at least in part of the management literature, with deeply embedded cultural characteristics, specifically the top-down ethos and authoritarianism that Taylorism and Fordism nurtured more than a century ago, and which continue to exert a millstone influence on modern practitioner thinking (Peters and Waterman, 1982; Kanter, 1984; Deal and Kennedy, 1999; Notter and Grant, 2011).

From here, too many people are locked into 'them and us' values and priorities, to a 'command and control' logic that threatens to destabilize any gains that can be achieved with the restructuring of work. This necessitates a rather more fundamental challenge to the way that people think about empowerment and organizational change. Measures that target job structures may be solid and sensible given current competitive conditions yet are liable to fail when fastened to organizations that cherish the values of the old industrial order. By this reasoning, the promise of empowerment is to be realized not so much by altering structures but by winning hearts and minds. Innovation becomes a cultural as much as a structural intervention. It means changing the corporate ethos, the core values, attitudes and beliefs that influence behaviour, socializing people into the role of 'team players' and over-coming any ingrained tendency towards low trust, adversarial relations.

This is very much a product of the excellence tradition of the 1980s, a movement that was stimulated by the publication of Peters and Water-man's book *In Search of Excellence* (1982) and fuelled by the pronounce-ments of like-minded consultants and management gurus who were eager to jettison any cultural baggage that inhibited performance (Deal and Kennedy, 1982; Robson, 1988; Kotter and Heskett, 1992; Chan Kim and Mauborgne, 2005). At a time of industrial upheaval and dislocation, when many Western companies were coming to terms with the economic ascendancy of their Japanese competitors, this case for cultural renewal struck a chord with prominent executives and senior managers, notably in the car industry and in consumer electronics (Starkey and McKinlay, 1994). The success of Japanese manufacturers seemed to underline the significance of common values and a consensual approach to work organization. These companies were evidently adding value to their structural arrangements by enlisting the help and cooperation of their people in a purposeful, family-like fashion (Pascale and Athos, 1986; Mouer and Kawanishi, 2005).

The putative virtues of homogeneous values and the consensual Japanese corporation may be less compelling since the Asian economic crises of 1998 and 1999 revealed tensions, when admired innovators such as Nissan and Mazda were dismantling the 'golden principles' of job and contract security and staff welfare provision (BBC, 2000). However, in the context of the 1980s, these were potent symbols in the campaign for 'strong' cultures and 'turned on' corporate citizens. Politicians and wider interest groups were also reinforcing the message, expressing policy initiatives in cultural terms and, most obviously in Britain, associating renewal with prosperity under the banner of an 'enterprise culture'.

Not that employer attempts to influence culture originated during this period. When faced with problems of absenteeism and labour turnover in the early twentieth century, Henry Ford had tried to manipulate working class values so that that staff would be more inclined to accept the pressures of his harsh regime. Various measures were devised, from bonus schemes to an Americanization programme for immigrants, all of them aiming to move people on an emotional and patriotic level, to 'help' them internalize Ford's vision of an appropriate work ethic and instil a greater collective sense of efficiency and industrial discipline (Littler and Salaman, 1984; Ford and Crowther, 1926).

As it was portrayed from the 1980s, however, culture management is a more seductive and seemingly neutral (less ethically charged) prospect, the excellence gurus investing it with an elixir-like potential to transform the fortunes of ailing companies (Thompson and McHugh, 1995; Collins, 2000). Cultural change became the solution to organizational ills. It was, and still is, prescribed as an antidote to the effects of disparate thinking and behaviour, an essential way of uniting corporate citizens behind irreproachable goals (Deal and Kennedy, 1982 and 1999; Chan Kim and Mauborgne, 2005; Notter and Grant, 2011). The resulting mantra is that excellent companies thrive because they engage in restructuring while at that same time enthusing people to be co-operative and creative. Their 'change masters' (Kanter, 1984) simultaneously humanize structures and 'unfreeze' the status quo, decentralizing work arrangements while creating a culture that is conducive to the change.

Yet in this project, culture carries a very specific meaning (Johnson and Duberley, 2011). It is the product of management decision-making, an expression of the way that senior figures define the character and purpose of an organization. It is, in other words, the official view, the sense of itself that is generated from the top, or as Deal and Kennedy (1982) more (in)famously put it, 'the way we do things around here'.

Culture is the 'higher cause' that glues the various communities of organizational life together (Deal and Kennedy, 1999), the 'software of the mind' (Hofstede, 1991) or 'collective mental programming' (Schein, 1985) that connects people to organizational goals.

Executives are told that to nurture innovation this 'hot wiring' must privilege humanistic concerns, putting people first and foremost on the corporate agenda. The lesson drawn from excellent companies is that supportive cultures gather strength by expressing anti-authoritarian sentiments, demonstrating a concern for employee welfare and cultivating a reciprocal identification with the needs of the organization. On this reading, shared values are established by driving fear out of the workplace and creating an atmosphere of openness, trust and cohesion (Peters and Waterman, 1982; Deal and Kennedy, 1999).

So how does an organization develop and solidify this strong culture of mutual care and concern? For most of these authors, and certainly the more consultancy-minded commentators (including Martin and Nicholls, 1987; Kotter and Heskett, 1992; Roth, 1997; Ward, 1996; Nicholls, 1995; Chan Kim and Mauborgne, 2005; DuBois, 2012), the process is reasonably straightforward. As a first step, transformational leaders are charged with creating a clear vision and corresponding 'umbrella of beliefs' (Deal and Kennedy, 1999), mining company history for suitable signals, benchmarking elements of this against admired organizations, and ensuring that the final package is consistent with the environment and characteristics of the business or service. Procedures, rituals and ceremonies are then devised to 'summon the collective spirit'. Corporate symbols are created and a distinctive language contrived to engender feelings of identification and shared mission.

Inspirational leadership is at the centre of the process. All of the main gurus agree that the ability of an organization to be culturally progressive is crucially dependent upon enlightened leaders who have a clear vision of how to put people first, and a determination to follow through, 'walking the walk and talking the talk' (Deal and Kennedy, 1999). With such a thrusting and dynamic image of leadership roles at the heart of the recipe, it is perhaps unsurprising that a large population of senior executives appear to have taken the advice. There are many examples of corporate 'change masters' rehearsing the case for cultural renewal, and attaching their personal seal of approval to moulding and socializing programmes (Robson, 1988; Jones, 2000; McCabe, 2002; Brannan and Hawkins, 2007). Yet their efforts reveal a remarkable sameness and monotony of practice.

The imprint of the guru schemes is discernible in all sorts of initiatives and settings, with their vocabulary and measures reproduced to a standard format. The 'Values Framework' at the BBC is similar to the 'Visions and Values' scheme at Collins publishing, which is much the same as the 'Hewlett-Packard Way', the 'Microsoft Way' and the Scottish Power statement of 'commandments' setting out what it will and will not do. These organizations, like many others, are keen to present their people-friendly credentials for attention, to project cohesive cultural characteristics and exemplify progressive leadership. Their web sites and promotional documents, both for internal and external consumption, proclaim that their purpose is to enrich the lives of staff and clients, to be creative at whatever they do, to build trust and respect with integrity and genuine conviction. In the aftermath of the Great Recession, and especially the associated scandals in the financial sector, this is a message that major companies are presenting more enthusiastically. Some, such as Google, have even introduced 'culture keepers' or 'chief culture officers' at an executive level to promote and protect cohesive corporate values (DuBois, 2012).

Claims about the essence of these 'culturally integrated' organizations (Johnson and Duberley, 2011), what they stand for and represent, are typically reinforced with policies and procedures, symbols and imagery that attempt to make the message convincing. The details are usually modelled on arrangements associated with the showcase organizations and exemplary cultures on Peters and Waterman's original list, reaching back to IBM, Disney, Hewlett-Packard and others. The efforts of these 'pioneering' companies in packaging and presenting their mission, translating it into dress codes, logos and corporate jargon, connecting it to stories and legends about charismatic founders and heroic managers, are absorbed and replicated.

Human resource programmes aim to induct people deliberately and often elaborately into the life of the organization, cultivating their commitment through subsequent performance appraisal and development programmes that re-emphasize values and expectations. Work locations are designed and coloured to reflect humanistic concerns, to be ergonomically pleasing and conducive to a positive experience, with windows and views or rest areas, rather than regimented cubicles and ill-considered lighting that contributes to a sense of drudgery. Walls are decorated with posters and slogans that help people to feel proud of their organization, to identify with the pronouncements of their leaders, share in their hopes for the future and recognize that they are valued members of an inclusive community.

Clearly, these measures are introduced with the intention of fusing people together, of moulding and socializing their commitment so that they welcome innovation, responding positively on a consensual basis and without the disruptive influence of fractured judgements about its significance (Notter and Grant, 2011). Whether culture is really amenable to such managerial shaping is a matter of intense controversy, however.

For some people in the research community and within organizations, culture management constitutes a potent force. The recipe targets the emotions of managers and workers in a way that renders them more susceptible to the pronouncements and priorities of senior figures. Without really being conscious of the effects, by some accounts, their identity begins to merge with the interests of the organization. They surrender a greater part of themselves and their independent influence as they become equivalent to "Beamers" at IBM (Willmott, 1993; Strangleman and Roberts, 1999).

For others, the formula is simply too crude, trite and faddish, with little or no substance to command serious attention. A large number of reviews are caustic and dismissive. *In Search of Excellence* was savaged by critics in both the business and academic communities who found plenty of ammunition in the performance figures subsequently delivered by companies on the list, and the dramatic fall from grace of American 'institutions' like IBM. It was described as 'the epitome of eighties shallowness' in *Business Age* magazine, 'a book for juveniles' (by Drucker, quoted in Silver, 1987), and 'dead wrong' by agents of the United States Justice Department (Delamarter, 1988).

Others again complain that culture has been commercialized by this treatment, that something valuable has been lost through accounts that reduce it to a corporate resource or communication device (Johnson and Duberley, 2011). By this reading, the culture management movement is at best a red herring, or worse, a disruptive influence that has stifled analysis and applied research, deflecting attention from richer source material that can help to clarify key concepts and contextualize innovation.

CRITICAL EVALUATIONS

The main worry for some critics is that culture management succeeds. They fear that it may limit and contain human experience, raising disturbing questions about distortion, manipulation and the servicing of elite interests. Some find it offensive, equating cultural change programmes with subjugation, the insidious control of subjectivity and nascent totalitarianism (Willmott, 1993; Grey, 1994; Ray, 1986). From here, culture begins to blend with surveillance as employees internalize the values of the organization to the point where they police their own activities, and management control is exercised through worker self-discipline (Brannan and Hawkins, 2007). Smith and Wilkinson (1996) detect such an outcome at Sherwoods, a company that ostensibly followed the prescriptive guidelines enthusiastically with integrative, non-authoritarian initiatives that delivered harmony and zealous conformity on management terms. By this evidence, culture management is a warped and malevolent project, a variation on Taylorism and Fordism and not, as publicized, the key to a humanistic alternative. It caters for elite interests, dominating rather than empowering, overwhelming instead of respecting people and their contributions.

This literature offers a potent antidote to upbeat managerialism. It provides an effective inducement to critical thinking and even a sceptical disposition, which is healthy when confronting the positive claims made for management recipes and 'universal' solutions in this area, as in others. However, there are grounds for caution, and for applying critical scrutiny to this bleak interpretation of culture management. In fact, there is a close correspondence between this treatment of culture and the stance taken by some of the critical writers on power and managerialism that were reviewed in the first chapter. At that stage, the contrasts between resource models, or capacity-outcome views, of power were found to be less significant than the similarities between them, which deflected attention away from relations of interdependence. The same applies to the analytical divisions between these opposing accounts of culture management. The critics share some key conceptual difficulties with the authors they seek to challenge.

Culture is more complex than either account permits. By concentrating on strength and control, integration and uniformity, consensus and value internalization, they oversimplify the subjectivities, processes and uncertainties involved. The most telling critiques of culture management point to the impossibility of creating truly uniform corporate cultures, and the limited effect of identity-building and symbolic conditioning measures of the sort advocated by the gurus. This is not to suggest that culture is beyond influence. On the contrary, the point is to promote a dynamic appreciation of culture, connecting it to a relational understanding of power and interaction as a feature of life that is continually negotiated rather than malleable and determinate.

The fearful view of culture management sides with the gurus in assuming that leaders are capable of creating culture. In this respect, both camps overstate their case. They work with an impression of senior executives that is unrealistic. As some other authors have noted (Thompson and McHugh, 1995; Collins, 2000), they seem to be taken in by the image of themselves that prominent executives and corporate personalities often cultivate, as 'masters of the universe' who command allegiance and preside over cohesive entities that have been forged in their own image. Their accounts differ mainly on the motives, ethics and interests that are attributed to these able and focused leaders.

Yet those at the top of organizational hierarchies have never been able to wield such authority, or to marginalize other interests and influences to the point where they become irrelevant to the nature and understanding of everyday events. The images traded by the gurus, and by this constituency of critical commentators, exaggerate the capabilities of corporate leaders, and also the receptiveness (or gullibility) of the managers and staff who operate below them in the official pecking order. No matter how charismatic, focused or active they may be in deploying the prescriptive techniques of culture management, leaders are simply unable to exert a totalizing influence on culture. Accounts that suggest otherwise crucially ignore both the strength and diversity of interests and affiliations that influence organizational life.

Workplace behaviour is variously framed, inspired and constrained by a complex mix of values, orientations and attachments, many of them transcending organizational boundaries (Beirne, 2011). Members of work organizations are typically drawn from different geographical areas, social classes, sexes, ethnic groups and religions. These aspects of existence are not suspended or removed when people pass through the gates of their employing organization. They inevitably approach their work in a way that reflects their upbringing, early socialization and wider life experiences, blending these together with occupational and professional influences, and others from within the organization, including those from hierarchical, functional, and specialist associations.

References to a uniform, all-embracing and monolithic corporate culture are difficult to sustain when this level of diversity is called into the analysis. These 'other' influences cannot be said to operate beyond, underneath or alongside the official culture because they interlock with it in a dynamic and often unpredictable manner. As Fincham and Rhodes (1992, p. 420) effectively phrase it, they 'form the basis of distinctive subcultures and counter-cultures that compete to define the reality of the organization'. Despite the efforts of the corporate culture gurus and their prominent followers, organizations are multicultural. They consist of various constellations of values and impulses that sometimes overlap or coincide, occasionally clash, and at other times exert a more subtle influence on events. This multicultural mix ensures that a large population is involved in framing the nature and identity of an organization. It is not an attribute of leadership or something that lies within the gift of executives, no matter how enlightened their approach.

A number of classic studies have underlined the importance of workplace subcultures, establishing their potential for influence, explaining how this is reproduced, and pointing to their resilience (Roy, 1973; Jones, 2000; Eastman and Fulop, 1997). Informal behaviour patterns and experiences with esoteric language figure prominently in accounts of cultural processes, especially those that flourish unofficially or in spite of management opposition. During the course of their work, individuals encounter forms of banter, humour and behavioural regularities that reinforce existing subcultures and counter-cultures. These are initially filtered and interpreted through norms and values that have already been assimilated, and which make the surrounding events seem more or less sensible, perhaps shocking, irrelevant and pointless, or possibly just a variation on taken-for-granted aspects of social engagement. People respond in a way that reflects their personal history and the constraints of the situation, gravitating towards some affiliations while spurning others with varying degrees of diplomacy. Yet the emerging pattern of association, affiliation, tolerance and avoidance is fluid and dynamic rather than consciously settled. Multicultural influences are subject to negotiation over time and in light of experience, resisting definitive classification or rational separation into categories that either support or challenge officialdom (Hatch, 1997).

In fact, people are capable of expressing distinctly different and seemingly contradictory values, of identifying with competing subcultures on an everyday basis. Jones (2000) provides a telling example from his personal experience of employment with work-study engineers at a Hotpoint domestic appliance factory in North Wales. He was assigned to a small group of some 15 individuals who shared a Taylorist outlook on work roles and formal relationships, exhibiting a mutual intolerance for operator slacking, which they regarded as a key management issue, and by extension a collective allegiance to machine pacing and work measurement as vital means of maintaining control. Yet these engineers had multiple identities, some of them based around sports, drinking and music that contributed to subcultures that straddled Taylorist demarcation lines between 'them and us'. There were regular patterns of social interaction between the engineers and shop floor workers that had a bearing upon exchanges between them. Although these engineers were part of a subculture that disparaged and fostered conflict with operators, some of them had established another identity as 'one of the boys'.

By this reckoning, the lines of influence between affiliation and expression are occasionally surprising, though seldom straightforward. Yet enthusiasts for culture management continue to present a unifying agenda based on programming from the top. Where subcultures are acknowledged, in the second of Deal and Kennedy's books, for example, discussion centres on the management challenge of 'knitting them together', of creating 'umbrella beliefs to unite disparate subcultures ... into a coherent and cohesive whole' (1999, p. 203). The assumption that leaders can apply the chosen message and appeal to people over and above other influences and orientations persists. An abundance of empirical evidence now supports the theoretical case for dismissing this proposition, however.

The work-study engineers at Hotpoint were able to maintain their sense of purpose and relevance, and indeed their capacity to exert an influence on work organization, despite a cultural change programme that explicitly challenged their position (Jones, 2000). The arrival of a new managing director marked a watershed in official thinking about work and employee relations, with 'humanistic' innovations introduced and traditional Tayloristic ideas openly criticized. Here was a new management regime with focused believers who were apparently putting the recipe for cultural renewal to work.

Time studies and stopwatch measurements were rejected as techniques that were 'demeaning to operators', and a payment by results scheme dismantled on the grounds that it encouraged 'sloppy work'. Yet their subjective sense of management priorities and necessary behaviour moved the work-study group to resist, and to carry on regardless of the signals and initiatives from above. They held on to the belief that productivity levels were modest, that worker discretion would be taken as a licence for slacking, and that the leadership line had not really been thought through or related to operational conditions at their factory.

Crucially, the subjectivities that sustained the work-study subculture were reinforced rather than undermined by the changes, because the self-image of the engineers as custodians of efficiency actually hardened. On their terms, the new leaders had a poor grasp of management realities, and were governed by fashionable notions or misplaced idealism. They were the only managers with any real understanding of efficiency, so it was important for them collectively to sustain their commitment despite the regime and until their contribution was verified or appreciated. This was an oppositional subculture that had been 'tightened' by the experience of culture management. Group members were highly sensitive to their engineering subjectivities, and more likely to spark conflict with workers and senior executives as a result.

Other case evidence registers similar doubts about managerial responsiveness, although highlighting different forms of resistance. Various researchers have called attention to distancing, acting and role-playing behaviour that enables people on the receiving end of culture management to counteract unpalatable or uncomfortable effects (Ogbonna and

Wilkinson, 1990; Anthony, 1994; McCabe, 2002). There are reports of managers feeling exposed by the antics of leaders who stage-manage cultural events and launch quirky initiatives, and then expect them to rehearse embarrassing slogans and sell the 'concept' to staff. Many baulk at the gimmickry and 'novelty' of culture management, and feel uncomfortable with the clichéd language of innovation spouted by their leaders and imported by consultants (Beirne, 2011).

For these managers, the apparatus of culture management is not intrinsically motivating or uplifting. Their identity and sense of self is challenged. Nonetheless, feelings of personal unease and the perception that credibility with staff is at risk have to be set against the expectation from above that policy will be implemented. Impression management is the answer for some, 'going through the motions', acting out roles for each constituency, and resorting to an older and more 'natural' discourse whenever possible (Ogbonna and Wilkinson, 1990; McCabe, 2002). These reactions signal something other than value internalization. Managerial subjectivities here, as in the previous example, produce varied and competing lines of influence.

Counter-cultures are also discernible at leadership level. In fact, senior figures in companies that profess to have inclusive and progressive cultures have been widely criticized for not adhering to the officially cherished values, of 'not practising what they preach', of exhibiting subcultural tendencies of their own that contradict the corporate culture. The debates around financial participation and outcry in Britain about 'fat cat' salaries provide a useful illustration.

As indicated in Chapter 4, the most common complaint levelled against executive share-ownership schemes is that they fragment team behaviour and reinforce 'them and us' attitudes by seeming to reward the self-serving behaviour of elite groups of executives. The accusations of greed and hypocrisy that have been captured by researchers and reported in the media centre on what various employees and managers consider to be the 'do as I say and not as I do' subculture in many of Britain's major companies (*The Daily Record*, 1998; *Scotland on Sunday*, 1999; Caulkin, 2012; *The Daily Mail*, 2012; Flint, 2012). Hence, perceptions about unfair practice and the divisiveness of schemes that seem to be 'rigged' in favour of executives are at odds with the declarations about openness, trust and shared values that frequently populate corporate web sites and official documents (Baddon et al., 1989; O'Connell-Davidson and Nichols, 1991; *The Herald*, 1996). The corollary is that the attitudes and behaviour that leaders have tried to mould and shape through culture management have actually been undermined by aspects of their own personal and subcultural identities. While these are considered to be quite separate (and are formally removed) from culture management processes, they nonetheless trigger negative judgements that affect reactions among wider groups of managers and employees.

These examples demonstrate the vulnerability of imposed cultural change programmes and expose the limited grasp of theory and empirical evidence that informs a lot of prescriptive managerial and fearful critical commentary about cultural engineering and the moulding of human subjectivity. Executive influences on organizational culture are neither uniform nor decisive, exhibiting contrasting and even contradictory tendencies that are mediated by other subjectivities. This is something that senior figures in a growing list of companies that have followed the recipe have come to appreciate. The official rhetoric of their corporate culture is far removed from the everyday meanings and understandings captured by in-house attitude surveys and by independent research studies that have tracked staff reactions to culture-shaping programmes (Thompson and Findlay, 1996). Significant investments of time, energy and resources have failed to impress, exacerbating tensions and raising the reported levels of dissatisfaction and distrust.

The British Airways slide from confident culture management to conflict, strife and managerial fire fighting is one of the most dramatic and widely recognized. Despite many years of cultural conditioning from the 1980s – 'Putting People First', 'Managing People First', 'Visioning the Future', fostering pride and the service ethic through 'Customer First Teams' in the 'World's Favourite Airline' (Bruce, 1987; Robson, 1988; Hopfl et al., 1992; Grugulis and Wilkinson, 2002) – members of staff were still forming and expressing their own views about company life, and these were persistently critical. The idealized view from the top was regularly punctured by grassroots experiences and understandings, back-firing quite spectacularly in the late 1990s during disputes with cabin crew and catering staff that exposed the less palatable propensities of key executives and functional managers.

New terms and conditions were imposed, cutting overtime, mileage and unsocial hours allowances, allocating some services to outside contractors, and introducing tighter controls and monitoring systems to improve staff performance. Accusations about intimidatory tactics and heavy-handed management captured headlines, and support from some unlikely sources. There was a general outcry about the 'shop-a-mate' money saving initiative that encouraged staff to blow the whistle on colleagues who were squandering or stealing resources, for example (*The Daily Record*, 1996). The British Medical Association complained to the company that a new requirement for staff to obtain a medical certificate for missing a single working day through ill health was unacceptable, placing significant burdens upon General Practitioners and asking them to be "industrial policemen" (*The Guardian*, 1997). Guidelines governing the height and weight of cabin staff attracted additional and very public criticism as pressure from within and beyond the company mounted on then Chief Executive, Bob Ayling, to improve morale and service to customers (*The Daily Record*, 1996; *The Guardian*, 1997; *The Herald*, 1997).

This was all in stark contrast with the view of itself that the company sought to promote, and the irony was not lost on large numbers of front-line managers and employees (Hopfl, Smith and Spencer, 1992; *The Guardian*, 1997; Grugulis and Wilkinson, 2002). Not that they were completely dismissive of the culture management initiatives. Some aspects were applauded and appreciated, though people were making discriminating judgements, seeing through the spin and calling upon wider and deeper reference points. For example, an event that was initiated in 1985 and entitled 'A Day in the Life' was credited by staff as offering a potentially useful means of cultivating participative awareness and respect for other contributions (Robson, 1988). Essentially, with this activity, representatives from different functional areas devised and delivered presentations, explaining what they do and claiming space for their role.

The wider significance of this was picked up and developed by managers at an NHS staff development course hosted by the University of Glasgow in 1999. An acute sense of status differentials and frustration with elitism and hospital politics was translated into a campaign for fair treatment and mutual respect that had groups from porters and filing staff at medical records to managers, doctors and other professionals using a similar sort of approach to reflect on work roles and relationships. Back at British Airways, however, many employees were saddened that the scope for reflectively developing such helpful activities was overridden by more fundamental difficulties and tensions in employment relations.

CULTURE, STRUCTURE AND ARENAS OF STRUGGLE

Critical social science provides an important corrective to the culture management movement, bringing diversity sharply into focus and underlining the value of a relational approach. Clearly, culture is not a management resource. The cultural life of an organization is collectively produced and reproduced by a wide range of constituents and in ways that are beyond management control. Yet framing and positioning people within contrasting and overlapping subcultures and patterns of socialization does not by itself account for the dynamics of cultural formation, nor capture its significance for empowerment and workplace innovation.

As emphasized in Chapter 1, the processes that enable people to derive meanings, to form interpretations and exercise judgement, must be explicitly connected to structure, to the effects of markets, commerce and technology, for example. Culture and subjectivity cannot be separated out from the structural context in which meanings are produced and reproduced. The openness of subjectivity to local networks and subcultures, and to broader influences from upbringing, education, geography, gender, ethnicity, religion and so forth, should not deflect attention from the regularities of economy or the legal and institutional frameworks in which these processes are embedded (Beirne et al., 2004).

It is necessary to consider the relational interdependencies between culture and structure, and to track their mutual influence on the inequalities and struggles that characterize organizational life. This is the dynamic context in which innovation occurs, develops, falters or fails. It is simultaneously fostered and constrained within arenas of struggle in which culture and subjectivity give meaning to, and at the same time reflect, structural tendencies.

Two classic case studies exemplify this integrative treatment of empowerment and innovation. McCabe (2002) and Foster and Hoggett (1999) explain how dimensions of subjectivity connect with structural factors to influence innovation in particular arenas of struggle. Focusing on developments within an insurance company and at three branches of the British Benefits Agency, they demonstrate that correlations of culture and structure produce various coexisting and cross-cutting axes of struggle that reflect the past while reshaping it through innovative episodes, with results that are negotiated and often unanticipated rather than given or predefined.

McCabe contextualizes the subjectivities and struggles of middle to senior managers at AB Insurance during a period of departmental restructuring and computer-based job redesign. These developments were influenced by commercial concerns to improve quality and efficiency while reducing costs. Yet managerial and territorial subcultures were as important to the processes and outcomes of innovation as economics and technology.

The sectional interpretations, allegiances and promotional activities of three managers, of the Life Department, information technology and training, figure prominently in this analysis. Their respective expressions of contrasting and competing values, and attempts to secure personal status, identity and advantage, added impetus to internal politicking and manoeuvring as each tried to gain an edge and curry favour within the broader management community.

The Life Manager was steeped in the traditions of work-study that were ingrained within the company and perpetuated through subcultural ties of the sort that Jones (2000) identified at Hotpoint. However, at AB Insurance, representatives of this subculture had risen through the ranks to formal positions that gave work-study values and preoccupations higher status and apparent credibility, conferring prestige upon those who were actively cutting costs, tightening controls and securing greater efficiencies. This manager was exemplifying these attitudes and concerns in his approach to innovation, and through this to career building, pushing the technology programme towards work-tracking, task simplification and systems that would reduce the number of staff employed.

This reinforced political tensions and magnified some significant differences between AB subcultures. The IT Manager articulated concerns about a perceived challenge to the prerogatives, role and approach of the technology community, and was also moved to a personal defence of his identity and reputation for competence at senior levels as setbacks and technical difficulties were acknowledged and scrutinized. By contrast, the Training Manager adopted an offensive posture, attempting to bolster his status and identity by speaking to staff concerns about the employment effects of change, and highlighting the damaging impact of deskilling and disaffection on job performance.

As they engaged in the processes of navigating meanings and negotiating their positions, all three managers were constrained by broader managerial structures and subjectivities, however. Winning allies and mobilizing support within the management hierarchy was crucial to their respective struggles, and this obliged them to observe other norms and inter-subjective realities. The Training Manager acknowledged that seeming to criticize work-study would be extremely damaging, and that pointing fingers or blaming colleagues for problems would be counterproductive. The patterns of struggle were even affected by language, with influence slipping through the use of terminology or by articulating a case that was perceived to be crass or outside of the established traditions of management expression.

Many of the managers and supervisors at AB were described as 'old school', promoted through the ranks for their diligence and knowledge of insurance, and holding on to a view of the company as paternalistic, genteel, respectable and stable. There was a shared antipathy towards novelty and managerial radicalism that had a bearing upon the struggles, and indeed was variously endorsed by the three managers since they had multiple identities, again as indicated by Jones (2000), straddling the subcultures noted above and the wider managerial community of which they were a part. McCabe (2002, p. 529) acknowledges the analytical significance of this, quoting Young (1989) to reinforce the message that 'unity and division exist in tandem', reflecting relational interdependencies, influencing struggles and the way that people interpret and act upon their situations.

Unfortunately, there is little in this account to indicate how the struggles at AB affected staff, or for that matter the fortunes of the Life, IT and Training Managers. In fairness, McCabe's priority was to account for processes rather than outcomes, to demonstrate that innovation is constituted through struggles that reflect particular cultural and structural contexts. Foster and Hoggett (1999) have more to say about the working through of alternative possibilities, about the interrelated effects of local labour markets and gendered office cultures on teamworking and empowerment at the Benefits Agency.

This research explains why proposals emanating from the centre of the organization had very different local results. An empowerment programme that devolved staffing and budgetary responsibilities to middle and junior managers, encouraging them to provide an integrated 'one stop' service to clients via multidisciplinary teamworking, had a variable impact on struggles and patterns of organization and management. The authors tracked developments at three offices within the same district. The first was located in a deprived inner-city area, the second in a more desirable part of the city centre, while the third was situated in a conservative seaside town. Although there were similarities in terms of the initial scepticism and concerns expressed by staff at each office, there were also significant differences, notably in labour market conditions, the physical layout of buildings and local office cultures.

Collaborative teamworking was only really endorsed and developed at the out-of-city branch, where there was clear evidence that previous demarcation lines between tasks, relationships and working areas had been altered, and that groups of people were sharing knowledge, skills and the same office space to cover a wider range of issues affecting each claimant. The researchers attribute this to the interrelated effects of structure and culture on local struggles. They point specifically to working ties and managerial sensitivities that were influenced by steady staffing under a depressed local labour market, a predominantly female workforce drawn from the surrounding community and with commitments that made the Agency's flexible working arrangements attractive, and also a Cinderella identity founded on perceptions that staff at other branches treated them as the poor relations in this particular district.

Not that this was a settled situation, or that the struggles behind multidisciplinary teamworking had run their course. Tensions were discernible, when some of the younger women expressed subcultural concerns about a status-hierarchy based on age, for example. Nonetheless, when the research was conducted, the members of staff at this office generally acknowledged the benefits of an approach to innovation that their counterparts in the city dismissed as impracticably radical. Hostilities to multi-skilling and multidisciplinary working were pronounced (though not uniform) at the other sites, where the respective combinations of place, labour market and counter-cultures had a contrasting influence on struggles and outcomes. The city centre branch had developed 'co-located' teams, where clusters of specialists worked in greater proximity to each other. By contrast, the office in the deprived area was firmly attached to specialization, maintaining established boundaries with only very focused and informal teamworking among counter staff, who saw it as more of a support network for dealing with hostile claimants.

These studies conceptualize innovation as a variable quality of interdependent relations and cross-cutting struggles, embedding it within particular cultural and structural contexts. Clearly, managers and others are constantly orienting and reorienting themselves to unfolding processes, deriving meanings and interpreting events, with constrained options for acting, intervening and struggling. At one level, this underlines the problematics of empowerment and progressive intervention. Enthusiasts, and other actors, are caught up in dynamic arenas of struggle that are beyond personal influence and expressions of choice, commitment or inclination. Established structures, cultures and subjectivities inform and shape these struggles, yet are simultaneously re-shaped and reconstituted as they unfold. This helps to explain why practical episodes are rarely as radical as the prescriptive gurus suggest, although it also negates the continuity case rehearsed by critics who dismiss empowerment as a gloss on given inequalities of influence and ownership.

Again, the dynamic processes of organizational struggle and exchange variously reproduce and transform workplace relations and experiences in ways that resist prior design, that present unanticipated challenges and deliver unintended consequences. They simultaneously generate constraints on progressive intervention and opportunities for creative engagement, stimulating awareness and opening up conditions for reflective practice. As McCabe notes at the end of his analysis (2000, p. 533), the context of innovation provides an outlet for progressive thinking as well as the mobilization of conservative concerns, providing a reason and creating scope for those who are moved to intervene by the broader principles of empowerment and workplace reform.

PART II

Enabling, enacting and regulating

7.   Sustaining a voluntary commitment

The research reported in previous chapters demonstrates that empowerment is a highly charged, often fraught and inherently problematical process. Taking a panoramic view of the evidence, it is difficult to avoid the conclusion that progress towards any sort of authentic empowerment has been hesitant and subject to frequent back-sliding and deterioration. We are not, as citizens and members of organizations, cumulatively better off as a result of either the recurring interest in direct participation or the broad range of supposedly empowering initiatives that have been introduced.

Many companies that claim to empower employees in practice do nothing of the sort. There is evidence of window dressing and appearance management, with lots of schemes in various contexts favouring rhetoric over substance. They offer an impression that progressive management is at work, yet fail seriously to challenge, or regularly slip back to, more conventional values and command structures. Hopes have often been raised and then dashed, while legitimate concerns have been dismissed out of hand. From their own experiences, a large number of managers and employees consider empowerment schemes to be hollow or unpalatable, variously expressing scepticism, cynicism, frustration and distrust. As previously discussed, the legacy of the past remains potent, generating significant obstacles and constraints. To paraphrase an oft-quoted remark by Tom Burns from the 1970s, the workplace continues to be one of the most authoritarian environments in democratic society.

Yet there is a danger of slipping from this sort of sober assessment to debilitating pessimism, and even negativity. The accumulated evidence of restricted or curtailed participation needs to be set against some recognized benefits, even if their impact to date has been sectional or fleeting. The sharp-end evaluations that were reviewed through earlier chapters point to valued aspects and positive features, although judgements tend to be cautious, acknowledging that favourable outcomes are unevenly distributed, and by no means straightforward or secure.

There was also evidence of creative thinking, of innovative ideas and techniques, many of them devised by principled managers and workers who are collectively pushing the boundaries of possibility for meaningful change. There were solid proposals for structuring work in new and liberating ways. There was evidence of fresh thinking about viable ways of challenging sectionalism and elitism, including the 'Day in the Life' scenario at British Airways, which lends itself to a less dogmatic application than culture management, as argued in the last chapter. These developments highlight opportunities as well as constraints, useful lines of influence as well as dilemmas. They show that empowerment is potentially progressive, a worthwhile if struggle-suffused pursuit. They also confirm that actors, at whatever level, are never so rigidly constrained or hemmed in that progressive interventions are impossible.

That said, conflict is inherently part of the politics of progressive management, and can be expected to find an outlet in everyday encounters. Given the range of experiences and reactions discernible to date, people remain to be convinced, and are more likely to question or challenge innovations than commit themselves wholeheartedly on the assumption that subsequent initiatives will mark an improvement in their situation. Even the best of intentions will encounter opposition, although there is no reason to regard it as absolute or decisive. There is an abundance of evidence to demonstrate the folly of bracketing workplace opinion rigidly, or assigning people to hard and fast categories of outlook and behaviour (McCabe, 2000; Vidal, 2007; Beirne, 2011).

This lesson became obvious with reactions to Fordism, although the workers who confront such an approach are still considered to exhibit an instrumental orientation to work. There is a continuing belief that manual workers are preoccupied with making money for a quality of life that is judged by factors beyond the workplace itself. In fact, this is frequently cited as a reason for not empowering staff, that the beneficiaries will not appreciate the efforts taken on their behalf, or will squander the opportunities. This line is rehearsed regularly in MBA classes and during research interviews (Hagen et al., 2003), usually with the pronouncements of insensitive managers who assert that their own staff do not want it, or will not respond to it, because they take a calculating attitude to their work.

While the expression 'we're only in it for the money' can regularly be heard from workers, there is evidence that it does not represent a full or decisive view, or provide a reliable guide to behaviour. It is, in some cases, a defence mechanism, an internalized way of dealing with regimes that treat them as little more than 'pairs of hands' with no worthwhile brains to support a creative contribution. Consequently, people can warm to initiatives when they feel it safe to take them seriously. Just as Goldthorpe and Lockwood's (1968) Vauxhall workers dramatically exploded the myths about their apathy and instrumentalism by taking strike action, so grassroots caution about work reform has occasionally given way to significant contributions by thoughtful and energetic people who can believe that there are genuine opportunities to make a difference (Blackburn, 1967; Beirne et al., 1998a).

The struggles involved in developing this positive view of empowerment can be intense, however, generating frustration and calling for resilience and coping activities as much as an enlightened sense of engagement. Even the best of intentions can be tested by difficulties felt in dealing with contrasting views and challenging activities on a daily basis. The hassle factor can take a serious toll on committed actors and managers, as well as employees, wearing them down and threatening their contribution.

Certainly, there have been casualties among forward thinking managers. Talent has been lost to organizations that begin to experiment with empowerment, and to the broader movement for emancipatory management. Alan Pearson provides a notable example. He was the pioneering influence behind a broad range of team-based nursing initiatives within the NHS, including primary nursing (Beirne, 1999; Pearson, 1988). Sectional disputes and traditional decision-making prerogatives produced a level of disappointment and frustration that made it easier for him to take his insights and abilities to Australia (Channel 4, 1993; Beirne, 2011).

There are also powerful examples of local managers who feel intimidated or stifled to the extent that they restrict their input, abandon enabling activities and even make career choices that allow them to escape from uncomfortable pressures. A recent case comes to mind, where a junior manager at a utility company was called to account by his immediate superiors after encouraging meter-reading crews to manage their own time and client contacts, without the need to 'sign in' or observe conventional and time-consuming controls. He reported that two other managers, including 'a twenty-two stone bully', told him 'not to be so bloody stupid' and to 'stop rocking the boat'. At this point, the spark went out of him. His response was to retreat, to deal with the situation in a very personal way, holding on to the belief that he would still be working with the company 'when these dinosaurs are long gone'. In the meantime, he would simply tread water, avoiding the pain and discomfort of 'sticking his neck out'.

Other managers, notably young graduates, use their qualifications to find an escape from such unpalatable experiences, even trying to put some distance between their own situation and the dilemmas involved in sustaining a progressive approach. A well-qualified graduate from the University of Glasgow recently resigned from a management position that was sought, on principle, with a major co-operative. After some two years of setbacks and difficulties in trying to articulate an empowering practice against an entrenched bureaucracy and traditional though inhibiting arrangements, she followed a very different route, resigning to promote brands of alcohol around the pubs and clubs of Central Scotland. The hassle attached to the management position was just too much for her to take, despite a strong commitment to grassroots empowerment and the expressed principles of the organization.

These unhappy accounts of life at the sharp end of potentially progressive management are just as compelling as employee reports about false starts, constraints and disappointments. So what can be done to support those with a positive outlook, to develop their capacity for principled action and their resilience under fire?

CRITICAL COMMENTARIES AND PROGRESSIVE IMAGES OF MANAGEMENT

Critical thinkers have produced a rich library of insights and empirical evidence that has applied relevance as a means of cultivating analytical and interpretive capabilities. As noted at the outset, and laboured through previous chapters, critical research can sharpen local knowledge and personal experience by adding measured and discriminating insights into the problematics of empowerment. It provides enthusiasts with the chance to cultivate a broad appreciation of the dynamic issues tied into empowerment and direct participation, magnifying difficulties and constraints and highlighting the tensions and imbalances that affect practical initiatives.

Post-mortem studies and accounts of schemes that have faltered or backfired are especially useful, marshalling evidence that can help practitioners to anticipate contradictory tendencies, acknowledge contrasting interests, appreciate genuine concerns and attend to the sort of inconsistencies that were belatedly recognized at Volvo and elsewhere (Berggren, 1995; Beirne, 1999; Foster and Hoggett, 1999). Since management is a subject that is frequently reduced to technology and technique by n-step prescriptions (Tracy, 1990) that attempt to remove values and reflective intelligence from the agenda (Collins, 2000), critical research provides a sensitizing rather than a numbing experience, raising personal awareness about the tensions and ambiguities involved, while building confidence and opening the sense of 'space for difference' among those who acknowledge progressive ideals. Yet management is also about activism and achievement. Liberated thinking and considered reflection are insufficient in themselves to secure collectively valued outcomes or deliver what a particular population might consider to be meaningful empowerment.

As argued in the Foreword and elsewhere (Beirne, 2008), critical commentators have been less than effective in speaking to the challenges that confront practitioners who identify with progressive ideals. Some are content to explain what they are against rather than what they favour, while others map out the characteristics of a critical approach (Alvesson and Willmott, 1992) or wrestle with the difficulties of cultivating an appreciation for it through management learning and cognitive development (Mingers, 2000; Currie and Knights, 2003; Hagen et al., 2003). Those with the most developed sense of practical activism have been working in specialist areas such as computing innovation, following the top-down approach of the driven theorist-practitioners identified in Chapter 3. For all the benefits that can be gleaned from this range of activity, there is a general need to attend directly to the practicalities of progressive management, to fill out the details of what it means to be critical and reflective, and to follow the logic of empowerment from the bottom up, giving everyday meaning to principled engagement.

This is where the traditions and conventions of collective art-making and community theatre may prove to be helpful. Historically, the visual and performing arts have made a significant contribution to critical management studies. There is a long and distinguished tradition of artists portraying the frustrations and harsh realities of working life and prompting critical scrutiny of difficult or oppressive management regimes. Diego Rivera's murals depicting work under Fordism and the renowned Frank McGuinness play, *The Factory Girls*, provide notable examples. There are also important parallels in the way that artists have challenged prescriptive management thinking and the influence of consultancy advice within their own organizations.

Artists and arts workers are now active members of the broad-ranging community that passionately objects to the influence of over-rationalized conceptions of management (Protherough and Pick, 2002). Many of their organizations have passively imported 'expert solutions' from the corporate sector, unreflectively endorsing top-down controls and narrow job boundaries with little sense of counterproductive consequences (Beirne and Knight, 2002a). The strings attached to arts funding have put a premium on demonstrably 'sound' management and the effective use of resources. Consultants have been hired and familiar prescriptions traded and visibly applied, delivering work specialization, promoting hierarchical control and putting a tight rein on resources, including staff. While satisfying the particular interests of funding agencies and showing a readiness 'to take management seriously', these developments have also had a damaging effect (Beirne and Knight, 2002a). Arguably the most significant, given prevailing levels of remuneration, is that the voluntary commitment that so many arts workers bring to their employment has been stifled, leaving them less inclined to be responsive to emerging needs or to work flexibly for positive results through their love of the art.

With the deliver-and-depart format of limited-budget management consulting, artistic directors and arts managers have been left to deal with the fallout from these episodes, including staff turnover, and are now among the most strident critics of rationalism (Beirne and Knight, 2002a; Protherough and Pick, 2002; Beirne, 2013). Indeed, their sense of annoyance has been heightened by the predatory nature of consultants who peddle universal prescriptions with little sensitivity to the distinctiveness of arts organizations while at the same time appropriating art, reducing classical drama and theatre conventions to quirky motivational techniques and teambuilding exercises, for example (Moshavi, 2001; Clark and Mangham, 2004).

Rejecting such rationalistic impulses, critical commentators in the arts have argued for a more liberating conception of the relationship between art and management. Community theatre practitioners are among the most vocal and persuasive, drawing a distinction between imported techniques and the management practices that are applied to produce art in their own area. Their contention is that arts organizations should draw managerial value more directly from their own traditions and creative practices. However, this case has wider applicability. Established community arts practices have significant potential, not only as a means of counteracting unreflective managerialism, but also as a stimulus to creative thinking about the practical activism of empowering management.

There is a fundamental correspondence between critical reactions to rationalism in community arts and the transformative movements that have their roots in engineering and technological innovation (Bjerknes et al., 1987; Greenbaum and Kyng, 1991) and in the critiques of management orthodoxy in the social sciences (including Alvesson and Willmott, 1992). They strike at rationalism from a common standpoint, rehearsing consistent themes and with dovetailing ideals that privilege active participation, reflective practice and negotiated learning (Beirne and Knight, 2002b). They stand for self-advocacy, ownership and equal access, favouring conditions that will enable people to develop their talent and realize their full potential. They are against authoritarianism, oppressiveness and hierarchical control, challenging the entrenched ideology that people are resources or commodities that function effectively when their opportunities for exercising discretion are restricted. Bringing their critical selves to the analysis of management, these commentators share a distaste for formats that privilege elite interests, highlighting problems of underrepresentation and taking silence in decision-making seriously as a cost, as a source of psychological, social, cultural and economic disadvantage.

Hence, community theatre, and more generally community arts, projects have largely developed in opposition to agency-led artistic programmes, certainly in Scotland where the latter have been criticized as patronizing forms of artistic social work (see Herbert, 2004). The issue here centres on respect for the participants as art-makers rather than for art as a civilizing influence on 'subjects' that can be developed or improved by exposure to it. From this angle, the artistic process is bound up with the challenge of enabling ordinary people to take control of their lives and to play a part in shaping their world, not only in terms of culture, but socially and economically.

During the 1960s and '70s in Scotland, community arts were radicalized as forms of political articulation, education and debate. 'Cultural democratization' became a rallying cry, not just for access to the arts but for socio-political activism and economic regeneration. The impetus came from the housing schemes of Edinburgh, Glasgow and Dundee, where locally produced art was a catalyst for community development. It combined cultural expression with self-determination, mobilizing the working class and other disadvantaged groups to present arguments for improving their situations or surroundings through art that was capable of 'touching' politicians and decision-makers (Crummy, 1992; Herbert, 2004). Here is a process of engagement that brings people out of themselves, building confidence, releasing talent and creative energy while fostering collaboration and respect for 'otherness'.

In terms of principles and driving logic, this movement is entirely consistent with critical management studies. What it adds, however, is a more developed sense of alternative practice. Community artists are reaching beyond the critique of rationalism to reflect upon their own role as managers, capturing, formalizing and generalizing information about the effective running of collective arts projects. Their introspection and efforts to draw management insights from their own traditions of reflective practice provide a means of connecting critical thinking with everyday management activities, and of anticipating a qualitatively different approach that is empowering, accountable and principled.

CONNECTING ART WITH MANAGEMENT

Community artists aim to liberate artistic talent in local settings, to find creative ways of enabling people to make their own art. As previously indicated, their purpose is not to cultivate an appreciation for art that already exists, or to adopt a missionary role in delivering art to neighbourhoods that lack culture. Nor do they attempt to fit people into approved systems that ostensibly generate quality-assured art for local consumption. The point is that participants themselves become artists, that members of the public figure in the creative process of, say, producing involving drama or engaging in theatre that speaks to social concerns or connects with local issues. Creativity in this area is not confined to the 'inner world' of actors and artistic directors. It is not dependent upon purveyors of independent expertise. Success requires the effective engagement of ordinary people, which means that the process must have relevance and authenticity. It needs to be grounded in the views, emotions and collective experience of the participants. The process is therefore relational, and the challenge of organizing it ensures that management activities form an essential part of collective art-making.

Effective community artists are also de facto managers, co-ordinating and enabling participants to articulate their own values and express their views in a telling and effective manner. However, in this realm of the arts very little can be achieved with a 'manager knows best' mentality. Successful outcomes depend upon the artist's ability to move and motivate participants, to harness their talent and energy and to promote shared learning and collective working. Active participation, critical reflection and negotiated learning are crucial managerial capabilities.

So what does this mean in practice? These artists often work with groups of people that are disadvantaged, vulnerable or troubled in some way. Progress is conditional upon nurturing and supporting their input, drawing them out of themselves, appreciating worries and concerns, and establishing the social ties that can support collaboration. By contrast with managerial preoccupations in work situations where the role of employees is often taken for granted, the participants in these empowerment schemes are the key reference points, the central focus of attention. Management only has meaning as a contextualized process of local learning and negotiated exchange as the arts practitioner endeavours to reach the participants, to appreciate their knowledge and experience, and respect their often unarticulated ability to perform in powerful or beautiful drama. This means finding the words, gestures and patterns of interaction that make their own contributions sincere and convincing. It means devising and developing collaborative arrangements as the work unfolds, continuously negotiating, reviewing and revisiting the terms of engagement with and between the participants. Management is therefore reconstituted as a sensitive, situated and relational activity that has nothing whatever to do with the transmission of abstract or universal expertise.

When interviewed about their practice, community artists often refer to the 'wealth' concept of negotiated learning as an underlying principle (Beirne and Knight, 2002a, 2004). This, again, puts the participants centre stage, acknowledging that people are generally capable, sensible and insightful, and therefore have a right to make decisions for themselves. The wealth conceptualization puts the onus on the artist-as-manager to help participants collectively discover their best route to expression, and to provide them with 'an uncensored space' for artistic development. As one theatre practitioner recently explained:

Each time we meet, we discuss our thinking and our reflections about the work ... We are constantly trying to find the best way to make the story work. We endeavour to make sure that everyone's contribution is valued and heard as clearly as everyone else's. (Cited in Beirne and Knight, 2004, p. 38)

This model of engagement aims to uphold the dignity of the participants by creating safe structures and viable conditions for fruitful collaboration. These are purposefully created through active reflection and from a grounded understanding of the real-life concerns of the contributors and the dynamics of the situation. To quote one of the aphorisms of community theatre, 'the context is half the work'.

A recently published example should help to put this approach in perspective, to indicate the repertoire of ideas and possibilities that it encapsulates and to establish its practicality beyond the many vague and unhelpful references to coaching and facilitating that characterize the empowerment literature (Beirne and Knight, 2004). Over a 15-month period, the Tuesday Afternoon Women's Theatre Group met in Edinburgh to devise and deliver a performance that celebrated their collective resilience and ability to struggle through life. The participants were all survivors of incest and sexual abuse, and were dealing with a very precarious, fragile and vulnerable existence. Their lives were shaped by risk and by the irregularities of being homeless, needing to hide and to avoid predictable patterns of living. Yet they had developed an interest in drama, having been encouraged to take part in a community arts programme, and were pushing for a project that would keep them involved. Their situations made it difficult to guarantee any sort of full and continuous collaboration, and there was always a danger of people falling out of the process for lengthy periods of time as other events took over their lives. Nonetheless, there was serious interest and a strong feeling that the experience could be helpful, so a team of community theatre practitioners developed a positive response.

As managers, their first task was to support the participants, to sustain their interest while keeping them secure and focused on activities that could deliver their ambition, to perform their own work in front of a live audience. This was a delicate challenge, encouraging the women to share their knowledge, to release insights and express views that had been forged through very painful experiences. Empowerment was conditional upon managerial sensitivity and reflective engagement. It required the artists-as-managers to read, interpret and respond to situations as events unfolded, and to reflect almost continuously upon the impact that their own activities had on others.

The initial priority was to find practical ways of establishing a safe working environment. Considerable effort was invested in building trust, and convincing the participants that they were not regarded as 'victims' by the artists or theatre crew. They were young women interested in making theatre, a message that was heavily reinforced with clear statements, regularly voiced, and with careful briefings for technical staff as they joined the production *en route* to performance. Other management tools were devised to establish an explicit consensus on the aims of the project and to cement working ties and relationships.

Early attention was given to a learning contract, and to openly negotiating its contents. Collective agreements and formal understandings of this nature figure prominently in community arts projects, synthesizing principles with ground rules and written standards of acceptable behaviour that increase the likelihood of productive collaboration. In this case, it was a flip-chart list of points summarizing why they were coming together, where they wanted to go, what they wanted to achieve, and how they would go about it. Given the sensitivities here, the emphasis was firmly on nurturing, sharing and supporting aspects, specifying landmarks and achievements that were to be celebrated along the way, and agreeing what people should do when they needed time out or a release from project work, for example. The list also included statements to reassure individuals that there was space for their input: 'everybody's contribution is valued'; 'everybody's ideas will be heard'.

Participants who had missed sessions or experienced difficulties with the process were brought back into the project by means of a drama exercise that gave them 'valuable gifts for reflection' from every other participant. These were offered from an imaginary basket of options, and would either emphasize the qualities they brought to the group or reveal hints and tips that would enable them to catch up with the others. Conversation would follow, with the core group talking through the latest deliberations and, significantly, explaining how the collective had held on to the individual's contribution since the last time they were together.

This case offers powerful and very practical examples of how mutual learning about people and situations can be combined with reflective thinking and a capacity for innovation to produce an enabling approach to management and organization. These managers are breathing life into the alternative agenda, finding creative ways of engaging with people so that empowerment has meaning, so that participants can believe that their values and interests are shaping events, without the stifling interference of elitist, hierarchical or other debilitating influences.

The achievements of the women reached far beyond the hopes and expectations of anyone involved, including the survivors themselves. Their own accounts are quite candid in acknowledging the achievements of the artists-as-managers in nurturing their interests and enabling them to express hidden talents with positive results (Beirne and Knight, 2004). Keeping in touch with the situation proved crucial, investing the time and energy to develop an informed understanding and establish mutual respect, rather than assuming the mantle of aloof experts. This allowed the managers to recognize and accentuate key moments in the process and to add momentum.

About five months into the project, one young woman, who was having a particularly tough time coping with the attention of pursuers and official agencies, including the police, told the group how she had uncovered information about street children in Brazil. She explained that she would love to be able to teach them to survive as she had. The compassion she displayed during her own time of distress was transformational for the group. Recognizing a turning point, the managers went into overdrive, searching for relevant images and stories, improvising ideas, and prompting the group to devise scenarios and develop characters. A consensus had emerged about the storyline. Survival was now regarded as something to be celebrated.

Other theatre professionals were increasingly called into the process, although their introduction was carefully managed so that they could blend in without disrupting the flow. Most were women, including a costume designer, stage manager and scenic artist. Alex, the lighting man, was the most obvious exception, and he came to be trusted as 'a woman with a beard'. As the various parts of the project came together, the participants finally realized their ambition, performing their work for an audience drawn from their own communities, and including other survivors groups. By all accounts, it was a moving and emotional occasion, attracting fulsome praise and admiration for the strength, resilience and creative achievements of the group (Beirne and Knight, 2004).

Again, the survivor's story offers a valuable insight into the practicalities and advantages of critical reflection and progressive management. It accentuates the nurturing and developmental role of management, although community theatre also casts light on less palatable, though equally important, aspects of alternative practice. There are other dilemmas and sources of unease in empowerment, such as whether and to what extent forceful and restricting activity is permissible.

This is not to be confused with a defence of managerial prerogatives, an endorsement of positional authority or a justification for commanding and controlling manoeuvres. It is a matter of counteracting factors that threaten, destabilize or otherwise undermine empowerment schemes, of containing divisive and disruptive influences, and of intervening to sustain open and effective collaboration. Of course, this raises very thorny questions about compromise, slippage and even contradiction that utopian discussions avoid (for example, Hirschheim and Klein, 1994) yet practitioners confront on a regular basis. Threats to the integrity of empowerment arise not just from hierarchy, rationalism or traditional management preoccupations. They filter through from other sources of elitism and narrowly constituted sectionalism that challenge progressive managers, creating dilemmas of conscience and choice as they try to balance directly supportive activities with more forceful and restricting interventions.

In community arts, the problems posed by disruptive influences can be very obvious, especially in youth theatre and with drama projects for young offenders where the challenges and the possibilities for sustaining principled engagement have been tested for some time (Giesekam and Knight, 2000). Horseplay and chauvinistic posturing regularly command attention here, along with more disturbing examples of intimidating, distancing and vulgar behaviour. Clashing egos and sensitivities can inhibit collaboration, producing tensions and flashpoints that require careful handling. Contrasting interpretations about what it means to participate in drama, and what sort of engagement enhances or detracts from personal standing and credibility, can generate conflict among participants, or create an atmosphere in which some are hesitant, uneasy or fearful of ridicule and abuse.

By contrast with the survivor's case, collaborative working under these conditions requires a level of self-restraint and respect for others that does not always come easily to those involved. It also presents the arts practitioner with an immensely difficult situation to manage, in which to build supportive group ties, cultivate talent and secure positive outcomes from genuine collaboration. In this context, the responsibilities attached to empowerment, as well as the rights and opportunities, come sharply into focus. Success can depend upon the artist-as-manager encouraging people to accept in others certain qualities or viewpoints that are not initially valued or even tolerated. It can be a matter of holding up a mirror to the outlook, orientation and even prejudice that participants bring to the activity, protecting some while connecting them to others.

While writers who express a Foucauldian allegiance may interpret this as providing approval for the reconstitution of subjects, for the shaping of identity so that people become more passive, compliant and willing (see Beirne et al., 2004, for a discussion of this tendency), it is a basic and practical matter of struggling to engender dialogue and active collaboration. Again, the logic is to create safe structures, to establish uncensored space for negotiated learning and development, and to do so by tackling sources of oppression and suppression that lie beyond management orthodoxy. There are dilemmas and dangers in this, as indicated above. However, the issues are real and pressing for those at the sharp end of principled management, where mutual respect and open collaboration are problematic objectives rather than given qualities. In any case, as previous chapters have argued, there is no reason to believe that social actors are so easily manipulated or purged of their priorities, values and reflective capabilities.

Health and safety provides an obvious management issue where intervention on behalf of employees or project participants, that forcibly disrupts autonomous working in the interests of collective welfare, is legitimate. Whatever the level of sophistication or maturity achieved with empowerment, positive action to evacuate a burning building or disable dangerous equipment is as much of a priority for principled management as grassroots decision-making. Under these circumstances, forceful intervention can be liberating rather than threatening, assuming, of course, that it is based on accurate information about the physical dangers and viable escape routes.

Since it encapsulates a basic principle of engagement, this logic of intervention or interruption applies as much to internally as to externally generated threats, and to emotional as well as physical safety. The corollary is that management as principled activism involves manoeuvring and politicking, partly to inspire and enthuse, though also to structure the processes of exchange and engagement by acting against impediments, including those that emanate from the participant community itself.

During a recent young offenders' project in Edinburgh, community artists used a variation of the learning contract mentioned earlier to challenge disruptive behaviour that was apparent from the outset, and to prevent it from getting out of hand. The flip-chart agreement eventually became a typed document that was copied and distributed to all participants, reinforcing the message that 'violent behaviour will not be tolerated' and that there would be 'no fisticuffs or slagging off in workshops'.

This may be an extreme situation in management terms, yet it highlights the importance of imaginative responsibility, of developing inventive ways of shaping reciprocal exchanges to knit people together. This means acknowledging differences and tensions, and even asymmetrical qualities and forms of expression. Moreover, it means tackling them so that people are encouraged to expand their outlook, to relate personal development to collective engagement, and collaborate within a free and open discourse. Mobilizing for safe structures, or at least acting to reduce feelings of vulnerability, will, in some situations, involve painful management interventions to marginalize or outmanoeuvre interests that are incommensurable yet find expression in ways that threaten the collective endeavour. Where efforts to apply non-elitist values and establish terms of fair engagement are seriously undermined, say by violent or oppressive sectionalism, or by the restoration of Fordist controlling tendencies, the principles of managing for empowerment become entangled with the practicalities of defending the group.

Clearly, for community artists, empowerment is not a licence for participants to create chaos, so balancing liberating activities with restricting, curtailing and even removing interventions is an essential element of reflective and creative practice. With the young offenders initiative, there was a mixture of subtle and very forceful manoeuvres to remove persistent images of guns and weaponry from the drama, and to disempower some individuals who intimidated others and exploited the process for personal aggrandizement. Critical reflection called for unpalatable, difficult and often charged forms of practice that were reconciled with, or at least evaluated against, broader principles and the negotiated priorities of the wider community. Through this lens, empowerment is purged of its mythical status as a straightforward practice and a condition in which everyone gains. Woolly references to coaching, facilitating and even democratic engagement become irrelevant, floating free from any practical sense of the dilemmas that confront principled managers, and from any meaningful understanding of empowerment as a potentially contradictory and struggle-suffused approach to collaborative working.

NO METHOD, NO GURU, NO ILLUSIONS

Through their approach to collective art-making, community artists offer a glimpse of the liberating and transformative potential of reflective management. What is attractive, and what they envisage, is an intimate connection between accomplished art and responsive, context-sensitive management. There are no recipes here, or prescriptions that free the artists-as-managers from self-conscious reflection about the values they bring to situations and the qualities they release in others. It is this situated blending of principle and practice, this balancing of learning, thinking and creative acting that has wider applicability as a means of enlarging our sense of what is possible in managing to manage.

For those committed to empowerment and innovation, there is inspiration here to bring the alternative agenda to life, to lift the critiques of rationalism and dominating elites away from the bookshelves and out of the academic networks, and into the everyday experience of practising managers and enthusiasts for change. Successful community artists are able to move well beyond the classroom endorsement that 'decency matters', some of them finding very practical expressions of personal and collective empowerment. To borrow some terminology from Nord and Jermier (1992), these artists are finding ways to increase the congruence between humanistic values and everyday job performance. In some respects, the issue is forced for them as projects would fail and participants move rapidly on if declared principles were not apparent in the work. Yet the means of aligning beliefs with situated learning and creative forms of engagement is instructive.

Thinking back to the local experiences and predicaments identified at the beginning of this chapter, many potential and actual managers are actively seeking the sort of congruence that these artists achieve. For this constituency of critical thinkers, reflective art-making holds the promise of viable insights, resources and practical pointers to innovative behaviour that may help them to 'keep the faith', and perhaps recognize more of themselves in their everyday managerial work. It offers a cautiously optimistic agenda that can help managers to challenge established arrangements and elite interests, and bring progressive ideas to life in their own situations. There is a practical demonstration here of the scope for action in difficult circumstances, of the possibilities for creative engagement and mutual learning, despite pressing constraints and opposing or difficult behaviour by others.

Not that this is a model for management training. Community theatre practitioners are relying on improvisation and patterns of creative engagement that have been learned in practice and by networking with colleagues and, crucially, participants under particular project conditions. They draw not on formulas and prescriptions but on repertoires of established knowledge and emerging insights that they apply, appraise and develop in the context of unique situations. This is what gives their work authenticity and wider significance. By consciously and regularly relating their activities to the situated experiences of the people involved, these artist-managers demonstrate both the importance of reflective, interpretive and creative abilities, and the scope for others to develop and apply them. In this respect, their contribution expands the meaning that can be attached to 'reflection-in-action'.

In a frequently cited account of personal and professional sense-making, Schon (1983) uses this term to demonstrate that managers are self-aware people who actively think about their situations and experiences. Watson (1994) expands on this with an image of managers having debates within themselves as they make sense of what is happening around them and endeavour to exert some control over events. From here, reflective practice is a matter of sectional influence and advantage, of coping and thriving under prevailing conditions rather than developing a critique or principled activism that might challenge the status quo. With community theatre, reflection is more obviously connected to principles and collective engagement, and to the critical evaluation of how unfolding events stack up against them.

When reviewing their approach, theatre practitioners have talked about layers of learning and engagement that straddle the emotional, intellectual, creative and critical dimensions of their work (Beirne and Knight, 2004). At one level, they aim to be innovative, to become purposeful creators rather than users of managerial knowledge, exploring, improvising and trying things out. Experiential knowledge and networked information is applied as they structure encounters intuitively with ideas and behaviour that realized performances elsewhere and in the past. At the same time, they are trying to be systematic about their analysis, to stand back and consider reactions and developments, evaluating how principles and practice are coming together and using creative intelligence to address contradictions or emerging difficulties.

The advantage, when it all comes together, is that management is enacted in a way that contributes to empowerment and to valuable outcomes while maintaining a critical, and even attractively subversive, sense of identity. At a time when being critical is fashionable in management studies (Beirne, 2008), and when few writers and researchers adopt non-critical positions, these artists offer a grounded and very practical view of what it means to be critical. They are active, both in deconstructing conventional concepts and categories, and in exploring alternative possibilities. They find space to reject narrow views and to pose other options, thereby engendering a sense of activism and awareness that is missing from a great deal of critical commentary.

The artist-managers discussed in this chapter are not unusual in working with conscious, responsive, purposeful and thinking human beings, although the women survivors and young offenders possibly provide a more compelling demonstration of human sensitivities than most employees at work. Nonetheless, managers in other contexts confront similar daily challenges in trying to operationalize their principles, give meaning to empowerment and enable the people around them to develop their potential. The insights afforded by community theatre provide these principled actors with positive images, constructive reference points and a realistic sense of difficulties and dilemmas. During the darker moments, when frustration grows and the pressures mount, the image of these managers and their struggles to maintain a consistent approach may help others to feel that they have room for manoeuvre and scope to express progressive values through management activity.

8. Public policy and regulatory initiatives

Although there are genuine opportunities to nurture progressive thinking, support creative engagement and promote meaningful empowerment, committed practitioners face an uphill struggle to secure lasting change, for many of the reasons already indicated. Preoccupations with hierarchy, authority and decision-making prerogatives continue to exert a potent influence in management circles. Many employers, especially in Britain, remain tied to low-cost, limited-innovation strategies that privilege outsourcing, regimentation and high-intensity working, aided and abetted, of course, by influential consultants who present a view of 'modernization' that is at odds with progressive images of empowerment.

The argument that employees are unhappy with responsibility, prefer routine jobs and take an instrumental approach to work is still rehearsed with remarkable regularity, asserted almost by reflex as a stock response to pressures for innovation. Moreover, in cases where the logic and momentum for change become irresistible, the suspicion and covert manoeuvring of managerial opponents frequently acts as a drag chain, hampering progress and promoting a snap-back to more conventional arrangements as conditions alter. As much of the evidence reported in this book confirms, workplace reform often amounts to a short-term, unsustained exercise that disappoints rather than inspires participants, reinforcing instead of transforming established attitudes, and adding bitter experiences that complicate the empowerment project.

Clearly, against this background and in light of these priorities, leaving progressive innovation to the voluntary commitment of principled actors may be insufficient to deliver lasting or generalized gains. Not that this renders their engagement pointless or futile, of course. The previous chapter clearly established the value of a personal commitment. The point here is to assess the strength of available institutional support structures, to discover whether public policies, typically in the form of legislative or negotiated programmes, provide the necessary prerequisites for sustainable innovation. Contesting, negotiating and struggling at local level become that much easier for innovators if the broader framework in which they operate is conducive, if public policy acts as a catalyst for meaningful empowerment and provides a viable resource base to 'lift' practitioners, build their resilience, encourage tenacity and offer them better opportunities to 'make a difference'.

Fortunately, in Europe, workplace participation has figured on the political agenda for a large number of years, certainly since the 1970s, and at worst as a background feature of employment policies and employee relations, as previous chapters have indicated. Some politicians and policy-makers have openly argued for state- and supra-state-sponsored programmes that are capable of promoting progressive innovation, and have kept their ideas alive in policy discussions even when other issues and ideologies have been in the ascendancy, when Conservative governments in 1980s Britain expressly rejected such an approach, for example.

Government sponsorship has been identified as a crucial conditioning influence by officials and lobbyists associated with various political, industrial, trade union and research institutions, especially in the Nordic countries and continental Europe, as subsequent sections will reveal. Some commentators argue more specifically for legislative backing, presenting this as an essential ingredient if local initiatives are to strike roots and flourish (for example, Bluestone, 1995, for the United States and Strauss, 1998, more generally). Guest expresses this position succinctly: 'In the absence of any legislative framework, we can hope but we cannot be optimistic that employers will pursue enlightened practices' (Guest, 1997, p. 351).

For justification, these commentators point to the operating arrangements of firms under different legal and institutional structures, noting how some readily dismantle or bypass participation schemes when requirements are eased or where they seem to be more relaxed, in managing labour in Spain, Britain or China as opposed to Germany and Sweden, for instance. From here, legislation is necessary to protect and encourage the advocates and practitioners of workplace reform, to create an environment in which they can maintain a strong voice, avail themselves of opportunities to innovate, and exert a progressive influence on the policies and regular activities of their organizations. So what have legal and political programmes delivered? How does public policy support empowerment and innovation? Have national and supranational initiatives been effective in speaking to the ambitions of progressive thinkers, or is decisive action required to 'move' policy-makers and create an enabling framework?

NATIONAL INITIATIVES

The economic preoccupations of policy-makers have added impetus to empowerment and workplace innovation, with a number of countries encouraging forms of participation and reorganization by law or exhortation, specifically as a means of boosting international competitiveness. In the 1970s, Western governments, as economic managers, were exercised by the damaging effects of employee disaffection under buoyant labour markets and were variously inclined to act on the view that absenteeism, labour turnover and damaging industrial relations were attributable to Taylorist job designs. Swedish, Norwegian and German administrations were among the most confident and purposeful, funding and co-ordinating programmes that promised to tackle these problems at their source by reorganizing work, improving working conditions, enlarging the content of jobs and adding opportunities for participative decision-making (Ennals and Gustavsen, 1999; Alasoini, 2003).

From the 1990s, trade liberalization, globalization and recession have introduced additional pressures, subjecting governments to new constraints and structural challenges that have stimulated concerns for creativity, innovation and enterprise as the most lucrative values that can be generated in Western economies. Knowledge-intensive growth is now a privileged political objective, the acknowledged key to economic regeneration and future prosperity in a wider world of low-cost, high-volume manufacturers and service providers. Counteracting the effects of traditional management thinking, 'quick-fix' cost-saving and cheap, high-intensity working, has been more of a political priority (Department of Trade and Industry, 1999; MacLeod and Clarke, 2009; Keep and Mayhew, 2010). Policy-makers have been openly and quite deliberately considering the role that governments and publicly supported programmes can play in developing workforce skills, counteracting recession, promoting workplace innovation and changing the way that companies compete on the global stage (Suff, 2009; Payne, 2010, 2012; Vaitilingam, 2011).

The scope and intensity of government activity varies substantially, however, reflecting different ideological positions, as well as pragmatic concerns for legitimacy and political standing. As previously indicated, the Scandinavian countries, along with Germany, have a much richer history of progressive framing and intervention, although there have been suggestions that this has slipped in recent years, and that regional authorities and institutions have taken the lead with 'enabling' arrangements, particularly in Sweden (Alasoini, 2003; Payne and Keep, 2003,

2005). Nonetheless, the belief that work involves more than a contractual agreement between employers and employees, that the state has an obligation to underwrite minimum standards of employment and cultivate collaboration, remains strong in these countries.

Ambitious multi-year development programmes were launched in Norway and Finland during the 1990s, moving them to the forefront of publicly sponsored innovation (Ennals and Gustavsen, 1999; Payne and Keep, 2005). This was also a decade in which the Irish government announced that it was making a similar long-term commitment to partnership and work reorganization. In Britain and the United States, by comparison, public policy debates followed a different course, betraying the influence of deregulatory interests in earlier Thatcher and Regan administrations. Patterns of state support for empowerment and employee relations were informed by very different values, by concerns for individualism rather than collectivism that challenged notions of partnership involving trades unions and nurtured a suspicion that regulatory proposals in this area would contradict the removal of trade barriers and inhibit the growth of free markets. These preoccupations jarred with ambitions to construct complementary legal and institutional structures, hence Britain and the United States lagged significantly behind Ireland, Germany and the Scandinavian countries in terms of infrastructure and the policy framework in which supportive arrangements could be devised, debated and advanced.

Successive Conservative governments in Britain during the 1980s and '90s sought to create a market-based employment relationship, defending the 'freedom' and decision-making prerogatives of employers, regardless of whether they favoured a 'low road', minimum cost and investment approach to staffing and work organization. These were matters for the private sector and market forces, not for governments, although intervention to bolster this particular version of empowerment was considered to be appropriate. Conservative government support for participation was confined to tax incentive legislation that granted relief on Inland Revenue-approved employee share-ownership and profit-sharing schemes, as discussed in Chapter 4. While these forms of financial participation grew significantly (Millward et al., 2000; Pendleton, 2005), policy-makers anticipated that this would be at the cost of collectivism and trade-union-based partnership arrangements. The point was to promote individualism through material involvement as opposed to decision-making rights and responsibilities, giving employees a direct stake in the fortunes of the employing organization, loosening the attachment to trade unions and demonstrating that benefits can be realized if managers are allowed to operate without 'interference'.

The election of New Labour governments from 1997 ostensibly marked a significant change of direction with British policy-makers finally expressing a commitment to workplace innovation and to enhancing the quality of working life (Department of Trade and Industry, 1999). From this point, government policy in Britain was more obviously in tune with the enabling approach promoted within the European Union. Shortly after taking office, New Labour symbolically signed up to the provisions of the European Social Charter and the Social Chapter of the Maastricht Treaty, for example, both of which encapsulate this logic (Ramsay, 1991). However, the contrast between rhetoric and substance is as pertinent here as in any other area of debate on empowerment and workplace innovation.

Payne and Keep (2005) argue that the Blair government basically failed to alter the policy trajectory set by the Conservatives in the 1980s. Lobbying institutions such as the UK Work Organisation Network (UKWON) seem to agree, complaining that their representations made little impression on policy and practice through the turn of the millennium (Cressey, 2003; Payne and Keep, 2005). Continuities can certainly be identified in the association of markets and globalization with organizational restructuring and the changing nature of work. Surprisingly for Labour politicians, faith in the 'invisible hand' of competition seemed to be a surrogate for purposeful intervention. The assumption that markets can push firms towards empowerment, to reduce hierarchies and challenge 'low road' preferences remains strong within contemporary Left political thinking, although with New Labour there was a determination to eschew policies which could upset the business community or trigger conflict with employers.

Other factors were also important, however. New Labour reticence could be interpreted as a matter of political conviction, rather than signalling a lack of it. Support for the representational empowerment of trade unions, and for the partnership role they fulfil in Northern Europe, was distinctly muted during the Blair and Brown periods of leadership. Strengthening the position of unions – or indeed removing the legal constraints that were imposed upon them in the 1980s – was not a policy objective. New Labour was keen to court business approval and respect managerial prerogatives as a pragmatic part of its broader political strategy. The endorsement of progressive framing and workplace innovation therefore conceals a particular view of partnership that contrasts with the approach taken in other European countries. Unions were kept at arm's length while Labour administrations sustained the so-called voluntarist system of industrial relations in Britain, effectively distancing them from an interventionist agenda on empowerment and workplace participation.

There was more of an appetite to force the issue with employers in previous Labour governments, especially in the 1970s when policy-makers were engaged in struggles to change the governance structures of British companies. Ministers in the Callaghan administration that held office until 1979 favoured legislation to extend participative management into central areas of decision-making, notably by adding worker directors to the boards of major companies. The election that brought them to power in 1974 was contested on a manifesto commitment to legislate for 'industrial democracy', the phrase that focused debate and magnified different opinions about work and organization at that time (Coates and Topham, 1980).

Looking to the experience of neighbouring countries, particularly Sweden and West Germany, and actively pursuing the tripartite model of partnership (between unions, employers and the state), this Labour government established a Committee of Inquiry under Lord Bullock in 1975 to find practical ways of introducing worker directors. Controversy raged through the deliberations, splitting the committee along conventional lines as the 'two sides of industry', employers and unions, expressed very different views on the logic, structure and extent of board level participation, on whether there should be single- or two-tier arrangements and a separation of policy from supervisory matters, for example.

One of the employer representatives resigned, while the remaining three presented a minority report conceding that employees could legitimately be granted a presence in the boardroom as part of a participation agreement, though rejecting imposition. The consensus among other committee members, trades unionists and independents, was that the legislative case had merit, however. Their majority report, delivered in January of 1977, rehearsed arguments that resonate with more familiar, contemporary claims for employee empowerment:

> During our inquiry ... we found a widespread conviction, which we share, that the problem of Britain as an industrial nation is not a lack of native capacity in its working population so much as a failure to draw out their energies and skill to anything like their full potential. (Report of the Committee of Enquiry on Industrial Democracy, 1977, p. 160)

Although greeted with consternation in management circles, a watered-down version of the majority report's recommendations was translated into legislative proposals through a White Paper published in May of

1978. The government was apparently keen to appease some of the critics and take a 'responsive' approach to partnership, yet it was also flexing its muscles, demonstrating a willingness to intervene and to secure workplace innovation with an explicit regulatory framework. An election defeat in 1979 marked the end of this particular initiative, deflecting attention away from its relative strengths and weaknesses, since the incoming Conservative government, the first under Margaret Thatcher's premiership, had no intention of enacting legislation in this area, and was actually moving away from notions of partnership involving unions. The contrasts between the Labour administrations of Callaghan and those of Blair and Brown remain instructive, however, especially as they relate to contemporary developments in the countries noted for government intervention. There was no evidence with New Labour of an equivalent stand on employee empowerment or workplace reform, nor the same commitment to trade union channels of representation. Indeed, since New Labour gave way to the coalition government of Conservatives and Liberal Democrats, and Ed Miliband became leader of the Labour Party, there is no sign of a similar regulatory commitment influencing British policy-making any time soon.

Arguably, this reflects a more sceptical turn in popular thinking about trade unionism, which on matters of empowerment and direct participation may indeed be warranted, as the earlier chapter on gender inequality ventured to suggest. Union movements in Scandinavian countries have a much better record of mobilizing, through partnership arrangements, to secure changes in the nature of work, and have rallied behind Quality of Working Life principles and initiatives, as illustrated in Chapters 2 and 3. Historically, British trade unions have shown very little interest in driving or shaping workplace reform schemes, confining their efforts to collective bargaining over wages and entitlements in employment.

This is not to say that strong unions with determined shop stewards and well-supported local organizations have been unable to influence job content and the introduction of work technology, or set constraints on managerial authority. There are examples of steward involvement in productivity agreements and of national officials (especially those representing clerical and white-collar workers) taking an interest in redesign episodes, with positive results arising from this in terms of work rate, environment and health and safety, for example (Flanders, 1964; Kelly, 1985). There is also contemporary evidence of local union representatives using partnership arrangements to limit unpalatable aspects of modernization programmes and influence local job revisions, for example in the Royal Mail (Stuart and Martinez Lucio, 2005; Beirne, 2011). It would be stretching credibility, however, to equate this with a challenge to Taylorist orthodoxy, or as anything more than reactive and opportunistic intervention.

While union activity has undoubtedly limited the diffusion of Taylorism in Britain, especially during the early decades of the twentieth century, officials and negotiators have traditionally accepted and worked within its terms of reference, conceding managerial prerogatives and deferring to line-management specialists on matters of work organization (Loveridge, 1980; Littler, 1982). Hierarchy, job fragmentation and the principles of Taylorism and Fordism have generally been taken for granted, providing a context instead of a target for union activism. At the core of this lies a fundamental belief about the role and responsibilities of trade unions.

Officials, activists and many commentators in Britain, tend towards the view that unions are opponents, not of authoritarianism, rationalism or unitary conceptions, but of management per se. They endorse an adversarial system of industrial relations, lumping managers and trade unionists into clear cut categories of allegiance, regardless of any values, orientations or dispositions that cut across the divide between employers and employees on the one hand, and their respective agents, managers and union officials, on the other. This perpetuates a reactive form of unionism that turns away from joint responsibility and shared decision-making, undercutting collaborative notions of partnership and casting unions as the 'opposition that can never become a government' (Clegg, 1960).

By this account, independence is the key to effective representation, and the logic of trade unionism is to defend ground and bargain advantages from whatever management initiative comes along, be it Taylorism or participative job redesign. Accepting elements of management and sharing responsibility for the running of organizations increases the risks of incorporation, of unions assimilating management values and compromising their ability to secure the best deal for their members. As Clegg (1960) contends in the clearest statement of this position, participation has the potential to weaken unions, creating role confusion and neutralizing their capacity to mobilize in support of an alternative agenda.

This fear was evident in reactions to the majority report of the Bullock Committee, when moderate and radical unions joined forces to oppose the case for worker directors with a level of hostility that matched some on the employer side. The Annual Reports of the Trades Union Congress reveal sharp exchanges and wrecking amendments as member unions tried to block any collective commitment to the majority report or expression of support for Bullock recommendations, asserting that the primary purpose of trade unionism is to oppose and to bargain. Again, their fear was that negotiating positions would be undermined if worker directors were party to decisions that later became the focus of collective bargaining.

A variation on this oppositional view can also be detected in more recent critiques of the partnership arrangements developed within the European Union. Hyman (2005) argues that European integration is an elitist project that privileges economic interests while cheapening labour, creating unemployment and eroding social protection. By responding to overtures from the European Commission and accepting a role in regulatory projects, albeit to add a 'social dimension' to economic liberalization, unions are ostensibly acquiescing to principles and forms of governance that damage the interests of their members.

For Hyman, the achievements of the union movement are founded on contention. Historically, they have secured benefits and protection for their members by challenging the prevailing social and economic ortho-doxy, and mobilizing support for an alternative agenda. His concern is that this capacity to contradict elite interests has been eroded by the institutionalization of their relationships with employers, governments and more recently the European Union. Pragmatic and defensive interests have given impetus to partnership at the expense of contention, privileg-ing formal and legalistic ways of maintaining legitimacy and influence against a background of industrial restructuring, recruitment difficulties and legislative restrictions dating back to the Thatcher era. Though perhaps understandable, these survival instincts pose dangers for unions, according to Hyman. The pressure from an 'elitist embrace' (p. 24) weakens membership ties and the claims to moral legitimacy that were founded on contention.

Significantly, this opposition is connected to progressive struggling in Hyman's conceptualization. He is appealing for advocacy as much as contention, for unions to rediscover their radical roots, to recapture the 'sword of justice' and present an alternative, 'moral economy'. This has not been such an obvious feature of institutionalized collective bargain-ing, however. As the established format for oppositional trade unionism, this in itself has produced a tendency towards oligarchy and union sovereignty (Michels, 1949; Loveridge, 1980), privileging procedural regularity, and through this survival, while discouraging principled action either *against* Taylorism or *for* direct participation. Institutionalized contention, by this approach, is not self-evidently an ethical project. Nor does it signal the sort of progressive trade unionism that Hyman associates with previous epochs. In fact, it exhibits contradictory tendencies, seeming to favour rather than counteract elitism by reproducing union channels of indirect representation and accepting authoritarian principles of work organization at the expense of direct empowerment.

Oppositionalism has been less of a barrier in Scandinavian countries, where contention transparently ranges beyond ideology to practical matters of progress, outcomes and reform. Unions, employers and governments have repeatedly committed themselves to decentralized workplace developments and to jointly governed regulatory initiatives. There is a long history of dialogue and collaboration in Norway, Sweden and Finland that has given meaning and purpose to tripartite notions of partnership, focusing policy and practice and adding impetus to innovation. Rather than simply contributing to discussions, representatives of employers' organizations and union confederations have worked alongside government officials, initiating, co-ordinating and managing development programmes, as well as sharing in some of the funding (Gustavsen et al., 1996; Alasoini, 2003; Payne and Keep, 2005).

Although activity levels have fluctuated with national political trends and economic conditions, this framework has reinforced the legitimacy of workplace reform while establishing conducive conditions for successive waves of innovation, from the Norwegian Industrial Democracy programme of the 1960s and '70s, through humanistic manufacturing and alternative technology movements in Sweden, and on to national innovation projects that connect empowerment and job restructuring to enterprise and organizational renewal (such as Enterprise Development 2000 and Value Creation 2010 in Norway). These programmes have captured international interest and approval, claiming space for partnership as a potentially viable arena in which to mobilize in favour of reform and against orthodoxy.

Studies of supported projects point to workplace gains in teamworking and cooperation within and across the traditional boundaries between employees, managers and specialists, leading to improvements in productivity, quality and flexibility (Alasoini, 2003; Payne and Keep, 2005). Though reliant on survey data and the recollections and impressions of key stakeholders, the available research offers a very positive assessment, with impressive approval ratings reported per category of respondent. Trade unionists have been a little more restrained than managerial and employee grades, yet a high proportion of those affected by publicly sponsored programmes across the various countries evidently take partnership to be a constructive rather than a threatening development (Gustavsen et al., 1996; Alasoini, 2003).

The effects on infrastructure and the broader environment in which activists operate are considered to be particularly significant. The Scandinavian programmes have traditionally given partnership roles to research institutes and social scientists as a means of expanding the boundaries on innovation, of posing fresh options and looking beyond existing assumptions and business preconceptions. Ideas and experiences have been shared as the relationships between the research and practitioner communities have developed, adding to the stock of available knowledge that innovators can call upon, creating interactive learning networks that foster dialogue and cooperation across wider communities, and building a 'critical mass' in favour of empowerment and innovation (Alasoini, 2003; Payne and Keep, 2005).

Not that progress is assured, even under these ostensibly propitious conditions. There have been setbacks and difficulties in capitalizing upon the local achievements of the major national programmes, with evidence underlining concerns about diffusion and sustainability. Innovations within particular areas or facilities have failed to secure wider support, or trigger general changes across sectors or organizations (Alasoini, 2003; Qvale, 2002). Enthusiasts have confronted major problems in moving the wider population of employers and stakeholders beyond expressions of interest, and in translating awareness into broader-ranging capacities for action. Doubts have also been expressed about directed change, echoing earlier Swedish critiques of top-down approaches that contradict the logic of empowerment and risk employee disaffection, as indicated in Chapter 3 (Payne and Keep, 2005). For these reasons, judgements about the value of national programmes have been tempered with disappointment, and frustration at the continuing difficulty of agreeing terms and establishing criteria for consistent local initiatives. These persistent concerns apply to more than just national regulatory schemes, however.

THE ROLE OF THE EUROPEAN UNION

Arguably, the European Union provides the most significant regulatory stimulus to workplace reform, specifically through the social provisions that aim to protect citizens from the deleterious effects of unrestrained competition (European Commission, 1998, 2010, 2011; Gill et al., 1999; Gill and Krieger, 2000). Claims for wider employee participation have influenced the European social agenda since the beginning of the 1970s, with an influential community of policy-makers articulating a vision of participative management and corporate governance that is consistent with Quality of Working Life principles and sympathetic to trade union representation. Their efforts have been controversial, however, provoking heated debates and triggering political compromises that have restricted the scope of practical initiatives. As Hyman (2005) has observed, Europe is a contested territory, where the momentum behind economic integration has not been matched by a consensual politics of workplace development and organizational renewal. Reports about the impact of 'Social Europe' in this direction tend to be highly qualified, and subject to regular expressions of frustration from enthusiasts for reform.

Yet, there have been some very ambitions attempts to structure empowerment and promote innovation at the European level. Reflecting the broad interest in industrial democracy during the 1970s, the European Commission sought to legislate for employee rights to formal representation on the governing bodies of public limited companies. The draft Fifth Directive, presented in October of 1972, proposed a two-tier structure of supervisory and management boards, backed by statute, that would grant decision-making influence to the grassroots in undertakings with 50 or more staff. This was followed in 1980 by the Vredeling Directive, named after then Social Affairs Commissioner, Henk Vredeling, which sought greater levels of transparency around corporate affairs, with formal rights to information and consultation for employees of multinational companies.

These proposals sparked intense controversy, having little impact in the face of concerted opposition from business interests and lobby groups acting on behalf of many multinationals (Ramsay, 1991). European legislators were not moved to ratify them at this stage, although by the end of the 1980s policy-makers were more amenable to action on this front, anticipating the creation of a potent regulatory framework that was capable of advancing participation.

This renewal of interest, and even determination, was founded upon the realization that economic liberalization and the arrival of the single European market in the 1990s would pose problems and generate tensions if the market-making mission was not counterbalanced by suitably sensitive social and employment policies. This sense was heightened by events within multinationals such as Hoover, where executives were setting plants against each other to force changes in working practices, threatening redundancies or actually concentrating operations in areas where employees were prepared to accept more 'flexible' jobs, 'no-strike agreements' and far-reaching changes in terms, conditions and their psychological contract. 'Social dumping' was a particular worry for politicians and trade unionists in Germany and France, where pressure mounted to counteract any flight of capital to countries that could offer cost advantages by reducing the social responsibilities and regulatory requirements on firms. The preference here was to 'level-up' in terms of standards and regulatory provisions, and to improve competitive performance across Europe with enhanced forms of work organization, skill development and collaboration between the social partners, employers, employees and trade unions.

Out of this came the Social Charter and the idea of a basic platform of fundamental rights and protections that would complement emerging commercial opportunities and generate employee consent for performance improvements by securing effective channels of influence. Workers' rights to life-long learning, vocational training, freedom of association and movement between jobs, health and safety protection, and an 'equitable' wage, sit alongside benefit entitlements to 'adequate' social security and income after retirement in a framework that was endorsed in December 1989, and reinforced by the Social Chapter of the 1993 Maastricht Treaty. Through this period, policy-makers at the centre of the European project were aiming to accelerate the passage of legislation that would deliver the rights enshrined in the Charter, clearing obstacles to the legislative package (the Social Action Programme, as it is formally designated) as part of a movement towards closer European Union.

At that stage, the blocking policy of successive British Conservative governments (that were steadfastly against 'Social Europe' on the grounds that it compromised trade liberalization, the operation of the Single Market and the restrictions that Thatcher administrations applied to British trade unionism) was targeted, and apparently by-passed, with a rule change that brought Qualified Majority Voting to employment matters, meaning that no single state could prevent the passage of a law to which it alone objected. This provoked intense debate about the impact of European regulation at the time, especially when then Prime Minister John Major claimed to have negotiated an exemption from the Social Chapter. Judgements about the significance or otherwise of this for British companies, managers and workers became redundant, however, when New Labour embraced the Social Chapter and Charter shortly after taking office in 1997.

With this development and seemingly wide consensus on regulation, the pan-European approach promised meaningful progress. For some commentators, the Charter, Chapter and accompanying Action Programme represent the high-water mark of regulatory achievement (Gill et al., 1999, p. 315). Extending workers' rights to information, consultation and participation over matters that directly affect their employment is central to the framework and to the most significant achievement of the legislative programme so far. The aspirations that were invested in the

Vredeling and draft Fifth Directives were given new form and focus with the European Works Councils Directive of 1994.

This requires the creation of a European Works Council (EWC) or, alternatively, some other agreed procedure for informing and consulting workers in every 'community-scale' multinational company, defined as one with more than 1000 employees within the European Union and at least 150 in each of two member states. With this Directive, European policy-makers finally established the legal foundations for a transnational approach to participative management, giving employee representatives information and consultation rights on organizational changes, investments, the introduction of new technologies, processes and working methods, production transfers and plant closures, mergers, cutbacks and redundancies. Estimates vary on the proliferation of EWCs since the Directive came into force (outside Britain) in September 1996, although reliable indicators point to steady early growth, from approximately 550 by mid-1999 (Gill and Krieger, 2000) to around 700 in 2003 (Cressey, 2003; Hall and Marginson, 2005) from a projected total of 1850 eligible companies. This was prior to the last major enlargement of the Union in 2004, which brought an additional ten countries within the scope of the Directive (Hall and Marginson, 2005).

There has been a discernible shift in European thinking about participation and regulation since this period, however, possibly moderating its impact. Since the late 1990s, policy pronouncements have favoured direct forms of participation and, perhaps more significantly, 'softer' methods of leadership and 'steering' over imposition by recourse to directives (Gill et al., 1999; Hyman, 2005). This is evident in European Commission publications, beginning with the 1997 Green Paper 'Partnership for a new organisation of work', continuing with its 1998 communication, 'Modernising the organisation of work: a positive approach to change', and on to more recent variations on this output with 'Restructuring in Europe' (2010) and 'Adapting to change' (2011). These rehearse familiar arguments about the association of workplace innovation with competitive success, extolling the virtues of upskilling, flexible working and the benefits to be gleaned from investing in local empowerment and direct participation. They call for new working relationships and meaningful departures from the traditional forms of hierarchy and specialization that are rooted in adversarial Taylorism, though putting the onus firmly on managers to prioritize and drive change programmes at the level of the firm.

Of course, there is a recognition that many managers will struggle with this sort of adjustment, and that progress will be uneven and occasionally fraught. This has been weighed against employer suspicions of statutory intervention, however, and a history of dismissive and often hostile reactions to regulation through indirect participation involving unions and third party agencies (Gill and Krieger, 2000). The upshot is that European policy-makers now regularly accentuate the voluntary and negotiated aspects of change. By comparison with the approach taken during 1980s and early 1990s, there is a stronger emphasis on agreements that are in tune with local circumstances. Europe is presented as an arena populated by opinion formers, leaders and co-ordinators.

This is not to suggest that the European Commission has rejected regulation, or abandoned purposeful action for a relatively passive stance. The point is rather that legislative intervention is now predominantly regarded as a matter of last resort, as a fall back where voluntary agreements prove to be elusive. The prevailing vocabulary of European policy-making reflects this shift, with references to 'soft law' and 'social benchmarking' presented to cultivate a user-friendly image and counter-act any worries that the social partners may have about enforcement or the imposition of a standard European regime.

The EWC Directive itself asserts the primacy of negotiations between the social partners. By contrast with the 1970s proposals, it makes a point of avoiding 'hard law' regulation, allowing representatives of employees and employers to specify the precise nature, composition, function and procedures of EWCs, and the financial resources necessary to sustain them. They can even decide that councils are inappropriate, so long as they reach agreement about alternative procedures for informing and consulting staff. It would only be after three years of stalemate or inactivity that the directive's 'subsidiary requirements' would take effect, imposing the minimum standard of an EWC with between 3 and 30 members, fully representing the member states in which the company operates, meeting at least once a year to exchange information, or under the exceptional circumstances of plant closure, relocation or collective redundancies. Significantly, employee representatives on these councils have no rights to challenge managerial prerogatives or obstruct manage-ment decision-taking.

This 'soft touch' approach to innovation, together with the minimalist, 'pick and mix' flexibility of the EWC Directive, has attracted regular criticism from commentators and council members who detect some slippage from original principles and a shortfall in achievements relative to aspirations and declared intentions (Waddington, 2003; Cressey, 2003; Hyman, 2005; Hall and Marginson, 2005). Although early reports from the Trades Union Congress and Labour Research Department were positive, especially about the forerunner voluntary EWCs (introduced prior to September, 1996) that were ostensibly fulfilling their role of informing and consulting (Gill et al., 1999; Hall and Marginson, 2005), substantial grassroots benefits are difficult to detect. In fact, there is considerable dissatisfaction and a growing sense that EWCs in practice amount to rather empty talking shops that pose difficulties for the future of empowerment, rather than securing genuine influence.

With the leeway afforded to managers, it is difficult to be strongly optimistic that EWCs constitute a truly effective means of combating traditional constraints on empowerment. Surveys of managerial opinion suggest that a narrow view of their role and relevance predominates, that outright opposition is not necessarily the tactic that traditionalists pursue *against* EWCs, and that those who are inclined to defend managerial prerogatives have been able to bend them to their own advantage (Wills, 1999; Cressey, 2003). Wills (1999) discovered a tendency for EWCs in practice to strengthen hierarchical management, to be used as an additional means of corporate communication, and even to be absorbed within a culture management agenda as an extra conduit for promulgating official values across European operations. She also found that instead of accommodating or responding to input from employee representatives, some companies were using council arrangements to contain union influence, pitting trade unionists against non-union delegates or nominees for council seats.

This evidence is consistent with the findings from case study investigations conducted by Waddington (2003) and also by Marginson, Hall, Hoffmann and Muller (2004). These authors point to variations in the impact of EWCs between companies headquartered in Britain and the United States and those based in continental Europe. However, the overall effects are judged to be modest, the differences relating to the implementation of management decisions rather than their substance. The prevalence of a more restrictive approach among British and American nationals, even on these very contained terms, is largely attributed to Anglo-Saxon management traditions and the hold that essentially Taylorist values and preoccupations continue to have on practitioners. The case study councils tended to reflect and reproduce these aspects rather than challenge them, although the effects were moderated to some degree when arrangements were handled by European nationals and within the management structures of continental operations. Established traditions also have a bearing upon the perceptions of employee representatives, those from Anglo-Saxon companies registering lower levels of dissatisfaction than their continental, and especially Nordic, equivalents, partly because they start with weaker expectations founded upon previous experience. Nonetheless, the role of the councils, the scope for discussion and the information tabled are more obviously and heavily circumscribed in these cases, especially in multinationals headquartered in Britain.

Clearly, on this evidence, there is wide-ranging scope for management traditionalists to thrive within the European regulatory framework. Only a small minority of respondents associated EWCs with negotiated change and meaningful empowerment. This is not to say that limited outcomes are inevitable or that struggles are somehow neutralized within this arena. There are some encouraging reports of participative practice and substantive joint decision-making, of EWCs that reach beyond the limited rights enshrined in the Directive and hold their ground fairly well (Lecher et al., 2001; Hall and Marginson, 2005). The agency of committed participants seems to have been critical in these cases, with employee representatives in particular given credit for imaginative practice, recognizing new opportunities for networking and collective engagement on a wider scale. This marks the exception rather than the rule, however, with workforce representatives generally failing to 'punch their weight within EWCs', certainly in the case of British trade unionists (Hall and Marginson, 2005, p. 215).

That said, the representatives covered by Waddington's study (2005) broadly welcomed the principle of EWCs and European regulation. Their dissatisfaction with tactical management and limited information was channelled into calls for additional regulation, for a revision and general tightening of the Directive to deliver meaningful participation. This is patently a trade union position, however, which does not of necessity resonate with opinions on the shop floor. Social Europe undoubtedly appeals to trade unionists, promising a formal role through prevailing notions of partnership and indirect participation that may help them to consolidate their position and claim space for relevance in turbulent times (Hyman, 2005). Expressions of indifference or irrelevance are more likely at workforce level since EWCs have evidently not fulfilled a transformative role or secured general improvements in the daily experience of working life.

BEYOND 'SOFT LAW' POLITICS

Available opportunities to extend the scope of progressive management and enact a principled commitment to empowerment and workplace innovation are undoubtedly influenced by wider political movements that operate to structure organizational relations. Developmental issues have clearly captured attention and provided a focus for the mobilization of resources within these, policy-makers demonstrating awareness, allied to variable capacities for action, at national and supranational levels.

Yet the existing regulatory architecture across the areas reviewed in this chapter is generally weak, and too easily compromised or ignored by those who either regard empowerment and participative management as inimical to their interests, or seek to bend and contain these concepts within tight boundaries. Of course, it would be crass to deny the sincerity of the politics behind these regulatory initiatives, or condemn them as empty gestures. Any tendency towards symbolic posturing has to be set against the determined struggles of the policy-makers who advanced the national workplace development programmes and European initiatives considered here, usually against significant opposition and rearguard politicking. Their efforts have taken the empowerment project forward, though mainly in a supportive, incremental and non-regulatory fashion, through exhortation and encouragement, by keeping the agenda alive for front-line enthusiasts, adding momentum to networking and coalition building, and by fostering a climate that is conducive to the cross-fertilization of ideas (Alasoini, 2003; Hall and Marginson, 2005; Hyman, 2005; Payne and Keep, 2005).

However, there is more to progress than positive statements and solemn declarations of the sort invested in the Social Charter, important as these are in contextualizing innovation. Nor is it a matter of creating propitious conditions and outline structures, especially when these slip to minimalism in applied content, providing an outlet for token participation, reluctantly enforced when employers simply refuse to observe due process (for example, with EWCs). Supportive programmes need to make a difference at the grassroots, where practitioners confront constraints on a regular basis. In this respect, the regulatory initiatives developed in Britain, across Europe and even in the Scandinavian countries (according to the research reported in this book) have not been radical enough.

Front-line enthusiasts remain vulnerable and exposed, relying upon their own agency and collaborative ties, with insufficient protection from enlightened regulatory sources. Under these conditions, casualties of the sort described in Chapters 3, 5 and 7 are likely to grow in number. This is the hard end of 'soft law' politics. If innovators are to flourish and advance empowerment rather than succumb to the pressures from orthodoxy, legal and institutional provisions need to be fixed at the centre of publicly sponsored programmes, not mildly or tentatively included as a backdrop to persuasion and dialogue. Considering the available evidence, it seems difficult to avoid the conclusion that regulatory interventions need to be more focused and much sharper. Of course, this intensifies the politics of empowerment and innovation, putting a premium on reflective abilities, capacity building and determined struggling, in policy-making as much as management.

References

ACAS (2011), *The People Factor: Engaging Your Employees for Business Success*, London, UK: ACAS.

Ackers, P., M. Marchington, A. Wilkinson and J. Goodman (1992), 'The use of cycles? Explaining employee involvement in the 1990s', *Industrial Relations Journal*, **23**, 268–283.

Adler, N. and A. Harzing (2009), 'When knowledge wins: transcending the sense of and nonsense of academic rankings', *Academy of Management Learning and Education*, **8** (1), 72–95.

Adler, P. (1993), 'Time and motion regained', *Harvard Business Review*, January, 97–108.

Adler, P. (1995), '"Democratic Taylorism": the Toyota production system at NUMMI', in S. Babson (ed.), *Lean Work: Empowerment and Exploitation in the Global Auto Industry*, Detroit, MI: Wayne State University Press.

Adler, P. and R. Cole (1993), 'Designed for learning: a tale of two plants', *Sloan Management Review*, Spring, 85–91.

Al-Ahmadi, H. (2011), 'Challenges facing women leaders in Saudi Arabia', *Human Resource Development International*, **14** (2), 149–166.

Alasoini, T. (2003), 'Promotion of workplace innovation on the public policy agenda: reflections on the Finnish workplace development programme', UK Work Organisation Network, Working paper number 5.

Alvesson, M. and Y. Billings (2009), *Understanding Gender and Organizations*, London, UK: Sage.

Alvesson, M. and H. Willmott (eds) (1992), *Critical Management Studies*, London, UK: Sage.

Anderson, D., S. Vinnicombe and V. Singh (2010), 'Women partners leaving the firm: choice, what choice?', *Gender in Management: An International Journal*, **25**, 170–183.

Anthony, P. (1977), *The Conduct of Industrial Relations*, London, UK: Institute of Personnel Management.

Anthony, P. (1994), *Managing Culture*, Buckingham, UK: Open University Press.

Appelbaum, S., D. Hebert and S. Leroux (1999), 'Empowerment: power, culture and leadership: a strategy or fad for the millennium?', *Journal of Workplace Learning: Employee Counselling Today*, **11** (7), 233–254.

Argyris, C. (1998), 'Empowerment: the emperor's new clothes', *Harvard Business Review*, **76**, 98–105.

Audi (2007a), *The Audi Magazine*, Summer, Audi UK.

Audi (2007b), *The Audi Magazine*, Winter, Audi UK.

Bachrach, P. and A. Botwinick (1992), *Power and Empowerment: A Radical Theory of Participatory Democracy*, Philadelphia, PA: Temple University Press.

Baddon, L., L. Hunter, J. Hyman, J. Leopold and H. Ramsay (1989), *People's Capitalism: A Critical Analysis of Profit-sharing and Employee Share Ownership*, London, UK: Routledge.

Bansler, J. and K. Bodker (1993), 'A reappraisal of structured analysis: design in an organisational context', *Transactions on Information Systems*, **11** (2), 165–193.

Barboza, D. (2010), 'A night at the electronics factory', *The New York Times*, 20 June, 3.

Barker, J. (1993), 'Tightening the iron cage: concertive control in self-managed teams', *Administrative Science Quarterly*, **38**, 408–437.

Barry, J., J. Chandler and H. Clark (2001), 'Between the ivory tower and the academic assembly line', *Journal of Management Studies*, **38** (1), 87–101.

BBC (1994), 'The computer triangle', *The Money Programme*, BBC2, 16 January.

BBC (1995), 'Videoprint', *Sid's Heroes*, BBC1, 14 May.

BBC (2000), 'Changing the Japanese way', *Bubble Trouble*, BBC2, January.

BBC (2002), 'Production methods', *Working Lunch Business Education*, BBC1, 31 January.

BBC (2009), 'Can't deliver, won't deliver', *Panorama*, 14 December.

BBC (2010), 'Foxconn suicides: "workers feel quite lonely"', *Asia-Pacific News*, 28 May.

BBC (2012a), 'Nick Clegg plans more employee ownership', *BBC News*, 16 January.

BBC (2012b), 'RBS chairman says bankers' pay high for too long', *BBC News*, 3 February.

BBC (2012c), 'Birmingham city council loses equal pay appeal bid', *BBC News*, 24 October.

Beale, D. (2003), 'Engaged in battle: exploring the sources of workplace union militancy at Royal Mail', *Industrial Relations Journal*, **34** (1), 82–95.

Beath, C. and W. Orlikowski (1994), 'The contradictory structure of systems development methodologies: deconstructing the IS–user relationship in information engineering', *Information Systems Research*, **5** (4), 350–377.

Becker, G. (1985), 'Human capital, effort, and the sexual division of labor', *Journal of Labor Economics*, **3** (1/2), 33–58.

Beirne, M. (1999), 'Managing to empower: a healthy review of resources and constraints', *European Management Journal*, **17** (2), 218–225.

Beirne, M. (2008), 'Idealism and the applied relevance of research on employee participation', *Work, Employment and Society*, **22** (4), 675–693.

Beirne, M. (2011), 'Managers, workers, their union and modernization: challenging interpretations of management and change at the Royal Mail', *Organizational Change Stream. Seventh International Critical Management Studies Conference*, Naples, 13 July.

Beirne, M. (2013), 'Creative tension? Negotiating the space between management and the arts', *Journal of Arts and Communities*, **4** (2).

Beirne, M. and C. Cromack (2009), 'Managing creative coalitions: reflections on the social side of services innovation', *European Management Journal*, **27**, 83–89.

Beirne, M. and S. Knight (2002a), 'Principles and consistent management in the arts: lessons from British theatre', *The International Journal of Cultural Policy*, **8** (1), 75–89.

Beirne, M. and S. Knight (2002b), 'Principles and the practice of reflective management', *Proceedings of the First International Art of Management and Organisation Conference*, Kings College, London, UK, September.

Beirne, M. and S. Knight (2004), 'The art of reflective management: dramatic insights from Scottish community theatre', *The International Journal of Arts Management*, **6** (2), 33–43.

Beirne, M. and H. Ramsay (1988), 'Computer redesign and labour process theory: towards a critical appraisal', in D. Knights and H. Willmott (eds), *New Technology and the Labour Process*, London, UK: Macmillan, pp. 197–229.

Beirne, M. and H. Ramsay (1992), 'A creative offensive? Participative systems design and the question of control', in M. Beirne and H. Ramsay (eds), *Information Technology and Workplace Democracy*, London, UK: Routledge, pp. 92–120.

Beirne, M., H. Ramsay and N. Panteli (1998a), 'Participating informally: opportunities and dilemmas in user-driven design', *Behaviour and Information Technology*, **17** (5), 301–310.

Beirne. M., H. Ramsay and N. Panteli (1998b), 'Developments in computing work: control and contradiction on the software labour process', in P. Thompson and C. Warhurst (eds), *Workplaces of the Future*, London, UK: Macmillan, pp. 142–162.

Beirne, M., K. Riach and F. Wilson (2004), 'Controlling business? Agency and constraint in call centre working', *New Technology, Work and Employment*, **19** (2), 96–109.

Belt, V. (2002), 'A female ghetto? Women's careers in call centres', *Human Resource Management Journal*, **12** (4), 51–66.

Benders, J., P. Hoeken, R. Batenburg and R. Schouteten (2006), 'First organise, then automate: a modern socio-technical view on ERP systems and teamworking', *New Technology, Work and Employment*, **21** (3), 242–251.

Berggren, C. (1992), *The Volvo Experience: Alternatives to Lean Production in the Swedish Auto Industry*, Basingstoke, UK: Macmillan.

Berggren, C. (1995), 'Are assembly lines just more efficient? Reflections on Volvo's "humanistic" manufacturing', in S. Babson (ed.), *Lean Work: Empowerment and Exploitation in the Global Auto Industry*, Detroit, MI: Wayne State University Press, pp. 277–291.

Berner, B. (2008), 'Working knowledge as performance: on the practical understanding of machines', *Work, Employment and Society*, **22** (2), 319–336.

Beynon, H. (1973), *Working for Ford*, London, UK: Allen Lane.

Bhatnagar, J. (2005), 'The power of psychological empowerment as an antecedent to organizational commitment in Indian managers', *Human Resource Development International*, **8** (4), 419–433.

Bjerknes, G., P. Ehn and M. Kyng (eds) (1987), *Computers and Democracy: A Scandinavian Challenge*, Aldershot, UK: Avebury/Gower.

Blackburn, R. (1967), 'The unequal struggle', in R. Blackburn and A. Cockburn (eds), *The Incompatibles: Trade Union Militancy and the Consensus*, Harmondsworth, UK: Penguin, pp. 48–51.

Blanchard, K., J. Carlos and A. Randolph (1999), *The Three Keys to Empowerment*, San Francisco, CA: Barrett-Koehler Publishers.

Blomberg, J., F. Kensing and E. Dykstra-Erickson (1996), *PDC'96: Proceedings of the Participatory Design Conference*, Cambridge, MA: CPSR.

Bluestone, I. (1999), 'Public Policy and the Evolution of Change in Industrial Relations', in S. Babbson (ed.), *Lean Work: Empowerment and Exploitation in the Global Auto Industry*, pp. 350–361.

Blum, B. (1996), *Beyond Programming: To a New Era of Design*, New York: Oxford University Press.

Blumberg, P. (1968), *Industrial Democracy: The Sociology of Participation*, London, UK: Constable.

Boguslaw, R. (1965), *The New Utopians: A Study of System Design and Social Change*, Englewood Cliffs, NJ: Prentice Hall.

Bossen, C., C. Dindler and O.S. Iversen (2012), 'Impediments to user gains: experiences from a critical participatory design project', *Proceedings of the Twelfth Participatory Design Conference*, Roskilde, Denmark, August.

Brannan, M. and B. Hawkins (2007), 'London calling: selection as a pre-emptive strategy for cultural control', *Employee Relations*, **29** (2), 178–191.

Bratteteig, T. and I. Wagner (2012), 'Disentangling power and decision-making in participatory design', *Proceedings of the Twelfth Participatory Design Conference*, Roskilde, Denmark, August.

Briefs, U., C. Ciborra and L. Schneider (eds) (1983), *Systems Design, For, With and By the Users*, Amsterdam, the Netherlands: North Holland.

Broadbridge, A. and R. Simpson (2011), '25 years on: reflecting on the past and looking to the future in gender and management research', *British Journal of Management*, **22**, 470–483.

Brown, R. (1967), 'Research and consultancy in industrial enterprises: a review of the contribution of the Tavistock Institute of Human Relations to the development of industrial sociology', *Sociology*, **1** (1), 33–60.

Brown, R. (1984), 'BSA Presidential Address: working on work', *Sociology*, **18** (3), 311–323.

Bruce, M. (1987), 'Managing people first: bringing the service concept into British Airways', *Industrial and Commercial Training*, March/April, 21–26.

Buchanan, D. (2000), 'An eager and enduring embrace: the ongoing rediscovery of teamworking as a management idea', in S. Procter and F. Mueller (eds), *Teamworking*, **25**, 3.

Buchanan, D. and D. Preston (1992), 'Life in a cell: supervision and teamwork in a manufacturing systems engineering environment', *Human Resource Management Journal*, **2** (4), 55–76.

Burnes, B. (1998), 'Recipes for organisational effectiveness: mad, bad or just dangerous to know?', *Career Development International*, **3** (3), 100–106.

Burns, T. (1967), 'Sociological explanation', *British Journal of Sociology*, **18** (4), 353–369.

Business Week (2011), 'Boards of directors need quotas for women', February.

Butler, P. (2012), 'Birmingham equal pay victory for women may impact city of London', *The Guardian*, 24 October.

Carter, J.D.T. (2009), 'Managers empowering employees', *American Journal of Economics and Business Admininstration*, **1** (2), 41–46.

Castiglione, J. (2007), 'Self-managing work teams and their external leadership: a primer for library administrators', *Library Management*, **28** (6), 379–393.

Caudron, S. (1995), 'Create an empowering environment', *Personnel Journal*, September, 28–36.

Caulkin, S. (2012), 'Taking the lid off CEO pay', *Management Today*, April, 40–43.

Channel 4 (1993), *The Pulse*, Series 1, Programme 10, 5 May, London: Diverse Productions.

Channel 4 (2010), 'Post Office undercover', *Dispatches*, 8 February.

Chan Kim, W. and R. Mauborgne (2005), *Blue Ocean Strategy*, Boston, MA: Harvard Publishing.

Charles, M. (2005), 'National skill regimes, postindustrialism and sex segregation', *Social Politics*, **12** (2), 289–316.

Chen, C., T. Steiner and A.M. Whyte (2006), 'Does stock option-based executive compensation induce risk taking? An analysis of the banking industry', *Journal of Banking and Finance*, **30**, 915–945.

Cho, Y. and D. Newhouse (2011), 'How did the Great Recession affect different types of workers?', The World Bank, Policy Research Working Paper 5636, April, Washington DC: World Bank.

Ciulla, J. (2000), *The Working Life: The Promise and Betrayal of Modern Work*, New York: Random House.

Clark, T. and I. Mangham (2004), 'From dramaturgy to theatre as technology: the case of corporate theatre', *Journal of Management Studies*, **41** (1), 37–59.

Clegg, H. (1960), *A New Approach to Industrial Democracy*, London, UK: Blackwell.

Clement, A. (1993), 'Looking for the designers: transforming the 'invisible' infrastructure of computerised office work', *AI and Society*, **7**, 323–344.

Clement, A. (1994), 'Computing at work: empowering action by low-level users', *Communications of the ACM*, **37** (1), 53–63.

Clemons, D. and M. Kroth (2011), *Managing the Mobile Workforce: Leading, Building and Sustaining Virtual Teams*, New York: McGraw-Hill.

Clutterbuck, D. (1998), 'Empowerment as mutuality of benefit', *Human Resource Development International*, **1** (1), 95–102.

Collins, D. (1998), 'Il a commence a penser avant d'avoir rien appris: a processual view of the construction of empowerment', *Employee Relations*, **20** (6), 594–609.

Collins, D. (1999), 'Born to fail? Empowerment, ambiguity and set overlap', *Personnel Review*, **28**, 208–221.

Collins, D. (2000), *Management Fads and Buzzwords: Critical-Practical Perspectives*, London, UK: Routledge.

Commission of the European Union (1998), *Modernising the Organisation of Work: A Positive Approach to Change*, Luxembourg: Office for the Official Publications of the European Union.

Conley, H. (2012), 'Using equality to challenge austerity: new actors, old paradigms', *Work, Employment and Society*, **26** (2), 349–359.

Conti, R. and M. Warner (1993), 'Taylorism, new technology and just-in-time systems in Japanese manufacturing', *New Technology, Work and Employment*, **8** (1), 31–42.

Cooley, M. (1980), *Architect or Bee?* Slough, UK: Langley Technical Services.

Cooper, C. (2011), 'Management research in the UK: a personal view', *British Journal of Management*, **22**, 343–346.

Cowan, T. (2011), *The Great Stagnation*, New York: Dutton.

Craven, J. (2009), 'The future is female: why the business world wants a women's touch', *The Mail Online*, 8 August.

Cressey, P. (2003), 'European works councils: transforming European industrial relations?', *UK Work Organisation Network Journal*, **1**, 2–4.

Crummy, H. (1992), *Let the People Sing!* Edinburgh, UK: Craigmillar Festival Society.

Crystal, G. (1991), *In Search of Excess: The Overcompensation of American Executives*, New York: Norton.

Cunningham, I. and J. Hyman (1999), 'The poverty of empowerment? A critical case study', *Personnel Review*, **28** (3), 192–207.

Cunningham, I., J. Hyman and C. Baldry (1996), 'Empowerment: the power to do what?', *Industrial Relations Journal*, **27**, 143–154.

Currie, G. and D. Knights (2003), 'Reflecting on a critical pedagogy in MBA education', *Management Learning*, **34** (1), 27–49.

Curtis, B., H. Krasner and N. Iscoe (1988), 'A field study of the software design process for large systems', *Commnications of the ACM*, **31** (11), 1268–1287.

The Daily Record (1996), 'BA in shop-a-mate storm', 12 October, 9.

The Daily Record (1998), 'Make fat cats pay', 23 July, 8.

The Daily Record (2003), 'Fatcats trouser 288% rise', 10 October, 2.

The Daily Mail (2012), 'TUC urges revolt over fat cat pay', *Mail Online*, 9 February.

Danford, A. (1997), 'Teamworking and labour regulation: a case study of shop floor disempowerment', *Proceedings of the 15th International Labour Process Conference*, Edinburgh, UK.

D'Annunzio-Green, N. and J. Macandrew (1999), 'Re-empowering the empowered: the ultimate challenge?', *Personnel Review*, **28** (3), 258–278.

D'Art, D. (1992), *Economic Democracy and Financial Participation*, London, UK: Routledge.

D'Art, D. and T. Turner (2004), 'Profit sharing, firm performance and union influence in selected European countries', *Personnel Review*, **33** (3), 335–350.

Davidson, C. (2007), 'The future is female, BT predicts', *BBC Newsonline*, 23 April.

Davis, L. and J. Taylor (eds) (1972), *The Design of Jobs*, Harmondsworth, UK: Penguin.

Deal, T. and A. Kennedy (1982), *Corporate Cultures: The Rites and Rituals of Corporate Life*, Harmondsworth, UK: Penguin.

Deal, T. and A. Kennedy (1999), *The New Corporate Cultures: Revitalising the Workplace after Downsizing, Mergers and Reengineering*, Cambridge, MA: Perseus.

Delamarter, R. (1988), *Big Blue: IBM's Use and Abuse of Power*, London, UK: Pan Books.

Denham, N., P. Ackers and C. Travers (1997), 'Doing yourself out of a job? How middle managers cope with empowerment', *Employee Relations*, **19**, 147–159.

De Nijs, W. and E. Poutsma (2006), 'Financial participation revisited', *Economic and Industrial Democracy*, **27** (4), 539–542.

Department of Trade and Industry (1999), *Working for the Future: The Changing Face of Work Practices*, London, UK: HMSO.

Dong, A., C. Wang and F. Xie (2010), 'Do executive stock options induce excessive risk taking?', *Journal of Banking and Finance*, **34**, 2518–2529.

DuBois, S. (2012), 'The rise of the chief culture officer', *CNN Money*, 30 July.

Eastman, C. and L. Fulop (1997), 'Management for clinicians or the case of "bringing the mountain to Mohammed"', *International Journal of Production Economics*, **52**, 15–30.

The Economist (2001), 'A long march', 14 July, 79–81.

Edmonstone, J. (2000), 'Empowerment in the national health service: does shared governance offer a way forward', *Journal of Nursing Management*, **8**, 259–264.

Edwards, P. (2006), 'Power and ideology in the workplace: going beyond even the second version of the three dimensional view', *Work, Employment and Society*, **20** (3), 571–581.

Edwards, P. and M. Collinson (2002), 'Empowerment and managerial labour strategies: pragmatism regained', *Work and Occupations*, **29** (3), 272–299.

Ehn, P. (1988), *Work-Oriented Design of Computer Artifacts*, Stockholm, Sweden: Arbetslivscentrum.

Eldridge, J.E.T. (1981), 'Space for sociology', *Sociology*, **15** (1), 94–103.

Emery, F. and E. Thorsrud (1976), *Democracy at Work*, Leiden, the Netherlands: Martinus Nijhoff.

Ennals, R. and B. Gustavsen (1999), *Work Organisation and Europe as a Development Coalition*, Amsterdam, the Netherlands: John Benjamins.

Equality and Human Rights Commission (2008), *Sex and Power in Scotland*, Glasgow, UK: EOC Scotland.

European Commission (1997), 'Partnership for a new organisation of work', Green Paper, COM(97)128, Brussels, Belgium: European Commission.

European Commission (1998), *Modernising the Organisation of Work: A Positive Approach to Change*, COM(98)592, Brussels, Belgium: European Commission.

European Commission (2010), *Restructuring in Europe*, Brussels, Belgium: European Commission.

European Commission (2011), 'Adapting to change: the EU approach to re-structuring', *Social Agenda*, Issue No. 27, July, Brussels, Belgium: European Commission.

Fenton-O'Creevy, M. (1995), 'Empowerment', in N. Nicholson (ed.), *Blackwell Encyclopedic Dictionary of Organizational Behaviour*, Cambridge, MA: Blackwell, p. 155.

Fernandez, S. and T. Moldogaziev (2011), 'Empowering public sector employees to improve performance: does it work?', *The American Review of Public Administration*, **41** (1), 23–47.

The Financial Times (2003), 'A speedier route from order to camcorder', 12 February, 11.

The Financial Times (2004), 'Chief executive pay soars 168% in five years', 24 May, 9.

The Financial Times (2012), 'Investor anger boils over', 4 May, 1.

Fincham, R. (1989), 'Natural workgroups and the process of job design', *Employee Relations*, **11** (6), 17–22.

Fincham, R. and P. Rhodes (1992), *The Individual, Work and Organization: Behavioural Studies for Business and Management*, Oxford, UK: Oxford University Press.

Findlay, P., A. McKinlay, A. Marks and P. Thompson (2000), 'Flexible when it suits them: the use and abuse of teamwork skills', in S. Procter and F. Mueller (eds), *Teamworking*, Basingstoke, UK: Macmillan.

Flanders, A. (1964), *The Fawley Productivity Agreements*, London, UK: Faber.

Flint, M. (2012), 'Why is chief executives' pay not linked to performance', *BBC Radio 4 News*, 9 February.

Flowers, S. (1996), *Software Failure: Management Failure*, Chichester, UK; New York: Wiley.

Fondas, N. (1997), 'Feminization unveiled: management qualities in contemporary writings', *Academy of Management Review*, **22** (1), 257–282.

Ford, H. and S. Crowther (1926), *My Life and Work*, New York: Doubleday.

Foster, D. and P. Hoggett (1999), 'Change in the Benefits Agency: empowering the exhausted worker', *Work, Employment and Society*, **13**, 19–39.

Fox, A. (1971), *The Sociology of Work in Industry*, London, UK: Collier-Macmillan.

Foy, N. (1994), *Empowering People at Work*, Aldershot, UK: Gower.

Fracaro, K. (2006), 'The real meaning of empowerment', *Contract Management*, March.

Gadman, L. and C. Cooper (2009), *Open Source Leadership*, London, UK: Palgrave Macmillan.

Gall, G. (2003), *The Meaning of Militancy? Postal Workers and Industrial Relations*, Aldershot, UK: Ashgate.

Gall, G. (2005), 'Breaking with, and breaking, partnership', in M. Stuart and M. Martinez Lucio (eds), *Partnership and Modernisation in Employment Relations*, London, UK: Routledge, pp. 154–170.

Gandz, J. (1990), 'The employee empowerment era', *Business Quarterly*, **55** (2), 74–79.

Geary, J. (1993), 'New forms of work organisation and employee involvement in two case study sites: plural, mixed and protean', *Economic and Industrial Democracy*, **14**, 511–534.

Geary, J. (1995), 'Work practices: the structure of work', in P. Edwards (ed.), *Industrial Relations: Theory and Practice in Britain*, Oxford, UK: Blackwell, pp. 368–396.

Giesekam, G. and S. Knight (2000), *Luvvies and Rude Mechanicals? Amateur and Community Theatre in Scotland*, Edinburgh, UK: Scottish Arts Council.

Gill, C. and H. Krieger (2000), 'Recent survey evidence on participation in Europe: towards a European model?', *European Journal of Industrial Relations*, **6** (1), 109–132.

Gill, C., M. Gold and P. Cressey (1999), 'Social Europe: national initiatives and responses', *Industrial Relations Journal*, **30** (4), 313–329.

Goffman, E. (1961), *Asylums: Essays on the Social Situation of Mental Patients and Other Inmates*, New York: Anchor Books.

Goldthorpe, J., D. Lockwood, F. Bechofer and J. Platt (1968), *The Affluent Worker: Industrial Attitudes and Behaviour*, Cambridge, UK: Cambridge University Press.

Goulding, D. and D. Currie (eds) (2000), *Thinking About Management: A Reflective Practice Approach*, London, UK: Routledge.

Graham, L. (1994), 'How does the Japanese model transfer to the United States? A view from the line', in T. Elger and C. Smith (eds), *Global Japanisation? The Transnational Transformation of the Labour Process*, London, UK: Routledge.

Granath, J.A. (1998), 'Torslanda to Uddevalla via Kalmar: a journey in production practice in Volvo', *Seminario Internacional Reestruturacao Produtiva*, Rio de Janeiro, August.

Greasley, K., A. Bryman, A. Dainty, A. Price, R. Soetanto and N. King (2005), 'Employee perceptions of empowerment', *Employee Relations*, **27** (4), 354–368.

Greenbaum, J. and M. Kyng (eds) (1991), *Design at Work: Co-operative Design of Computer Systems*, Hillsdale, NJ: Lawrence Erlbaum.

Greenhouse, S. (2010), 'In Indiana city, an economic centrepiece closes and heads for Mexico', *The New York Times*, 20 June, 14, 19.

The Greenock Telegraph (2006), 'Gone by the end of the year', 3 April.

Grey, C. (1994), 'Career as a project of the self and labour process discipline', *Sociology*, **28** (2), 479–497.

Grugulis, I. and A. Wilkinson (2002), 'Managing culture at British Airways: hype, hope and reality', *Long Range Planning*, **35**, 179–194.

The Guardian (1997), 'Lost pay, lost time, lost expectations, lost trust', 11 July, 4.

The Guardian (1997), 'Doctors sick of cabin crew rush', 11 July, 4.

Guest, D. (1997), 'Towards jobs and justice in Europe: a research agenda', *Industrial Relations Journal*, **28** (4), 344–352.

Guidon, R. and B. Curtis (1988), 'Control of cognitive processes during design: what tools would support software designers?', *Conference Proceedings of CHI*, Washington DC; Chicago, IL: ACM Press.

Gustavsen, B. (1979), 'Liberation of work and the role of social research', in T. Burns, L.E. Karlsson and V. Rus (eds), *Work and Power*, London, UK: Sage, pp. 341–356.

Gustavsen, B., B. Hofmaier, M. Ekman Philips and A. Wikman (1996), *Concept-Driven Development and the Organisation of the Process of Change: An Evaluation of the Swedish Working Life Fund*, Amsterdam, the Netherlands: John Benjamins.

Hacker, S. (1990), *'Doing it the Hard Way': Investigations of Gender and Technology*, D. Smith and S. Turner (eds), London, UK: Unwin Hyman.

Hagen, R., S. Miller and M. Johnson (2003), 'The disruptive consequences of introducing a critical management perspective onto an MBA programme', *Management Learning*, **34** (2), 241–257.

Hakim, C. (1995), 'Five feminist myths about women's employment', *British Journal of Sociology*, **46** (3), 429–455.

Hakim, C. (2000), *Work-Lifestyle Choices in the 21st Century: Preference Theory*, Oxford, UK: Oxford University Press.

Hakim, C. (2004), *Key Issues in Women's Work: Female Diversity and the Polarisation of Women's Employment*, London, UK: Glass House.

Hales, C. (2000), 'Management and empowerment programmes', *Work, Employment and Society*, **14** (3), 501–519.

Hall, M. and P. Marginson (2005), 'Trojan horses or paper tigers? Assessing the significance of European works councils', in B. Harley, J. Hyman and P. Thompson (eds), *Participation and Democracy at Work: Essays in Honour of Harvie Ramsay*, Basingstoke, UK: Palgrave Macmillan, pp. 204–221.

Harding, S. and G. Gilbert (1993), 'Negotiating the take up of formal methods', in P. Quintas (ed.), *Social Dimensions of Systems Engineering: People, Processes, Policies and Software Development*, New York: Ellis Horwood.

Hardy, C. and S. Leiba-O'Sullivan (1998), 'The power behind empowerment: implications for research and practice', *Human Relations*, **51** (4), 451–483.

Harley, B. (1999), 'The myth of empowerment: work organisation, hierarchy and employee autonomy in contemporary Australian workplaces', *Work, Employment and Society*, **13** (1), 41–66.

Harley, B., J. Hyman and P. Thompson (2005), 'The paradoxes of participation', in B. Harley, J. Hyman and P. Thompson (eds), *Participation and Democracy at Work: Essays in Honour of Harvie Ramsay*, Basingstoke, UK: Palgrave Macmillan, pp. 1–19.

Harris, L., A. Tuckman, D. Watling and B. Downes (2011), 'Unlocking engagement: a review of the innovative workplaces initiative', *ACAS Research Summary*, London, UK: ACAS, March.

Harris, M. and H.R. Weistroffer (2009), 'A new look at the relationship between user involvement in systems development and system success', *Communications of the Association for Information Systems*, **24**, 739–756.

Hassard, J., L. McCann and J. Morris (2009), *Managing in the Modern Corporation: The Intensification of Managerial Work in the USA, UK and Japan*, Cambridge, UK: Cambridge University Press.

Hassard, J., J. Morris and L. McCann (2011), 'My brilliant career? New organizational forms and changing managerial careers in Japan, the UK and USA', *Journal of Management Studies*, **49** (3), 571–599.

Hatch, M. (1997), *Organisation Theory: Modern, Symbolic and Postmodern Perspectives*, Oxford, UK: Oxford University Press.

Heinbokel, T., S. Sonnentag, M. Frese, W. Stolte and F. Brodbeck (1996), 'Don't underestimate the problems of user centredness in software development projects: there are many', *Behaviour and Information Technology*, **15** (4), 226–236.

Heller, F. (1999), 'Is participation really working?', *Quality of Working Life News and Abstracts*, **138**, Spring, 6–10.

Heller, F. (2003), 'Participation and power: a critical assessment', *Applied Psychology*, **52** (1), 144–163.

The Herald (1996), 'Performance pay schemes backfire', 11 March.

The Herald (1997), 'Caterers' ballot turns up the heat on BA', 11 July, 2.

Herbert, S. (2004), *Arts in the Community, Scottish Parliament Information Centre Briefings*, Edinburgh, UK: Scottish Executive.

Herzberg, F. (1968), 'One more time: how do you motivate employees', *Harvard Business Review*, **46** (1), 53–62.

Hewett, J. (2008), 'Maytag closes Newton Iowa', *BBC World News*, May.

High Pay Commission (2011), *Cheques with Balances: Why Tackling High Pay is in the National Interest*, London, UK: Joseph Rowntree Charitable Trust.

Hindess, B. (1982), 'Power, interests and the outcomes of struggles', *Sociology*, **16** (4), 498–511.

Hirschheim, R. and H. Klein (1994), 'Realizing emancipatory principles in information systems development: the case for ETHICS', *MIS Quarterly*, March.

Hofstede, G. (1991), *Cultures and Organisations: Software of the Mind*, London, UK: McGraw-Hill.

Holden, L. (1999), 'The perception gap in employee empowerment: a comparative study of banks in Sweden and Britain', *Personnel Review*, **28** (3), 222–241.

Holme, C. (2000), 'Too few women mean business', *The Glasgow Herald*, 3 March, 8.

Holt, R. (2006), 'Principles and practice: rhetoric and the moral character of managers', *Human Relations*, **59** (12), 1659–1680.

Hooper, R. (2010), *Saving the Royal Mail's Universal Postal Service in the Digital Age*, Cm 7937, London, UK: Her Majesty's Stationery Office.

Hopfl, H., S. Smith and S. Spencer (1992), 'Values and valuations: corporate culture and job cuts', *Personnel Review*, **21** (1), 24–38.

Howcroft, D. and M. Wilson (2003), 'Participation: "bounded freedom" or hidden constraints on user involvement', *New Technology, Work and Employment*, **18** (1), 2–19.

Humphries, J. (1998), *Managing Successful Teams*, Oxford, UK: How to Books.

Huq, R. (2010), *Employee Empowerment: The Rhetoric and the Reality*, Devon, UK: Triarchy Press.

Hurd, F. (2012), 'Work innovations: transformation, micro-emancipation, or discursive shift?', *International Journal of Work Innovations*, **1** (1), 79–93.

Hyde, P., A. McBride, R. Young and K. Walshe (2005), 'Role redesign: new ways of working in the NHS', *Personnel Review*, **34** (6), 697–712.

Hyman J., H. Ramsay, J. Leopold, L. Baddon and L. Hunter (1989), 'The impact of employee share ownership', *Employee Relations*, **11** (4), 9–16.

Hyman, R. (2005), 'Trade unions and the politics of the European social model', *Economic and Industrial Democracy*, **26** (1), 9–40.

Ichniowski, C., T. Kochan, D. Levine, C. Olson and G. Strauss (1996), 'What works at work: overview and assessment', *Industrial Relations*, **35** (3), 299–333.

Jacobs, A. (2010), 'Honda strikers in China offered less than demanded', *The New York Times Business*, 19 June, B2.

Jenkins, G. and M. Poole (eds) (1990), *New Forms of Ownership*, London, UK: Routledge.

Jenkins, S., M. Martinez Lucio and M. Noon (2002), 'Return to gender: an analysis of women's disadvantage in postal work', *Gender, Work and Organization*, **9** (1), 81–104.

Johnson, D. and D. Redmond (1998), *The Art of Empowerment: The Profit and Pain of Employee Involvement*, London, UK: Pitman.

Johnson, P. (2006), 'Whence democracy? A review and critique of the conceptual dimensions and implications of the business case for organizational democracy', *Organization*, **13** (2), 245–274.

Johnson, P. and J. Duberley (2011), 'Anomie and culture management: reappraising Durkheim', *Organization*, **18** (4), 563–584.

Jones, O. (2000), 'Scientific management, culture and control: a first-hand account of Taylorism in practice', *Human Relations*, **53** (5), 631–653.

Kalmi, P., A. Pendleton and E. Poutsma (2005), 'Financial participation and performance in Europe', *Human Resource Management Journal*, **15** (4), 54–67.

Kanstrup, A.M. (2012), 'A small matter of design: an analysis of end users as designers', *Proceedings of the Twelfth Participatory Design Conference*, Roskilde, Denmark, August.

Kanter, R.M. (1977), *Men and Women of the Corporation*, New York: Basic Books.

Kanter, R.M. (1979), 'Power failure in management circuits', *Harvard Business Review*, **57** (4), 65–75.

Kanter, R.M. (1984), *The Change Masters: Corporate Entrepreneurs at Work*, London, UK: Routledge.

Kantor, J. (2012), 'Elite women put new spin on old debate', *The New York Times*, 22 June.

Kazlauskaite, R., I. Buciuniene and L. Turauskas (2012), 'Organizational and psychological empowerment in the HRM-performance linkage', *Employee Relations*, **34** (2), 138–158.

Keep, E. and K. Mayhew (2010), 'Moving beyond skills as a social and economic panacea', *Work, Employment and Society*, **24** (3), 565–577.

Kelan, E., L. Gratton, A. Mah and L. Walker (2009), *The Reflexive Generation: Young Professional's Perspective on Work, Career and Gender*, London, UK: London Business School.

Kelly, J. (1985), 'Managements redesign of work: labour process, labour markets and product markets', in D. Knights, H. Willmott and D. Collinson (eds), *Job Redesign*, Aldershot, UK: Gower, pp. 30–51.

Kenney, M. and R. Florida (1993), *Beyond Mass Production*, Oxford, UK: Oxfords University Press.

Kerr, J. and C. Tait (2008), 'Evaluation of tax-advantaged all-employee share schemes', *HM Revenue and Customs Research Report*, September, London, UK: Crown Copyright.

Khan, S. (1997), 'The key to being a leader company: empowerment', *Journal for Quality and Participation*, January–February, 44–50.

Kizilos, P. (1990), 'Crazy about empowerment?', *Training*, **27** (12), 47–56.

Klidas, A., P. van den Berg and C. Wilderom (2007), 'Managing employee empowerment in luxury hotels in Europe', *International Journal of Service Industry Management*, **18** (1), 70–88.

Korvajarvi, P. (1998), *Gendering Dynamics in White-Collar Work Organizations*, Tampere, Finland: University of Tampere.

Kotter, J. and D. Cohen (2002), *The Heart of Change*, Boston, MA: Harvard Business School Press.

Kotter, J. and J. Heskett (1992), *Corporate Culture and Performance*, New York: Free Press.

Kottke, J. and M. Agars (2005), 'Understanding the processes that facilitate and hinder efforts to advance women in organizations', *Career Development International*, **10**, 190–202.

Kuokkanen, L. and H. Leino-Kilpi (2001), 'The qualities of an empowered nurse and the factors involved', *Journal of Nursing Management*, **9**, 273–280.

Labour Research Department (2002), 'Another year of executive excess', press release, 27 August.

Lamb, N. (2012), 'Employee ownership: moving from niche to mainstream', *Liberal Democrat Voice*, 9 July.

Land, F. and R. Hirschheim (1983), 'Participative systems design: rationale, tools and techniques', *Journal of Applied Systems Analysis*, **10**, 100.

Lecher, W., H. Platzer, S. Rub and K. Weiner (2001), *European Works Councils: Developments, Types and Networking*, Aldershot, UK: Gower.

Legge, K. (1978), *Power, Innovation and Problem-solving in Personnel Management*, London, UK: McGraw-Hill.

Lencioni, P. (2002), *The Five Dysfunctions of a Team: A Leadership Fable*, San Francisco, CA: Jossey-Bass.

Levine, D. and L. D'Andrea Tyson (1990), 'Participation, productivity and the firm's environment', in A. Blinder (ed.) *Paying for Productivity: A Look at the Evidence*, Washington DC: Brookings.

Lewin, K. (1946), 'Action research and minority problems', in G. Lewin (ed.), *Resolving Social Conflict*, London, UK: Harper and Row, pp. 201–216.

Lewis, M. and J. Urmston (2000), 'Flogging the dead horse: the myth of nursing empowerment?', *Journal of Nursing Management*, **8** (4), 209–213.

Littler, C. (1982), *The Development of the Labour Process in Capitalist Societies*, London, UK: Heinemann.

Littler, C. (ed.) (1985), *The Experience of Work*, Aldershot, UK: Gower.

Littler, C. and G. Salaman (1984), *Class at Work: The Design, Allocation and Control of Jobs*, London, UK: Batsford.

Littrell, R. (2007), 'Influences on employee preferences for empowerment practices by the "ideal manager" in China', *International Journal of Intercultural Relations*, **31**, 87–110.

Long, R. (2000), 'Employee profit sharing: consequences and moderators', *Industrial Relations*, **55** (3), 477–503.

Loveridge, R. (1980), 'What is participation? A review of the literature and some methodological problems', *British Journal of Industrial Relations*, **18** (3), 297–317.

Lukes, S. (1974), *Power: A Radical View*, London, UK: Macmillan.

Lukes, S. (2005), *Power: A Radical View*, Second edition, Basingstoke, UK: Palgrave Macmillan.

MacLeod, D. and N. Clarke (2009), *Engaging for Success: Enhancing Performance through Employee Engagement. A Report to Government*, London, UK: Department for Business, Innovation and Skills.

Mandel, E. (1973), 'The debate on workers' control', in G. Hunnius, G. Garson and J. Case (eds), *Workers Control: A Reader in Labor and Social Change*, New York: Random House, pp. 344–373.

Marginson, P., M. Hall, A. Hoffmann and T. Muller (2004), 'The impact of European works councils on management decision-making in UK and US-based multinationals: a case study comparison', *British Journal of Industrial Relations*, **42** (2), 209–233.

Marginson, P., J. Arrowsmith and M. Grey (2007), 'Undermining or reframing collective bargaining: variable pay in two sectors compared', paper presented at the *Reward and Performance Conference*, Manchester, UK, March.

Martin, P. and J. Nicholls (1987), *Creating a Committed Workforce*, New York: McGraw-Hill.

Martin, R. and R. Fryer (1975), 'The deferential worker?', in M. Bulmer (ed.), *Working Class Images of Society*, London, UK: Routledge, pp. 98–115.

Mathieu, M. (2012), 'An open letter to HM Revenue and Customs', *The European Federation of Employee Share Ownership*, Brussels, Belgium, 22 August.

McCabe, D. (2000), 'The team dream: the meaning and experience of teamworking for employees in an automobile manufacturing company', in S. Proctor and F. Mueller (eds), *Teamworking*, Basingstoke, UK: Macmillan.

McCabe, D. (2002), 'Waiting for dead men's shoes: towards a cultural understanding of management innovation', *Human Relations*, **55** (5), 505–536.

McCarthy, D., E. Reeves and T. Turner (2010), 'The impact of privatization and employee share ownership on employee commitment and citizen behaviour', *Economic and Industrial Democracy*, **31** (3), 307–326.

McKenna, J. (1990), 'Smart scarecrows: the wizardry of empowerment', *Industry Week*, **239** (14), 8–19.

McKinlay, A. and P. Taylor (1996), 'Power, surveillance and resistance: inside the factory of the future', in P. Ackers, C. Smith and P. Smith (eds), *The New Workplace and Trade Unionism*, London, UK: Routledge, pp. 279–300.

Medland, D. (2012), 'The benefits of gender diversity put to the test', *The Financial Times*, 18 October, 4.

Men, L.R. (2011), 'How employee empowerment influences organization–employee relationship in China', *Public Relations Review*, **37**, 435–437.

Metz, I. and P. Tharenou (2001), 'Women's career advancement: the contribution of human and social capital', *Group and Organization Management*, **26** (3), 312–342.

Michels, R. (1949), *Political Parties*, Glencoe, UK: Free Press.

Miller, E. and A. Rice (1967), *Systems of Organisation: The Control of Task and Sentient Boundaries*, London, UK: Tavistock.

Mills, A. (2002), 'Studying the gendering of organizational culture over time: concerns, issues and strategies, *Gender, Work and Organization*, **9** (3), 286–307.

Millward, N., A. Bryson and J. Forth (2000), *All Change at Work? British Employment Relations 1980–1998, as Portrayed by the Workplace Industrial Relations Survey Series*, London, UK: Routledge.

Mingers, J. (2000), 'What is it to be critical? Teaching a critical approach to management undergraduates', *Management Learning*, **31** (2), 219–237.

Mingers, J. and H. Willmott (2010), 'Moulding the one-dimensional academic: the performative effects of journal ranking lists', *Kent Business School Working Paper No. 239*, December.

Mitrofanov, S. (1966), *Scientific Principles of Group Technology*, Boston Spa, UK: National Lending Library.

Morgan, J. (2012), 'No shortage of managers but academics bemoan a leadership lacuna', *Times Higher Education*, 5 April.

Morrell, K. and A. Wilkinson (2002), 'Empowerment: through the smoke and past the mirrors?', *Human Resource Development International*, **5** (1), 119–130.

Moshavi, D. (2001), '"Yes and...": introducing improvizational theatre techniques to the management classroom', *Journal of Management Education*, **25** (4), 437–449.

Mouer, R. and H. Kawanishi (2005), *A Sociology of Work in Japan*, Cambridge, UK: Cambridge University Press.

Mowshowitz, A. (1980), *Human Choice and Computers 2*, Amsterdam, the Netherlands: North Holland.

Mumford, E. (1979), 'The design of work: new approaches and new needs', in J.E. Rijnsdorp (ed.), *Case Studies in Automation Related to the Humanisation of Work*, Oxford, UK: Pergamon.

Mumford, E. (1980), 'The participative design of clerical information systems', in N. Bjorn-Andersen (ed.), *The Human Side of Information Processing*, Amsterdam, the Netherlands: North Holland.

Mumford, E. (1981), 'Participative systems design: structure and method', *Systems, Objectives, Solutions*, **1** (1), 5–19.

Mumford, E. (1983), 'Successful systems design', in H. Otway and M. Peltu (eds), *New Office Technology: Human and Organisational Aspects*, Leicester, UK: Pinter.

Mumford, E. (1996), *Systems Design: Ethical Tools for Ethical Change*, London, UK: Macmillan.

Mumford, E. (2003), *Redesigning Human Systems*, London, UK: Information Science Publishing.

Mumford, E. and C. Cooper (1979), *The Quality of Working Life in Western and Eastern Europe*, London, UK: Associated Business Press.

Mumford, E. and R. Hendricks (1996), 'Business process re-engineering RIP', *People Management*, 2 May, 22–27.

Mumford, E. and D. Henshall (1979), *A Participative Approach to Computer Systems Design*, London, UK: Associated Business Press.

Mumford, E, and B. MacDonald (1989), *XSEL's Progress: The Continuing Journey of an Expert System*, London, UK: Wiley.

Nardi, B. and J. Miller (1991), 'Twinkling lights and nested loops: distributed problem-solving and spreadsheet development', *International Journal of Man–Machine Studies*, **34**, 161–164.

Nicholls, J. (1995), 'Tackling hidden contempt', *People Management*, 30 November, 36.

Noon, M. (2010), 'The shackled runner: time to rethink positive discrimination?', *Work, Employment and Society*, **24** (4), 728–739.

Noon, M. and P. Blyton (1997), *The Realities of Work*, Basingstoke, UK: Macmillan.

Noon, M., S. Jenkins and M. Martinez Lucio (2000), 'Fads, techniques and control: the competing agendas of TPM and TECEX at the Royal Mail', *Journal of Management Studies*, **37** (4), 499–520.

Nord, W. and J. Jermier (1992), 'Critical social science for managers? Promising and perverse possibilities', in M. Alvesson and H. Willmott (eds), *Critical Management Studies*, London, UK: Sage.

Notter, J. and M. Grant (2011), *Humanize: How People-centric Organizations Succeed in a Social World*, Indianapolis, IN: Que.

Nuttall, G. (2012), *Sharing Success: The Nuttall Review of Employee Ownership*, London, UK: Crown Copyright.

Oakland, J. (1996), *Total Quality Management: a Practical Approach*, Bradford, UK: European Centre for Total Quality Management, University of Bradford Management Centre.

Oakland, J. (2004), *Oakland on Quality Management*, Oxford, UK: Elsevier Butterworth-Heinemann.

O'Connell-Davidson, J. and T. Nichols (1991), 'Privatisation and employee share ownership: it's still us and them', *Financial Times*, 7 March.

O'Connor, E. (1995), 'Paradoxes of participation: a literary analysis of case studies on employee involvement', *Organization Science*, **16** (5), 769–804.

Ogbonna, E. and B. Wilkinson (1990), 'Corporate strategy and corporate culture; the view from the checkout', *Personnel Review*, **19** (4), 9–15.

O'Reilly, N. (1995), 'Hero of the Hour', *Personnel Today*, 9 May, 41.

O'Reilly, J., D. Lain, M. Sheehan, B. Smale and M. Stuart (2011), 'Managing uncertainty: the crisis, its consequences and the global workforce', *Work, Employment and Society*, **25** (4), 581–595.

Owen, J. (2009), *The Death of Modern Management: How to Lead in the New World Disorder*, Chichester, UK: Wiley.

Parker, M. (1993), 'Industrial relations myth and shop floor reality: the team concept in the auto industry', in N. Lichtenstein and J. Howell (eds), *Industrial Democracy in America*, Cambridge, UK: Cambridge University Press.

Parker, M. and J. Slaughter (1988), *Choosing Sides: Unions and the Team Concept*, Boston, MA: South End Press.

Pascale, R. and A. Athos (1986), *The Art of Japanese Management*, London, UK: Sidgwick and Jackson.

Pateman, C. (1970), *Participation and Democratic Theory*, Cambridge, UK: Cambridge University Press.

Payne, J. (2010), 'Skill utilisation: towards a measurement and evaluation framework', *SKOPE Research Paper No. 93*, Cardiff University, UK.

Payne, J. (2011), 'Scotland's skills utilisation programme: an interim evaluation', *SKOPE Research Paper No. 101*, Cardiff University, UK.

Payne, J. (2012), 'Fronting up to skills utilisation: what can we learn from Scotland's skills utilisation project?', *Policy Studies*, 33 (5), 419–438.

Payne, J. and E. Keep (2003), 'Re-visiting the Nordic approaches to work re-organization and job redesign: lessons for UK skills policy', *Policy Studies*, 24 (4), 205–225.

Payne, J. and E. Keep (2005), 'Promoting workplace development: lessons for UK policy from Nordic approaches to job redesign and the Quality of Working Life', in B. Harley, J. Hyman and P. Thompson (eds), *Participation and Democracy at Work: Essays in Honour of Harvie Ramsay*, Basingstoke, UK: Palgrave Macmillan, pp. 146–165.

Pearson, A. (1988), *Primary Nursing: Nursing in the Burford and Oxford Nursing Development Units*, London, UK: Chapman and Hall.

Pedersen, V.B. and S. Lewis (2012), 'Flexible friends? Flexible working time arrangements, blurred work-life boundaries and friendship', *Work, Employment and Society*, 26 (3), 464–480.

Pendleton, A. (1995), 'The impact of employee share ownership plans on employee participation and industrial democracy', *Human Resource Management Journal*, 5, 44–60.

Pendleton, A. (2001), *Employee Ownership, Participation and Governance*, London, UK: Routledge.

Pendleton, A. (2005), 'Employee share ownership, employment relationships and corporate governance', in B. Harley, J. Hyman and P. Thompson (eds), *Participation and Democracy at Work: Essays in Honour of Harvie Ramsay*, Basingstoke, UK: Palgrave Macmillan, pp. 75–93.

Pendleton, A. and A. Robinson (2011), 'Employee share ownership and human capital development: complementarity in theory and practice', *Economic and Industrial Democracy*, 32 (3), 439–457.

Pendleton, A., N. Wilson and M. Wright (1998), 'The perception and effects of share ownership: empirical evidence from employee buy-outs', *British Journal of Industrial Relations*, 36 (1), 99–123.

Peters, T. (1987), *Thriving on Chaos: Handbook for a Management Revolution*, London, UK: Macmillan.

Peters, T. and R. Waterman (1982), *In Search of Excellence: Lessons from America's Best-Run Companies*, New York: Harper and Row.

Podro, S. (2011), 'The future of workplace relations: an ACAS view', *ACAS Policy Discussion Paper*, London, UK: ACAS, January.

Poling, S. (2005), 'Only women's work', *Frontline Scotland*, BBC One.

Pollert, A. (1996), 'Team work on the assembly line: contradiction and the dynamics of union resistance', in P. Ackers, C. Smith and P. Smith (eds), *The New Workplace and Trade Unionism*, London, UK: Routledge.

Poole, M. (1989), *The Origins of Economic Democracy: Profit-sharing and Employee-shareholding Schemes*, London, UK: Routledge.

Poutsma, E. (2001), *Recent Trends in Employee Financial Participation in the European Union*, Dublin, Ireland: European Foundation for the Improvement of Living and Working Conditions.

Poutsma, E., P. Kalmi and A. Pendleton (2006), 'The relationship between financial participation and other forms of employee participation: new survey evidence from Europe', *Economic and Industrial Democracy*, **27** (4), 637–667.

Procter, S. and F. Mueller (eds) (2000), *Teamworking*, London, UK: Macmillan.

Protherough, R. and J. Pick (2002), *Managing Britannia: Culture and Management in Modern Britain*, Norfolk, UK: Edgeways.

Purcell, J. (2010), 'Building employee engagement', *ACAS Policy Discussion Paper*, London, UK: ACAS, January.

Purcell, K. (1990), 'Research on gender: understanding the world in order to change it', *Work, Employment and Society*, **4** (4), 605–618.

Purser, R. and Cabana, S. (1998), *The Self-Managing Organization*, New York: Free Press.

Qvale, T. (2002), 'A case of slow learning? Recent trends in social partnership in Norway with particular emphasis on workplace democracy', *Concepts and Transformation*, **7** (1), 31–55.

Ramsay, H. (1977), 'Cycles of control: worker participation in sociological and historical perspective', *Sociology*, **11** (3), 481–506.

Ramsay, H. (1980), 'Phantom participation: patterns of power and conflict', *Industrial Relations Journal*, **11** (3), 46–58.

Ramsay, H. (1985), 'What is participation for? A critical evaluation of labour process analyses of job reform', in D. Knights, H. Willmott and D. Collinson (eds), *Job Redesign: Critical Perspectives on the Labour Process*, Aldershot, UK: Gower.

Ramsay, H. (1991), 'The community, the multinational, its workers and their charter: a modern tale of industrial democracy?', *Work, Employment and Society*, **5** (4), 541–566.

Ramsay, H. (1993), 'Recycled waste? Debating the analysis of worker participation: a response to Ackers et al.', *Industrial Relations Journal*, **24** (1), 76–80.

Ramsay, H. (1997), 'Fools gold? European works councils and workplace democracy', *Industrial Relations Journal*, **28** (4), 314–322.

Ramsay, H. and D. Scholarios (2005), 'Organizational participation and women: an attitude problem?', in B. Harley, J. Hyman and P. Thompson (eds), *Participation and Democracy at Work: Essays in Honour of Harvie Ramsay*, Basingstoke, UK: Palgrave Macmillan, pp. 113–144.

Randle, K. (1997), 'Rewarding failure: operating a performance-related pay system in pharmaceutical research', *Personnel Review*, **20** (3), 187–200.

Ray, C. (1986), 'Corporate culture: the last frontier of control', *Journal of Management Studies*, **23**, 287–297.

Report of the Committee of Inquiry on Industrial Democracy (1977), Cmnd 6706, Chairman: Lord Bullock, London, UK: HMSO.

Robson, M. (1988), *The Journey to Excellence*, Wantage, UK: MRA International.

Rosenbrock, H. (1990), *Machines with a Purpose*, Oxford, UK: Oxford University Press.

Roth, W. (1997), 'Going all the way with empowerment', *The TQM Magazine*, **9**, 42–45.

Roy, D. (1969), 'Making out: a counter-system of workers' control of work situation and relationship', in T. Burns (ed.), *Industrial Man*, London, UK: Penguin.

Roy, D. (1973), 'Banana time: job satisfaction and informal interaction', in G. Salaman and K. Thompson (eds), *People and Organisations*, Harlow, UK: Longman.

Royal College of Nursing (2007), *Developing and Sustaining Effective Teams*, London, UK: RCN.

Salzman, H. and S. Rosenthal (1994), *Software by Design*, New York: Oxford University Press.

Sandberg, A. (1993), 'Volvo human centred work organisation: the end of the road?', *New Technology, Work and Employment*, **8** (2), 83–87.

Sandberg, A. (1995), *Enriching Production: Perspectives on Volvo's Uddevalla Plant as an Alternative to Lean Production*, Aldershot, UK: Avebury.

Sayles, L. (1958), *Behaviour of Industrial Work Groups*, London, UK: Wiley.

Schein, E. (1985), *Organisational Culture and Leadership*, San Francisco, CA: Jossey-Bass.

Scholarios, D. and P. Taylor (2011), 'Beneath the glass ceiling: explaining gendered role segmentation in call centres', *Human Relations*, **64** (10), 1291–1319.

Schon, D. (1983), *The Reflective Practitioner*, Cambridge, MA: Basic Books.

Schuller, T. (1985), *Democracy at Work*, Oxford, UK: Oxford University Press.

Scotland on Sunday, (1999), 'Fat cats to be collared', 4 April, 5.

Scott, J., R. Crompton and C. Lyonette (eds) (2010), *Gender Inequalities in the 21st Century: New Barriers and Continuing Constraints*, Cheltenham, UK and Northampton, MA: Edward Elgar.

Segal, D. (2012), 'Army of fans finds working in Apple stores a letdown', *The New York Times*, 24 June, 18–19.

Selznick, P. (1966), *TVA and the Grass Roots*, New York: Harper and Row.

Semler, R. (1989), 'Managing without managers', *Harvard Business Review*, September–October.

Semler, R. (1993), *Maverick: The Success Story Behind the World's Most Unusual Workplace*, London, UK: Arrow.

Silver, J. (1987), 'The ideology of excellence: management and neoconservatism', *Studies in Political Economy*, **24**, 105–129.

Sirota, D., Mischkind, L. and M. Meltzer (2005), *The Enthusiastic Employee*, Upper Saddle River, NJ: Prentice Hall.

Slater, P. and W. Bennis (1964), 'Democracy is inevitable', *Harvard Business Review*, March–April.

Smith, S. and B. Wilkinson (1996), 'No doors on offices, no secrets; we are our own policemen: capitalism without conflict?', in S. Linstead, R. Grafton Small and P. Jeffcutt (eds), *Understanding Management*, London, UK: Sage.

Spreitzer, G. (1995), 'Psychological empowerment in the workplace: dimensions, measurement and validation', *Academy of Management Journal*, **38** (5), 1442–1465.

Spreitzer, G. and D. Doneson (2008), 'Musings on the past and future of employee empowerment', in T. Cummings (ed.), *The Handbook of Organization Development*, Thousand Oaks, CA: Sage, pp. 311–324.

Squires, J. (2009), 'Teamwork is vital in providing holistic care', *Nursing Times*, 27 January.

Starkey, K. and A. McKinlay (1994), 'Managing for Ford', *Sociology*, **28**, 975–990.

Storey, J. and K. Sisson (1993), *Managing Human Resources and Industrial Relations*, Milton Keynes, UK: Open University Press.

Strangleman, T. and I. Roberts (1999), 'Looking through the window of opportunity: the cultural cleansing of workplace identity', *Sociology*, **33**, 47–67.

Strauss, G. (1998), 'Participation works: if conditions are appropriate', in F. Heller, E. Pusic, G. Strauss and B. Wilpert (eds), *Organisational Participation: Myth or Reality*, Oxford, UK: Oxford University Press, pp. 190–219.

Street, S. (2010), 'In my opinion', *Management Today*, November, 66.

Stuart, M. and M. Martinez Lucio (eds) (2005), *Partnership and Modernization in Employment Relations*, London, UK: Routledge.

Subramanyam, R., F. Lee and M. Krishnan (2010), 'User participation in software development projects', *Communications of the ACM*, **53** (3), 137–141.

Suff, R. (2009), 'The recession: what the future holds for employment relations', *ACAS Policy Discussion Paper*, London, UK: ACAS, June.

The Sunday Telegraph (1993), 'Pay research shock for UK boardrooms', 26 September, 1.

Sward, K. (1948), *The Legend of Henry Ford*, New York: Rinehart.

Taylor, F.W. (1911), *The Principles of Scientific Management*, New York: W.W. Norton.

Thomas, K. and B. Velthouse (1990), 'Cognitive elements of empowerment: an interpretative model of intrinsic task motivation', *Academy of Management Review*, **15** (4), 666–681.

Thompson, P. (1986), 'Crawling from the wreckage: the labour process and the politics of production', *Proceedings of the Fourth Aston/UMIST Labour Process Conference*, April.

Thompson, P. and P. Findlay (1996), 'The mystery of the missing subject', *Proceedings of the Fourteenth International Labour Process Conference*, March.

Thompson, P. and D. McHugh (1995), *Work Organisation*, London, UK: Macmillan.

Tracy, D. (1990), *10 Steps to Empowerment*, New York: Quill.

Trist, E. and K. Bamforth (1951), 'Some social and psychological consequences of the longwall method of coal getting', *Human Relations*, **4** (1), 3–38.

Trist, E. and H. Murray (eds) (1993), *The Social Engagement of Social Science: A Tavistock Anthology, Vol. 2: The Socio-technical Perspective*, Philadephia, PA: University of Pennsylvania Press.

Trist, E., G. Higgin, H. Murray and A. Pollock (1963), *Organisational Choice: Capabilities of Groups at the Coal Face Under Changing Technologies: The Loss, Rediscovery and Transformation of a Work Tradition*, London, UK: Tavistock.

TUC (2012), *Worker Representation on Remuneration Committees*, Trades Union Congress Briefing Paper, London, UK, January.

Uchitelle, L. (2007), 'Is there (middle class) life after Maytag?', *The New York Times*, 26 August.

Upadhya, C. (2009), 'Controlling offshore knowledge workers: power and agency in India's software outsourcing industry', *New Technology, Work and Employment*, **24** (1), 2–18.

Vaitilingam, R. (2011), *Recovery Britain: Research Evidence to Underpin a Productive, Fair and Sustainable Return to Growth*, Swindon, UK: Economic and Social Research Council.

Vallas, S. (2003a), 'The adventures of managerial hegemony: teamworking, ideology and worker resistance', *Social Problems*, **50** (2), 204–225.

Vallas, S. (2003b), 'Why teamworking fails', *American Sociological Review*, **68** (2), 223–250.

Vidal, M. (2007), 'Manufacturing empowerment? Employee involvement in the labour process after Fordism', *Socio-Economic Review*, **5**, 197–232.

Vinnicombe, S., R. Sealy, J. Graham and E. Doldor (2010), *The Female FTSE Report 2010: Opening Up the Appointment Process*, Cranfield, UK: Cranfield University School of Management.

Waddington, J. (2003), 'What do representatives think of the practices of European works councils? Views from six countries', *European Journal of Industrial Relations*, **9** (3), 303–325.

Wagner, E. and G. Piccoli (2007), 'Moving beyond user participation to achieve successful IS design', *Communications of the ACM*, **50** (12), 51–55.

Wajcman, J. (1998), *Managing Like a Man: Women and Men in Corporate Management*, Oxford, UK: Polity.

Walby, S. (1990), *Theorising Patriarchy*, Oxford, UK: Blackwell.

Ward, B. (1996), 'How to empower', *Canadian Manager*, Winter, 20–22.

Watson, T.J. (1994), *In Search of Management: Culture, Chaos and Control in Managerial Work*, London, UK: Routledge.

Watson, T. and D. Watson (1999), 'Human resourcing in practice: managing employment issues in the university', *Journal of Management Studies*, **36** (4), 483–504.

Weidenfeller, N. (2012), 'Breaking through the glass wall: the experience of being a women enterprise leader', *Human Resource Development International*, iFirst, 1–10.

Weizenbaum, J. (1976), *Computer Power and Human Reason: From Judgement to Calculation*, New York: Freeman.

Welz, C. and E. Fernandez-Macias (2008), 'Financial participation of employees in the European Union: much ado about nothing?', *European Journal of Industrial Relations*, **14** (4), 479–497.

Wickens, P. (1993), 'Steering the middle road to car production', *Personnel Management*, June.

Willmott, H. (1993), 'Strength is ignorance; slavery is freedom: managing culture in modern organisations', *Journal of Management Studies*, **30** (5), 515–552.

Willmott, H. (1998), 'Commercialising higher education in the UK: the state, industry and peer review', *Proceedings of the Higher Education Close-Up Conference*, University of Central Lancashire, UK, July.

Willmott, H. (2012), 'Reframing relevance as social usefulness', *British Journal of Management*, Online First, August.

Wills, J. (1999), 'European works councils in British firms', *Human Resource Management Journal*, **9** (4), 19–38.

Wilson, D., P. Petocz and K. Roiter (1996), 'Software quality assurance in practice', *Software Quality Journal*, **5**, 53–59.

Wilson, J. and A. McKinlay (2010), 'Rethinking the assembly line: organization, performance and productivity in Ford Motor Company, c. 1908–27', *Business History*, **52** (5), 760–778.

Womack, J., D. Jones and D. Roos (1990), *The Machine that Changed the World: The Triumph of Lean Production*, New York: Rawson Macmillan.

Wong, E. and G. Tate (1996), 'A study of user participation in information systems development', *Journal of Information Technology*, **9**, 51–60.

Wooddell, V. (2009), 'Employee empowerment, action research and organizational change: a case study', *Organization Management Journal*, **6**, 13–20.

Wright, M. and P. Edwards (1998), 'Does teamworking work, and if so, why? A case study in the aluminium industry', *Economic and Industrial Democracy*, **19** (1), 59–90.

Wright Mills, C. (1973), *The Sociological Imagination*, Harmondsworth, UK: Pelican.

Yates, C., W. Lewchuk and P. Stewart (2001), 'Empowerment as a Trojan Horse: new systems of work organisation in the North Amercian automobile industry', *Economic and Industrial Democracy*, **22**, 517–541.

Yeates, D., M. Shields and D. Helmy (1994), *Systems Analysis and Design*, London, UK: Pitman.

Young, E. (1989), 'On the naming of the rose: interests and multiple meanings as elements of organisational culture', *Organization Studies*, **10** (2), 187–206.

Yukl, G. and W. Becker (2006), 'Effective empowerment in organizations', *Organization Management Journal*, **3** (3), 210–231.

Zhang, H. and E. Wu (2004), 'Human resource issues facing the hotel and travel industry in China', *The International Journal of Contemporary Hospitality Management*', **16** (7), 424–428.

Index